DRESSAGE FOR THE
21ST CENTURY

DRESSAGE FOR THE 21ST CENTURY

PAUL BELASIK

J. A. ALLEN

ISBN 0 85131 835 5

J.A. Allen
Clerkenwell House
Clerkenwell Green
London EC1R 0HT

J.A. Allen is an imprint of Robert Hale Ltd

British Library Cataloguing in Publication Data
A catalogue record for this book is available from the British Library

The extract from *American Psychologist* in the Conclusion to this book is reproduced with the permission of K. Anders Ericsson

Photographs by Karl Leck, except for photos 4–6, 17, 18, 20, 21, 84, 88, 89,
118, 119 (Lorell Jolliffe) and photos 1, 2, 3, 7–12, 22–24, 31, 32, 37, 39–41,
45, 57, 58, 72, 79, 90, 100–111,114,116,117 (by, or the property of, the author)

Artwork by Brian Tutlo, except for Figures 25–30, reproduced from
A General System of Horsemanship © J.A. Allen 2000

Design by Judy Linard
Edited by Martin Diggle
Printed in Hong Kong by Dah Hua International Printing Press Co. Ltd.

CONTENTS

ACKNOWLEDGEMENTS

I would like to thank Caroline Burt at J.A. Allen who initially prompted me to undertake this book. For many years, I have relied on her judgment and expertise, but more than that she is someone in whom I have complete trust.

I thank Jeanne Belasik for the many hours spent in preparing the typescript through its various drafts, and for helping with so much of the business of getting this book together.

I owe a great debt to my old friend Karl Leck, whom I have known as a world stage photographer for twenty-five years. Throughout the writing process, it was often trying to explain the details of Karl's photos that inspired me.

Brian Tutlo, the accomplished artist whose work appears in this book, is my next-door neighbor. You can't imagine what a comfort it is to wonder if something is possible and then have Brian come back in a week or two with an illustration that is better than one's own imagination.

How can I thank Lorell Jolliffe, my long-time assistant, who is now a trainer and teacher in her own right, for her years of hard work?

I feel I must also mention Hilda Nelson, a scholar whose books I refer to so often and whose work is quoted with permission in Chapter 7. Without her translations and explanations, we in the equestrian world would all be poorer.

I also want to thank Martin Diggle for his expert and sensitive editing and Judy Linard for all her design work.

To all my students, who have also been my teachers.

ABOUT THE HORSES

Although most of the photographs in this book were taken by Karl Leck, there are some that were not. These, I have included for historical or educational value. My intention was always to use the most illustrative examples, not necessarily the most complimentary. The choice of horses was also deliberate. Excelso, the gray ten-year-old pure Spanish stallion, is a horse not unlike the type of horses of Newcastle's and Pluvinel's time. St. Graal, a twelve-year-old Thoroughbred, is a much more modern type, almost too long, with a slightly high croup. The principles of classical dressage are not breed specific. Other horses used in the text are Mime, a seventeen-year-old Thoroughbred; Front Paige, a four-year-old Oldenburg; Rainy Lake, a six-year-old Canadian Sport Horse; and Santo Iago, a three-year-old Andalusian/Hanoverian cross.

INTRODUCTION

If, at the beginning of the twenty-first century, one takes a perspective view back to Pignatelli's School in Northern Italy in the late sixteenth century, it is easy to make an assumption that our riding has been considerably watered down. During the Renaissance, the exploits of Greek horsemen from an earlier era acted like a slow-burning catalyst and noblemen from all over Europe went to Pignatelli's School. 'Graduates' and colleagues such as Pluvinel of France, Löhneysen of Germany and the Austro-Hungarian empire, Vargas of Spain, the Duke of Newcastle from England, and La Broue of France, literally went on to inscribe the principles that formed the core and the genesis of dressage riding. There were no nationalistic differences between these riders: they were one. They were often obsessed with style, grace and virtue. They were engrossed with technique. They were both scientific and artistic. They collected their horses and they jumped – how they loved their airs above the ground!

A little later, in the Baroque era, their students, and students of their students, rode in lavish carousels and founded some schools so sound in their fundamentals that they are still alive today, and have not been 'improved' upon. This was the era that produced men such as Eisenberg, who was not only a great riding master employed by Charles VI (the sovereign who commissioned Fischer van Erlach to build the Spanish Riding School), but also author of a gorgeous book of artwork – some of which can still be seen today at Wilton House in England.

Nowadays, most equestrian professionals throughout the world work in utilitarian schools, often small and privately supported. If a school opens up today it will be lucky if it lasts as long as whoever founds it. Few people in the world train their horses in the airs above the ground. Even the chief trainers at the Spanish Riding School have more 'normal' private training stables. These function above and beyond the trainers' duties at the great 'Winter Riding School'. In the recent past, a European, World and Olympic Champion competition rider relied heavily on his family and produced his mounts under a demanding business schedule in a modest school.

Yet before we develop an inferiority complex in comparison to the Baroque, and earlier, specialists, we should perhaps consider another perspective. (In so doing, we should also remember that it was, in part, this exclusivity which eventually contributed to the end of the Baroque era.) If a rider/trainer takes up the figurative perspective from the Baroque, looking toward today, I think a case can be made that our current work is not inferior if we present our best efforts. From that viewpoint, then, our work of late may not seem diluted so much as distilled.

A certain consensus evolved from Xenophon, the students of Pignatelli, and their colleagues. This took place along academic, physical and spiritual lines. My intention is not to trace the historic advance from the Baroque era to the present. There are several outstanding books that have already done this. Instead, my intention is to produce a training manual for the horse and rider that could not exist without this consensus, which forms what are commonly known as the Classical Principles of Dressage. The ideals presented will not necessarily be my own, but some will be. In general, I feel that these principles need to be presented again because they are in great danger of being misunderstood and lost.

In a memorial eulogy for the great dressage rider Reiner Klimke, one of the more influential riders and trainers in the last hundred years, Col. L.. van Dierendonck said:

On the occasion of his last seminar symposium in the U.S., the point Reiner kept trying to make to Jan (my wife) and myself was that this generation of competitive dressage riders, instructors and trainers was lost… Too many gadgets, too many artificial aids, too much force, too much emphasis on winning and not enough emphasis on the basics…Too many ruined horses that are paying the price of personal egos and ambition. [1]

I don't want to think Reiner Klimke really believed this. He helped too many young people. His own children were riders – he had too much invested. I think this was and is a powerful warning precisely because he had so much invested. He did not stand alone in making this criticism.

In 1941, in his masterpiece *Horsemanship*, Waldemar Seunig stated that, outside the Spanish Riding School and the castle at Budapest, there were probably only one dozen Grand Prix horses. Now, some sixty years on, teams of Olympic level can be fielded in dozens of countries, and there are thousands of horses capable of Grand Prix movements.

In the last hundred years, there have been two main forces shaping dressage riding. The first, which is quite new, is the *Fédération Equestre Internationale* (FEI), the International Equestrian Federation. Formed in the early part of the twentieth century, this body developed the rules that are supposed to govern dressage competitions. These rules, now about eighty years old, were written by the Frenchman General Decarpentry and the German General von Holzing. Michel Henriquet, a world authority on classical riding, is a man who has severely criticized competitive riding. Nevertheless, he has said of Decarpentry and von Holzing (and I agree with him) that 'These two men gave a veritable synthesis for the rules which stated that there should be a code of conduct on the part of the judges and that this code should be respected. They have *even infused poetry* into these rules. Unfortunately, these rules are far from being followed.'

Within the long history of dressage, it is hard to overstate how revolutionary was the idea of turning it into a sport was. One might draw an analogy with a group of people getting together and deciding to make ballet a sport. In the introduction of Robert Greskovic's book, *Ballet a Complete Guide*, he talks about this matter:

Not for all its athletic dimensions and evident physical prowess, can we ever confuse the art of ballet with the act of any sport. Athletic activity aims for quantity; the winning score becomes the bottom line. Aesthetic activity aims for quality: a beguiling, fine grained experience motivates the going-on…In sports the form the athlete shows is sometimes taken into consideration but it is never THE consideration…The athlete will say to hell with form in order to achieve a quantitative result. The dancer will not.. [2]

Among a group of artists such an idea would, of course, have been rejected. Exhibitions –yes; recitals – yes; performances – yes. But a score card counting the number of pirouettes, or piaffe steps – impossible.

However, for a group of military men devoted to upholding rank regardless; men who lived and breathed, advanced or retreated on constant appraisal reports; whose own lives and those of others depended upon unconditional acceptance of orders that even detailed their daily tasks, this was not such a stretch. Showjumping could easily be calibrated to pick a winner. Cross-country followed from their familiar cavalry exercises. So why not dressage? This despite the fact that all the important precedents had insisted that school riding was an art. High school horses were not prepared for utilitarian purposes. High school was an end in itself. Guérinière has chapters on racing horses, carriage horses, and hunting horses. These are separate endeavors. He says: 'Can someone with even a little discernment contend that a rider capable of following the principles of a Good School is not also more capable of rendering obedient a horse intended for war, and for suppling and giving stamina to a horse adjudged suitable for the hunt.' [3] The principles of dressage reached

[1] CRC Newsletter, Autumn 1999.

[2] Greskovic, Robert, *Ballet, A Complete Guide* (Robert Hale 1998).
[3] De la Guérinière, F.R., *School of Horsemanship* (J.A. Allen 1994).

out to the utilitarian horses, not the other way around. Later, dressage training was even broken down to various levels so that a horse intended for other uses could stop at a more basic level.

Dressage as a scored sport went on to become the antithesis of Pluvinel's instruction, which instilled in the young nobleman such ideals as honor, courage, pride and virtue – the qualities of classical humanism. Furthermore, it became infected with the worst political viruses. In his book, *The Art of Dressage*, Alois Podhajsky chronicled the judging of dressage at the Olympic Games from its first appearance at Stockholm in 1912. The early equestrian Olympics were completely dominated by military men. Judging politics and jingoism quickly took over. Of the 1936 Olympics in Berlin, Podhajsky wrote:

Everyone of the five judges had one or more compatriots among the competitors. Three judges placed their countrymen first, three placed them second. One rider who was placed second by his fellow country-man ranked seventeenth, twentieth and twice in twenty-first place in the scores of the other four judges. This was in a group of twenty-nine contestants from eleven nations! Any further comment is superfluous.[4]

Incidents continued. Indignation ebbed and flowed until a point was reached after the 1956 Olympics where the International Olympic Committee was about to elimi-nate dressage altogether from the Olympic Games.

Ever higher political intrigues continued in order to reinstate it, but the problems continue to the present. International competitor John Winnett has written about the concept of 'red lining'[5] — a solid arrangement of the top ten competitors arrived at only after international judges see a combination many times at selected shows. This is a barrier so controlled that it is virtually unbreach-able by a newcomer. Preferential halo effects by well-known riders at small competitions are a phenomenon experienced by anyone who has gone to a horse show. Are dressage judges more corrupt than judges of jumpers? Or is it more a case of patching and repairing an old machine over and over — a machine that has a fundamental design flaw and cannot work correctly. Dressage as sport seemed to be a machine built (whether intentionally or not),

without the use of prior research, and it was built in the vacuum of the European militaries.

Just as revolutionary as the concept of scoring – if not more so – was the new type of horse being used at these competitions. In 1665, The Duke of Newcastle wrote: 'The Spanish horse possesses great strength and courage, is eager to learn and walks and trots with the most elegant and dignified movements. He has a proud gallop.' In 1588 Löhneysen had said, 'It would to be recognized moreover that of all the horses on earth, the Spanish are the most intelligent, the most likeable, and most gentle', while in 1600 La Broue wrote 'Comparing the best horses, I give the Spanish horse first place for its perfection, because it is the most beautiful, noble, graceful and courageous'. Pluvinel, Guérinière, and the riders throughout the Golden Age of Versailles (and sources back toward Xenophon) all hailed and promoted the 'Spanish' (Iberian) type of horse as the best in the world for dressage. Trainers universally sought a horse of average size, close-coupled, with quick reflexes, but good dispositions. They looked for 'uphill' horses that were naturally built for collection. In the late nineteenth and early twentieth centuries this changed. Constantly rearming, armies had collected large supplies of crossbred horses. Breeders across Europe were developing a horse in a 'rectangular' frame.[6] This was a horse that at first was heavily infused with Thoroughbred blood; one that could be multidisciplinary. It was a horse first for cavalry use, and then a horse that could run, jump and hunt as well as perform in dressage competitions. The proliferation of these horses was rapid. In 1938, for example, in just the Mid-European area of East Prussia, '...horses numbered 478,499. A surplus of thirty-two thousand horses were ANNUALLY sold away from the Country. These exported horses went to practically every country in Europe as well as North and South American, Africa, and the Far East.'[7]

It was the cavalry officers – now facing the mechaniza-tion of the armies – who began in the late nineteenth century, and then more formally in the early twentieth century, to compete against each other at dressage shows, among other disciplines. Quite naturally, the officers

[4]Podhajsky, A., *The Art of Dressage* (Doubleday 1976).
[5]Winnett, J., *Dressage as Art in Competition* (J.A. Allen 1993).

[6]Schilke, *Trakehner Horses* (American Trakehner Association 1977).
[7]Goodall, D.M., *Flight of the East Prussian Horses* (Arco 1973).

competed on their own horses. These new horses were generally larger than the old Spanish type, and often proportionally longer backed. As more carriage-type horses were used in breeding, the 'new' horse continued to develop a long suspended trot, which quite simply became the fashion of the entire century in the competition arena.

In part, the shift in horse types came about because of a strong German influence in the early years of competition dressage. A case can be made that winning these early competitions on the newer Warmblood horses was important for the promotion of the German horse. Good salesmanship by the German breeders was a factor here, but I think that the underlying situation was more complex than that. The reason why there was even a market for these horses had to do with major philosophical and political changes that were going on. There was still a strong, if not intensifying, backlash against collection and school riding because of their identification with aristocracies and their social abuses. There was also an increasing infatuation with sports of the field. The Italian Fedrico Caprilli's elegant jumping style was seen as revolutionary, being practically the diametric opposite of the school riding that started in his own country a few hundred years earlier.

In terms of competition dressage, the shift to the new 'rectangular' type of horse was very nearly universal. The FEI was essentially giving tacit approval through the markings of its judges, which were biased toward the new kind of horse. Read Podhajsky's accounts of trying to compete with his Lipizzaners and the response to them as opposed to the Thoroughbred types he had been so successful with. This kind of endorsement by the international body went a long way toward standardizing the type of horse that would be successful at their competitions. The breeders were only too happy to supply such horses to competitors — especially since they were being confronted with a dwindling demand by the armies of the world.

The second set of forces shaping dressage — that prevented a complete monopolistic shift to the modern horse — hailed from the traditional, historic lineage and included some non-competitive riders and some outstanding equestrian artists. It was primarily these people and their associated institutions that prevented the extinction of the traditional, classical riding style and horse. This was not easy. The great and powerful German rider, trainer and hipplogist Gustav Rau tried to install Hanoverian horses at the Spanish Riding School. It was Alois Podhajsky who fought, as he did all his life, to keep the Baroque horses as the centerpiece of the living museum-school that the whole world now admires. Along with Podhajsky, and eminent figures such as Nuno Oliveira and Egon von Neindorff, this second set of forces included artistic riders and teachers who, like musician's musicians, may be unfamiliar to the general public, but are admired by those who know them.

Many people seem intent on dividing these two forces that shape dressage. Perhaps they are correct, but perhaps they are not.

It seems ironic to me that a competitor of competitors, like Reiner Klimke, could not see this coming – this confusion of purpose in trying to make dressage a sport. As I said, it is my intention to prepare a manual of practice based on the evolving consensus of classical principles: a consensus which was fundamentally complete long before the invention of dressage as sport. Furthermore, it is my intention not to be involved in a more superficial debate, which will eventually settle itself. Listen to Oliveira himself in, speaking in 1983:

We do not speak of a superiority of any method (i.e., the German method), but it must be recognized that dressage is very popular in Germany and there are many junior riders capable of competing in Prix St. Georges. Of course, German riders are not all top class riders, having the tendency to ride and work their horses with a rigidity and harshness, which induced a very strong contact with the reins. But if you observe the top German riders, you will notice this is not what happens. They are not ignorant of the 'descente de main' (relaxing or releasing of the hands) which is the result and reward of real collection…In the 1982 World Championship at Lausanne, Reiner Klimke also demonstrated very often in his test this 'descente de main'. If a horse is not truly light, exercises such as the pirouette, the passage, the piaffe and especially the transition from passage to the piaffe are not really accurate and brilliant.[8]

Oliveira, Podhajsky, Decarpentry, *et al.* In fact all the best riders have said it in one way or another: that there is no parochial division at the top – there is a consensus.

Earlier, I talked about a distillation of dressage ideals in the last one hundred years. I have spoken repeatedly about

[8]Loch, S., *Dressage* (Trafalgar Square 1990).

the development over the years of a *clearer* consensus pertaining to the theory concerning and the execution of dressage movements. This does not mean that, even now, at the beginning of the twenty-first century, there are no nationalistic flavors in riding. There are. As with folk dancing, there are kinds of folk dressage in many areas of the world. Sometimes, in periods of complication, people long for a return to the uncomplicated and simple pursuits of the past. One often sees resurgence in things folkloric. A lot of the general appeal of riding is rooted in a kind of romance. More specifically, within the whole study of dressage, one sees parochial retreats away from the world-view. The fundamentalist movement permeates even dressage. Yet when one listens to the pinnacle riders who are scholars, or who are thinkers, from the different areas of the world, one often hears pronouncements about a form of dressage with universal principles. Such people rarely champion the differences in the dressage of different countries. They almost always accent the similarities. They know it comes through Pignatelli and Xenophon.

Today, there is a huge explosion of interest in dressage. Statistics show dressage to be one of the fastest-rising horse-related activities. However, explosions of interest are not always good for an activity, much less for an art form. They may be good for promoters and people selling things, but huge influxes of capital can corrupt a system unused to such attention.

Those who respect dressage must be careful. However, there is a lot of help. Although there have been no new dressage movements in the last hundred years, the core principles that have been codified in many writings have become clearer. In many cases the rarest of manuscripts have been revived. So much gratitude has to be given to visionary publishing companies and translators. They undertook financially unrewarding projects to clarify the traditions in dressage and present relatively inexpensive copies of great books for the students of dressage. There are also some new authors and books which have come out later in the twentieth century which have chronicled the historical development of dressage a little more evenhandedly than in the past.

At the beginning of the twenty-first century, we are in the midst of an information and communication explosion, chiefly generated by the use of computers. As true science continues to develop our knowledge about horses and riding, many untested sciences and theories are being presented by almost anyone with a book-making machine. As the great physicist and philosopher David Bohm warns, we in the West are notoriously prone to fragmentation. He cites a wonderful example of having an identical wrist-watch in each hand. One is smashed to pieces; the other is disassembled. While both contain all the pieces of the watch, only one is capable of being put together in a cohesive whole. Too many of us become obsessed with fragments and try to build theories around pieces of the watch, which can never yield a functional whole. The test of all theory must be a connection to practical reality. The only way someone will ride well is to practice riding. As they say in Zen, you can point your finger when talking about the moon, but you can get in a lot of trouble if you start thinking your finger is the moon. If there is one thing you learn in classical riding, it is that you must ride it as a whole. Lately, because of some of these new machines, we have seen more biomechanical descriptions and explanations. The difficulty here is that analysis of bad models may not explain anything about a desirable model. In a recent article, Dr. Hilary Clayton analyzes the movements of certain competition dressage horses. She says:

In many top dressage horses, the weight does not shift significantly from the front to the hind limbs as the horse becomes more collected. However, a few horses do show a marked weight shift, and seem to be the horses that are particularly well balanced. Therefore, balance may indeed be related to the horse's ability to carry more weight on the hind quarters, but the absence of the ability does not preclude a horse from competing successfully at the highest levels of competition.[9]

This comment sends us back to Robert Greskovic's statement about the difference between the art of ballet and the art of any sport: 'The athlete, however, will say to hell with form in order to achieve a quantative result. The dancer will not.'

If we accept the factual truth of Dr. Clayton's statement (and I personally do), then either someone has redefined collection in competition, or it has been deemed unimportant. There is no other possible explanation, if the horse

[9]Clayton, H. 'What is biomechanics', in *The American Hanoverian Magazine*, Fall 1999.

and rider can compete successfully at the highest levels without it.

If we were to compare the art of dressage with the art of painting, we might say that we can know the percentage of each color in a painting; we can know the chemical composition of that paint, but nothing really happens until an artist does something with this material. Always, always, reality is about dancing and not about a photograph of a dancer. It is about participation, process, doing it. It is easy today, because of our modern machines, to see performances of the highest quality in any activity. People see this and if they think too much about quantity and results, about sport and calibration, they say 'I can't do that, my horse will never beat that horse, I don't have a chance'. In this way, they self-select out of an activity on the basis of some genetic information or preconceptions about potential. This is a shame, especially in dressage, because it is often most valuable to the animals, both human and equine, who are not perfect specimens. It is the participation that is its own reward.

In terms of performance, the twentieth century rounded out the practice of dressage by placing more equal emphasis on all gaits, and collection *and* extension within every gait. Of course, as in all rounding, sharp edges disappear. The specialized jumps and airs above the ground, which were the fine edges of collection so often practiced in the previous centuries, are very rare and in some cases extinct today.

There is one ominous similarity between the Baroque times and (especially competitive) dressage at the beginning of the twenty-first century that requires observation. That similarity is money and its effects. The opulence of riding in the Baroque era eventually isolated and distanced its practitioners from the rest of the world. The social gulf, obviously not created by riding, but supported by it, certainly went onto affect equitation. Today, at a time when we talk constantly about dressage being for every horse, it costs more to campaign one horse for one season of FEI competitions in Europe than all the prize money issued at all the dressage competitions in all the world in a full year during the first half of the twentieth century. Financial exclusionary prerequisites of this kind are already building a gulf between practitioners of dressage. They need to be addressed before groups isolate

themselves. The real victim of all the backlashes will be dressage itself, just as in the fall of Versailles. (Today, two hundred years later, France's equestrianism has still not recovered from its fracture.)

A hard, objective look at the Baroque past and the present; the aesthetic schools and the sport schools, shows that there is no panacea that will promote the healthy evolution of dressage. All approaches had, and have, their plans. Pluvinel taught dancing, fencing, art, mathematics and philosophy to his students. He insisted on and promoted the combined development of the rider's mind and body. He was one of our brilliant forefathers. However, by his own admission, it took him some thirty-two lessons to teach the Spanish horse Soleil all the airs above the ground. Another pony called Sapourit was put to the courbettes and the terre-à-terre in less than a month. The horses of Guérinière didn't do flying changes at the canter. It is clear that in some areas of collection, the horses of those times may have reached a 'zenith' as noted horseman Michel Henriquet has said. However, one has to ask how completely, by our standards today, were these horses trained in such a short time?

If the horses of the past were under-trained by some modern standards, then certainly nowadays there are too many examples of modern sport horses being completely over-trained. Horses drilled and forced until there is not a spark of freshness in their whole being (which is ironic, since it is still always considered a mistake – witness frequent comments like 'how unfortunate that she has mistakes in the one-time changes.') Seemingly, we love our scientific precision so much that we allow any means to produce a mistake-free horse.

Late in the twentieth century, the musical freestyle was reinstituted in competitions with a lot of fanfare. It was hailed as a possible way out of the mechanistic hole into which we seemed to be riding ourselves. Curiously, I think that many of our older, wiser trainers and teachers wanted to applaud yet seemed to have reservations regarding their support. (For instance, H.L.M. van Schaik spoke to me about this many times.) I know that some of them feared its possible commercial exploitation, turning dressage riding into a fair, with the emphasis on palatable entertainment. Would the freestyle give riders more room for true expression? Would it be a way to bring art back in? Or would it simply turn dressage into a commercial circus?

In my opinion, there was and is one very big, overwhelming problem with the notion that the freestyle could help the art of riding. That problem is that no one ever asked where this high level of art would come from. It was assumed that, because riders could ride technically at the Grand Prix level, they would somehow be able to ride artistically at the Grand Prix level. They would somehow have the academic and spiritual balance to produce art. This was an incredible assumption, since many riders had never been trained on any academic or aesthetic level. When quizzed, they are unfamiliar with the history of equestrian art; with equestrian theory; with the construction of exercises from both their traditional/historical context and from their biomechanical, anatomical contexts. In terms of choreography, there is misunderstanding in combining cooperative and antagonistic exercises. There is often only a childlike knowledge of the art in riding and art in music. If a radio station were to play the synthetic, clichéd arrangements behind freestyles, it would be laughed off the air. Phillip Glass, the famous modern composer, tells a story of taking lessons from the sometimes terrifying but great French teacher, Nadia Boulanger. Already at that time an accomplished music student, he was studying advanced theory and composition with her. He said that one day, after two years, he finally realized what she was trying to do. He was having a lesson and he played a Mozart piece. She stopped him and said it was wrong. He said, 'But Madame Boulanger, it is right', and he cited 'the rules of voice leading, all these things are correct'. 'Yes, she said, but it is still wrong. If Mozart had played it, he would have played it like this.' And she showed him. The rules are right, but it is still wrong. He said, 'I realized then what she had been trying to teach me was the relationship between technique and style. The style of Mozart is a special case of style. Your ear can pick up a certain composer's predilection to resolve a technical problem in a highly personalized way. All within the rules.' He goes on to say that you cannot have a style without the basis of technique. There is your platform from which to make choices. Without technique there would be no style, only accidents. Riding artists have to follow the same rules. In too many cases, there is a downright resistance to learning and practicing this part of riding.

As I am writing, right before me on my desk I have a blue cup that I have used for years to hold my pens and pencils. It was one of the first pieces of art that my son ever made. He might be embarrassed by it now. It is a cup, but his first art teacher somehow made him aware that it was not just a cup, but that it was to be freely decorated by his own mind and body, and not necessarily ever to be used for drinking. So she began to show him the bridges between utility and creativity: the first rules of aesthetics. You cannot expect someone to go and see the works of Picasso late in their life and to appreciate them without some education. Picasso himself produced technical masterpieces very early in his own life. He went on. His work is not paint thrown on a wall. It is a serious progression. It is the careful work of a disciplined ever-expanding artist. Good aesthetic expression is original but understandable. It may be very sophisticated and difficult, but it is artfully communicative and can be different on many levels. To be your own Picasso requires a lot of work. It has to be learned – so it has to be taught.

If careful education in the aesthetics is not reintroduced to technical riding, the result will be the continuation of some very banal art. My hope for the future is that there is, in teaching, a more careful weaving of the academic, the artistic, the spiritual and the physical.

The technical aspects of the fundamental principles of dressage have to be studied more, so that there is not a constant reinvention of the biomechanics of dressage. This work is finished. Despite recent developments in breeding, horses have not evolved recently in any manner that requires a re-examination of the principles of Guérinière, Podhajsky, Steinbrecht, et al. The unbalancing forces of the rider's weight in the middle of the horse's back still have to be addressed primarily. All the riding and longeing exercises on the first level aim at: the non-injurious, harmonious and ethical development of the riding horse; overcoming physical and psychological faults and weaknesses and enhancing the horse's strength, elasticity and longevity. On the second level, these exercises can prepare horses aesthetically, deliberately altering their gaits with classical exercises to enhance their natural beauty. But never are the gaits to be made dysfunctional or turned into parodies of their natural movement.

'On the bit' is still a concept which describes a horse in

a physical and mental position. Proud, with its neck up, its poll as the highest point, its face at, or just in front of, a line perpendicular to the ground. It is still only in this position with its neck not crushed in or down that a horse can truly collect and extend its gaits. In this position, the neck is a longitudinal connector. Any exercises that disconnect, weaken or stiffen the neck are wrong. The position Steinbrecht has described, where the spinal vertebrae connect with the maximum surface area, thereby making a clean, strong line which energy can efficiently pass *through*, is a culmination of a training evolution – an evolution that passed by the 'pli' bends of Newcastle, and the flexions of Baucher. So today, the classically oriented rider/trainer realizes how important the proper neck form is to the balance, comfort and happiness of the horse. Whether we like it or not, we do not ride the horse entirely with the reins. If great care is not taken in training to position the neck correctly, it can be the site of many evasions.

Collection is still the concept of rebalancing weight toward the hind legs, thereby lightening the forehand. That this is rarely done, or is very difficult to accomplish, is no reason to accept less. When a competitor is heard to say 'Show me in the rules where it says a horse has to sit in the piaffe', it should make people shudder. Engagement of the haunches has to be based on impulsive, forward riding with a correct seat, otherwise attempts at collection present a real danger of hollowing the horse's back and disengaging the hind legs. Making a horse straight and riding it forward together are still THE elementary requirements, which address the natural crookedness in all horses.

All lateral exercises are governed by two basic rules. First, forwardness must always take precedence over sideways motion. The more energy is employed in crossing over, the less is left for true impulsion. Second, the direction in which the horse's mass is traveling off a centerline will determine which hind leg is doing more work.

The correct juxtaposition of exercises is often more valuable and more revealing than concentrating for too long on one set of muscles or on one kind of exercise. Correct transitions have always been the hallmark of great equitation. Impulsion without lightness is only workman-like riding at its best. A horse held up by the reins is still

the antithesis of a classical dressage horse. Dressage is a performance art. It is a practice in motion with complete harmonious use of the body.

So there are technical requirements. Yet there have been plenty of great technicians who had no spiritual development: their riding ended at the execution of technique. There are also academic requirements. Guérinière, Podhajsky – so many of the great riders warned that riding could never attain the level of art without a blend of theory and practice. The rider must understand the principles or be doomed to imitation. Yet, how many of us know riders who have 'read all the books', but cannot execute the simplest exercises, or have never really participated in the action.

Most of all there are the spiritual requirements – all those things connected with the forces of life, ethics, aesthetics and harmonies. Things that lift the spirit, and things that form the spirit., During the degree examinations for the martial arts, the great Zen Master, Taisen Deshimaru was asked, of the three things that are important: *shin*, *wasa*, and *tai* – mind or spirit, technique, and body – which is the most important? He replied: 'In the martial arts, as in the game GO, a thorough knowledge of *wasa*, technique, is useful. And it is certain that in a young person the body is the fundamental element, whereas in the older man technique and spirit predominate. In reality, *shin*, spirit, is what matters first.'[10] I think this is very important. The spiritual things first. The body will grow and strengthen with the exercises. Ardent study of technique can eventually lead to a personal style. From the beginning, though, the spirit has to be in control. The aesthetics belong there. So this is what we, as riders, have to try to do. This is our practice: to try to blend these things, to learn this classicism. Why? As a monument to the past? No. Precisely the opposite, because it is a prescription for the ills of the future. More than ever in the coming century, human beings will need to become a cohesive part of Nature. When riding is used as an art form, as a meditation, it is one of the greatest and most revolutionary relationships between species. From this friendship, we humans are offered a unique view of the natural world under the guidance of our horses. Today, humans design

[10]Deshimaru, *The Zen Way to Martial Arts* (Arkana 1982).

experiments to teach animals to talk like humans. In equitation, the best riders have put down their own native language to try to learn the horse's – and they have. To someone on the outside of these conversations, this long experiment might seem odd. Once you have made friends with horses, and have lived with them in this world without words, you begin to see words as less important than actions. Horses don't care about your words: they care about and respond to your actions. Riding will bring you into a world of action, of real living. It will show you how life is interconnected.

You might have already decided to take up the practice of dressage. You might think that I have implied that you will have to choose — picking sport or picking art. But this is not our real choice at all: a bad artist is as bankrupt as a bad athlete. Your decision has to be whether you will decide to do it right: without a desire for gain, for profit, for the reason of ego. Do it for the purity of the experience, wherever it takes you – for the love and excitement of the trip. If that is your decision, and if I can help, you don't know what an honor it is for me to serve you and your horse.

CHAPTER ONE
Longeing and In-hand Work

There are probably three major uses of longeing in classical equitation. The first is in breaking the young horse. We use longeing to prepare the young horse to be backed and ridden. Second, it is used with slight adjustments of equipment to teach the horse in-hand work. Finally, it is a common technique for what could broadly be described as remedial or rehabilitative work – the retraining of problem or injured horses.

Breaking the Young Horse

When the three-year-old horse is ready to begin training, it is brought into the stable. In the first few days it is accustomed to being groomed, cross-tied, and handled. Depending on its sensitivity, within one week it will be fitted with a snaffle bridle without reins, a longeing caves-son (one which has a thick, padded noseband and rings attached), a light saddle (usually without stirrups at first), a surcingle with multiple rings to adjust the height of the side reins, and a solid leather pair of side reins. A longe line and a long whip are also part of the equipment – see Photo 1.

This equipment has been virtually unchanged for at least five hundred years, but has been evolving for thousands. Especially with dominant horses, it is often an advantage to work quickly in the first few days, getting the equipment on the horse. Often, the young horse will be a little bewildered by the newness of all the attention, activity and change in routine. A trainer who is wise, firm and

fair, can slip smoothly into command while there is a lapse in ranking which has resulted from bringing the young horse out of the field and separating it from its friends.

For the next three months, the young horse will be longed nearly every day in order to condition it, to have it learn the longeing process, and the correct fundamentals in the walk, trot and canter. In this phase of training, the trainer is governed by two broad guidelines. These are the psychological objectives and the physical objectives. Within the fixed but broad classical framework, the trainer has to marry these objectives. Depending on the personality of the horse – and every horse will be different – the trainer will have to adjust the work and equipment constantly and creatively.

Photo 1. Three-year-old horse in full longeing equipment.

I think this is probably a good time to explain what I mean by working within a fixed but broad classical framework. Taking up the study of dressage riding is a little like taking up fly-fishing. You realize it may be possible to catch more and bigger fish with spinning tackle or nets or chemicals, but the end result is not the only thing that counts. It is not just the catching of the fish, but how the catching is done. In these cases *one deliberately limits the options of equipment to make the mind and body of the trainer the most important component of the process.* The elegance with which one pursues and accomplishes one's aims is important. Artistry may develop from this kind of practice, which is not governed necessarily by outcome. In fact, part of the artistry and strength is to develop self-control, discipline, confidence, and security – not to be wavered by temporary outcomes, which may have more to do with fate than with effort.

When the practice of dressage develops this way, a fascinating balance between form and function comes alive. The angler who catches the most fish often has very good form. The practical sets of checks and balances, the catching of a fish in fishing, the riding of a horse in riding, become functional proofs of one's art form. If there is no connection between action and result, theory and practice, the art can deviate into empty theater, or Bohm's fragmentation (see page 5 of Introduction). Countless independent researchers all over the world have replicated the experiment of classical dressage and its techniques, over hundreds of years. Its effectiveness in producing better horses and better riders is irrefutable.

Psychological Objectives

Dr. Jay F. Kirkpatrick, who has spent a considerable portion of his life studying feral horses and their behavior, has said:

> Wild horses are one of the most social animals in nature. The complexity of their social organization is extreme. Their social relationship and well-defined social order are based on the horses' knowing one another real well. We still do not understand all the nuances or origins of their behavior…. Perhaps just as important they also give us important messages if we take the time to listen about the social needs of their domestic cousins. [1]

In the first three months of training the young horse on the longe line, the trainer and the horse start to get to know each other very well. The trainer has to be constantly observing the young horse – its likes, its dislikes, whether or not it is sound-sensitive, afraid of strange sights, whether it is bold and fearless, timid and shy, aggressive and dominant, aggressive and insecure, big and clumsy, well balanced and athletic, or, for instance, whether or not it is going to challenge the trainer's rank. Almost everything that you, as trainer, do with the young horse yields information that can help you learn how to train that particular horse in the best way. How does it respond when you lead it past something strange? How about the first time you wash it with a hose? When your dog is near, does the horse move toward it or away? You must watch everything.

Over the years, studies have shown that horses are very social. If they are isolated and stall-bound, without interaction and communication, one should not be surprised when behavioral problems arise in training.

Horses have developed in a world of ranking. In training, if the rank of the trainer is unclear, this will confuse the horse. Throughout my career I have been amazed how seemingly placid horses will become vicious and dangerous when a rider/trainer displays no clear authority. Trainers must be clear and strong. (This does not, however, condone abuse.) They need to have empathy, but must understand that empathy means learning the needs of the horse, not necessarily its wants. It is possible that what a horse wants may be harmful. Studies have shown that dominance does not seem to be related to intelligence when defined as learning capacity. Intelligent, timid horses can be just as problematic as intelligent, dominant horses. It has been my experience that problems or challenges presented by issues of dominance or submission are less complicated to overcome than problems that center on intelligence. For example, is a horse avoiding working in a certain way because it doesn't understand? Or is it avoiding working in a certain way because it understands precisely? What is going on in its mind? Depending on the answer, the training could proceed on two very

[1] Kirkpatrick, Jay, *Into the Wind, Wild Horse of North America* (Northwind Press 1994).

different tracks, one requiring greater patience, the other requiring less patience.

Horses have many different personalities: they are very individualistic. The trainer who can get to know what kind of personality they are dealing with before backing the horse will have a huge advantage. Horses are strongly controlled by hormones. I have found, for example, that if mares have a reasonable amount of training before they become completely mature sexually, they rarely are unmanageable during estrus. If they have no early training and start as four-year-olds, they can be very difficult. As in humans, if education begins after maturation, it is too late. The Jesuits used to say, 'Give me that child until the age of eight, then you can have him back, because by then he will be trained in the proper principles for life.'

When a trainer begins longeing it can even be more disconcerting for some horses than the weaning process. The horse is now asked to put on the uniform of work. Being told what to do is often more of a problem than the new, uncomfortable equipment. Up until now, the young horse was led everywhere: it followed. But now the horse will be driven from the rear. It will be taught to go ahead of the trainer. A horse that is to do well in dressage will need to be bold. It will have to face things first. These are very big changes in perspective. They are not unnatural, however. In wild herds, all young stallions would be banished from their home herd as potential challengers. Even young mares are sometimes banished to prevent inbreeding. This push is not without force and can seem cruel. But it is the way of Nature. The best trainers must also push their young horses to an independent way of going. The smoother they make the process, the less the risk of physical injury to their prize prospects. The less traumatic the training, the more confidence one leaves in the horse.

If a stranger were to watch the longeing process, they might easily to read a lot of symbolism into it: the human holding a long whip, standing at the center of a confined, circling horse. The whole scene can reek of egotism. This would be a perfunctory assessment, however: two things prevent it from being true. The first is that any trainer who takes up this art of longeing must realize that the equipment and technique they use have gone unchanged for five hundred years. Probably every great dressage trainer

over that time – Pluvinel, La Broue, Guérinière, the Duke of Newcastle, and so on – has stood exactly as you or I stand. They have handled the same equipment. One cannot stand there without realizing the part one is playing in a great tradition. Imagine longeing in this company and it should place you in a proper state of humility. When you, as trainer, pick up the equipment and address the noble horse, treat the process with due importance and have respect for the tradition you are now a part of, remembering what people endured to bring it to you and me. Disrespect to any part of the process demeans its power – and ultimately your own as a trainer.

It is strange, the variations in the cultures of the world. In the East, a man is a hero if he relinquishes his ego, celebrates his inner connection with the world. In the West, a man is a hero if he leaves a singular mark – faster, richer, stronger than anyone else. He is trained to set himself apart, to make some distance, and then he suffers in his loneliness. Horses don't care about the singular achievements of a man. They are even less enthusiastic when a man's quest for such achievement is at their expense. If someone does not really like horses or their company, it is perverse to employ them like a personal Sherpa guide to egotistical summits. There is the climber who loves climbing, and the climber who loves summiting.

The second reason why longeing cannot be legitimately viewed as an exercise in egotism is that a perfunctory look at it would not even begin to recognize the incredible nuances of technique that are required in order to address its physical objectives. These are what we will discuss next.

Physical Objectives

The primary physical objective will be to prepare the horse to be ridden. This will involve preparing the horse to carry weight on its back and to be guided by the rider's influences on the back and around the torso. Any school or type of riding that prides itself on breaking the horse quickly is missing the point. Carrying weight correctly involves muscular conditioning. How we prepare that cylinder of the torso initially will have ramifications for the horse's entire ridden life.

In the first days, the focus of our attention will be primarily upon the safety of the horse and rider, which encompasses acclimatization to the equipment and place of work. Soon, it will shift to a more sophisticated analysis. It is very important that we start this work somewhere where there is good footing. Young horses don't necessarily have perfect balance, timing or obedience. Also, the feeling of the new equipment and surroundings usually distracts them. Nothing will upset them more than having their feet slip out from under them. They will feel that they are being punished for moving forward. If they feel they can't balance, they often run faster, with more risk.

Having broken many young horses with and without a round ring (Photo 2), I can tell you that, especially if you are alone, the whole process will go much more smoothly if you begin (even if only for the first few weeks) in such a ring. It need not and should not be too large. A 15 meter circle is fine. When the young horse can be pushed to follow a round fence, it allows the trainer to be much softer with the longe line. Since it is not needed to hold the horse on the circle, a lot of upsetting tugging on the cavesson is avoided. Furthermore, a round, fenced-in ring virtually eliminates the problem of young horses spinning their hindquarters out, to end up stopping facing the trainer, or trying to go in the other direction. Without a round ring this can be a nerve-racking problem, but, if the trainer does not have one, it must be solved by patient readjustment. It

Photo 2. Longeing in the round ring.

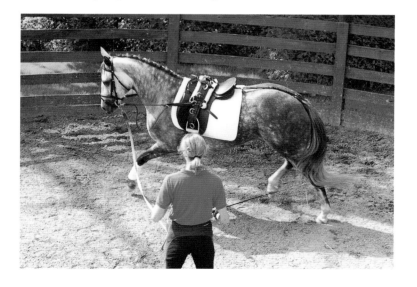

must never be addressed by attacking the young horse, compelling it to move on again out of control.

The horse must first be taught to move forward from the signal of the whip. As soon as this occurs, the side reins have to be attached. Without the restraining aids, the driving aids would have no regulation. Any push from behind could be all speed, thrust-propelling energy through a stiff back. Without restraining aids, we could not influence the longitudinal balance of the horse, which manifests itself physically in the horse's profile. A galloping racehorse, for example, has the longest of frames with the greatest weight being borne by the forehand. At the other extreme is a dressage horse in levade, carrying virtually one hundred percent of its weight on the two hind legs. In between are all the variations of balance. We don't learn this later. We start now.

In the first days it is important to hook up the side reins as soon as is safely possible, first one at a time. The inside rein is hooked up first. It is adjusted long, so there is very little pressure, should the horse fight it. Also, a horse who fights the one rein will just turn itself in a circle, rather than running into the chute of two reins (should both be hooked up at first), possibly causing a claustrophobic panic. Longeing the horse free, without side reins, is always risky. The young horse is at the most vulnerable stage, as it is in its weakest physical condition and yet most likely to misbehave with some explosive, wrenching bucks or caprioles. The sooner the trainer can get the horse in a sound working shape, the better. Once the trainer has the young horse trotting in circles with both side reins connected, it is time to take a well-deserved sigh of relief.

The trainer can now begin to form a strategy which will address faults of conformation or the individual behavior of each horse as it is longeing. Lengthening or shortening the side reins, or raising or lowering them on the different surcingle rings, will effect the bulk of these alternations. In some cases, the strategy may to adjust the size of the circle, making it small for instance, to keep a difficult horse under a little more scrutiny and control. In other cases, it may entail adjusting the tempo: more forward for horses looking for trouble, slower for certain nervous types; more transitions, less transitions, depending on the needs of each horse.

In the next months, we will teach the young horse to walk, trot and canter correctly, bent and on the bit in both directions.

Sometimes the first canter transitions can be difficult if the horse gets too excited. If the work is being done in a round pen this is rarely a problem: even if there is an exuberant strike-off initiated by the trainer's whip, the canter will usually settle, guided by the walls. However, if the trainer is in the open and the young horse is reluctant to strike off, or alternatively blasts off like a rocket, then control can be difficult. Eventually, if there is too much pressure on the longe line, the horse will stop and spin its haunches out. If this becomes a habit, the trainer may need to set up some jump poles to form a temporary barrier, or get an assistant to stand outside the longeing circle and help drive the horse forward, until it becomes honest again.

Once the trainer gets through any awkwardness in these first transitions, then all transitions will be practiced daily, so that the horse becomes very attentive to the voice commands.

We also teach the horse to respect but not fear the whip, to move forward immediately from a light signal on the big circle, and to yield to it by stepping sideways away from its touch on the ribs and flanks (the site of our future leg aids) -— if you will, a turn on the forehand at the walk.

Pignatelli and the World View

To my mind, all this work evolved from the legacy of Pignatelli's students and their colleagues in the late seventeenth and early eighteenth centuries. These people began an incredible study of bend and collection. Their work is amazing – no photographs, no films, no force plates – only their powers of perception. They produced lavish books characterized by a scientific approach, with experiments and exploration in lateral and longitudinal balance. They developed theories and prepared many illustrative engravings. Over three hundred years ago, the Duke of Newcastle wrote that the 'art of horsemanship was a very profitable science to learn' and that the horse 'ought always to be part of the circle in which he moves; and therefore he ought always to be bent on the inside and not

outside of it' and that 'these things ought to be well considered because they are the very foundation of horsemanship'; that 'art ought never be contrary to nature'.

The legacies of Pluvinel, the Duke of Newcastle, La Broue, Löhneysen, Eisenberg, and Guérinière are epitomized by careful exercises and analysis of bend, collection, and philosophy. Exquisite illustrative engravings of countless circles, movements, and diagrams of footfalls aim at educating the reader as to how to lighten the horse's shoulders; how to get submission and bend; and how to improve lateral balance. At the same time, there is convincing language repeating over and over that the 'quintessence of horsemanship is to put the horse upon his haunches'. Exercises to perfect this longitudinal shift of balance are illustrated and explained. Finely woven throughout is the advice that the rider must blend the study of theory with practice until, as Newcastle says: 'there is an elegance in horsemanship which is as if it was natural, though it proceeds from art', and 'the perfect horseman rides with art, that seems rather natural than acquired by practice'.

The highest achievement is to be a 'judicious horseman'. When, In 1626, the King of France asked about the difference between a graceful and a judicious horseman, Pluvinel told him that the seat and form describe the graceful horseman; but to be a judicious horseman one must automatically meet the qualifications of grace, but much more than this, it is necessary to determine:

by means of practice and reason, the manner of training all types of horses in all airs and movements; to totally understand their strength, their inclination, their habits, their perfections and imperfections as well as their nature. In addition to all these requirements one must activate the judgement to determine of what the horse is capable in order to undertake with him that which he can execute gracefully; and with this knowledge, one sets out, continues, and brings to completion the schooling of a horse with patience, resolution, gentleness, and the necessary force in order to arrive at the goal to which a sound horseman must aspire, qualities to be found in that man whom one can truly esteem as being a judicious horseman.[2]

A hundred years or so later we have, in Guérinière, a kind of patron saint of dressage. What was it in Guérinière that is so special? I think most people would say his inven-

[2]Pluvinel, Antoine de, *Le Maneige Royal* (J.A. Allen 1989).

tion of the shoulder-in. What is so important about the shoulder-in? The shoulder-in, in one exercise, marries these two great lines of technical study: lateral balance and longitudinal balance (Photo 3). Guérinière goes on to plait in a third strand of humanity – compassion – to come up with a beautiful braid, the art of dressage.

Photo 3. In one exercise, the shoulder-in marries two great technical lines of study: lateral balance and longitudinal balance.

All this work was not perfect in its science then, and it is not perfect in its science now. That part will continually evolve. What it was and remains, though, is a perfect art. It must have Nature as a partner. An egotistical person cannot do it. It requires a trained intellect to understand its physics and engineering. It requires a trained body to execute and perform its exercises. It requires a disciplined mind to accept things outside one's control.

Longitudinal Balance – The Quintessence of Horsemanship

Once we hook up the side reins to the snaffle bit, and we touch the horse with the long whip and then drive it forward from its signal, we have introduced the horse to

the driving and restraining aids. These are the two broad classes of riding aids that will develop and control longitudinal balance. Without some kind of bit, there is no dressage. The horse and rider use the bit as a reference point for propriocentric balancing, in the same way as a person walking through a dark room may need only to touch a chair back or handrail to help keep their balance. The muscle systems of the body, sensing a static reference point, balance the body over the feet. This is much the same as the way a person would hold on to a train strap for balance – they don't actually hang onto the strap and pull themselves off the floor and swing like a gibbon. These static points are used as solid references, enabling the body to redistribute weight over the feet in different ways.

However, before the bit can be used as a balancing reference point, the horse has to be trained to touch it, and must be comfortable with the feel of it. It cannot hide from it or be afraid of its pressure. It must learn to read any pressure of the bit and right itself with its legs and body. The neck will be a transmitter for any signals from the mouth to the torso and legs. If the neck is too stiff, the signal can't get through. If the neck is too weak and disconnected, it can't help in producing leverage. If the neck kinks the spine, it inhibits transmission of information along the nervous system, and will ultimately injure the body by contorting itself. (For thousands of years, humans have developed systems and practices to align the spine with muscular and psychological exercises. Kundalini yoga, acupuncture, chiropractic and martial arts all understand that injury, genetics, gravity and the like all affect the symmetry of the body, and ultimately health. In the horse as in man, the muscles can be trained to help keep the organs affected by gravity in healthy alignment.)

The bit itself should fit well. It should not pinch the corners of the mouth, or be so thin that it is uncomfortable. The thick, mild snaffles, well machined of composite metals, that get thinner toward the joint and thicker near the lips of the horse are really beautiful, simple tools. Despite their essential role in balancing, bits cannot balance any horse. They work best when they are simplest and do not distract the horse or the rider from the real work of training the body.

As I said earlier, we want to attach the solid leather side reins from a surcingle (fitted so that does not wobble) to the bit as quickly as is safely possible. The trainer watches the horse carefully for signs of stress and tightens them in a careful progression until the horse is on the bit. This is a position with the neck arched (see Photo 1, page11), the poll near the highest point, and the face of the horse approximately perpendicular to the ground. Working for only a few minutes at first, almost every day, the horse gets accustomed to carrying his head in this position. Horses that are ewe-necked, with no muscle at the top of their necks, might be kept a little shorter to encourage cresting, flexing the muscle and strengthening it. Horses that are too cresty might have longer side reins to encourage them to stretch out. Horses that carry their heads too high will have the side reins lower on the longeing surcingle. Horses that carry their heads too low will have the side reins raised. The judicious use of the side reins will help adjust any neck toward an ideal position whereby the nuchal ligament and the muscles of the cresting neck will lift the back with a kind of see-saw action, with the withers of the horse acting as a kind of fulcrum. It must be understood that side reins, like postural adjustments in humans, aim for a natural position which maximizes the ability to be in balance. Any horse that has not had a serious injury can be trained to be on the bit, since this position is as natural as two strange horses approaching each other in the field with crested necks. The body is never forced into a position, it is shaped over time.

Since almost all horses are already too much on the forehand, the practice of teaching long and low first is a mistake. After the horse learns the working form, then we can teach the stretching exercises. Of course, at a later stage, once we are sure the young horse respects the bit and will not use the lowered head and neck as an excuse to misbehave or to really overburden the forehand, this process will be reversed with stretching warm-ups always preceding heavier work.

Ideally, in all of this work, we keep the longe line attached to the padded longeing cavesson so as not to complicate the lessons of the mouth and bit with steering. However, in some cases, with very strong horses or control problems, the trainer will feel a need to be hooked directly to the bit. Once the horse is trained, there is very little pull on the line and this is not a problem (see Photo 2, page 14), but done too early there

is an obvious risk of creating problems with the mouth.

There are several ways of attaching the longe line without a cavesson. One common method is to thread the line in through the inside bit ring, over the crown piece and down to the other bit ring (Photo 4). Another is to thread the line through the inside bit ring under the chin and attach it to the outside bit ring (Photo 5). This is useful for horses that want to pull to the outside or keep lowering their heads. Arrets (arrests) from under the chin will raise the head to a more correct position. A third method is to attach the longe line directly to the inside bit ring (Photo 6), which is a common attachment for in-hand work. Care has to be taken not to pull on the outside ring of the bit, which will be invisible to the trainer. In all these examples, if there is too much weight on the line, the trainer has to slow the process down and calm the horse.

One more word about arrets: Often, trainers will try to physically lift the heads and necks of difficult horses that want to come behind the bit. This is impossible. The arrets work better if they snap and startle the horse. Startled horses will always raise their heads. If the coupling jangles with the bit, the sound and surprise will often be more effective than huge amounts of strength.

Photo 4. Attaching the longe line by what is often called the 'Continental method'.

Photo 5. Longe line through the inside bit ring, under the chin and attached to the outside bit ring.

Photo 6. Longe line attached directly to the inside bit ring.

In longeing the young horse I have found that there are two almost distinct kinds of going behind the bit. The first is the traditional curling and falling on the forehand. Usually, by adding a little more impulsion the rear end drives the forehand up and the problem is solved. In the second, the horse simply lowers its head rudely as if it saw a nice piece of grass on the way to being turned out. No groom would allow such behavior. The horse would be rebuked with the lead shank, would walk with its head up until they were in the paddock and then would be quietly let free. When young horses being longed go behind the bit in this manner, the trainer's response should be the same as the groom's.

Once the horse has accepted the bit and is approximately in the correct profile, we begin working on the hind legs. Eventually we use all gaits, transitions and tempo changes. There can be no thought of adjusting the imbalance perceived by the reference point of the bit unless the hind legs and body are strong enough and flexible enough to adjust themselves in relationship to the forehand. This work is first introduced unmounted on the longe. Later, it will be perfected with the additional weight and unbalancing vertical force of the rider sitting straight up on the horse's back.

We begin exercising daily in all three gaits to strengthen the back and legs, and to begin teaching controlled engagement, placing the hind legs further under the body, more toward the center of gravity. If the withers are a kind of fulcrum, with the neck drawing against the long spinal processes of the withers to lift the front part (thoracic) region of the back, then the lumbo-sacral joint is a second fulcrum. In this second fulcrum, the hips and hind limbs swing under to engage the ground toward the center of gravity, thereby lifting the lumbar region of the back behind the saddle. This whole motion, with complementary support and lift of the abdominal muscles, was coined the 'ring of muscle' in the nineteenth century. When formed or regulated by the bit, the complete forward drive creates a bascule, which is a way to balance or lever the forehand up by virtue of the 'ballast' of the hind, in much the same way as the long deck of a drawbridge can only be levered and lifted up over the water by virtue of great ballast back at the shore. This is not an obvious or completely natural phenomenon. Many horses like to use their necks to rebalance themselves – which can be fine if the horse is never ridden. But once we plan to ride the horse, we must train it to handle the forces of the rider's body on top. Then, the neck will not be strong enough to implement this rebalancing function.

In encouraging the horse to feel the bit, to reach for it without heavy leaning and to engage the hind legs, we introduce the horse to the concept of 'throughness'. This is the concept that energy, first generated by the hind legs, and later absorbed by the hind legs in a downward transition, will pass cleanly 'through' the back and through the neck of an athletic horse, right up to the bit. As the horse's education and strength progress, signals from the bit and the seat of the rider will need to pass equally cleanly back toward the hind legs and feet. It is my firm belief that, in the same way as human children can learn a language more easily than adults because of the stage of brain development, so young horses can learn to accept the bit and learn about bascule and balance more easily than older horses because they are more malleable mentally and physically. Trainers who miss this opportunity, for whatever the reason, can actually make this lesson much more difficult than it need be.

Lateral Balance: Inside Bend – the Unshakeable Principle

Let's say that we have our young horse circling on a 15 meter circle at the trot. The ideal we will be aiming for will be a form where the curve of the horse's body relatively matches the curve of the circle on the ground. As the Duke of Newcastle said, 'always the bend to the inside'. The horse's neck will also be curved gently to the inside and the profile shape will be an arch with poll near the highest point. (Sometimes, in a muscular neck, the muscle will be the highest point. One should not confuse this with the spine underneath – we try to approximate a shape we would like to ride.) The spine is extended. The underside of the neck is soft and raised upward from the base of the neck, not braced or puffed out like a pigeon. The neck is arched but not cramped. Free, powerful steps engage the hind legs. When this form is correct it seems harmonious,

balanced, and easy to achieve. In reality, it is almost never correct in a young horse – especially since our ideal asks for a perfect symmetry when going to the left and the right. 'I take it to be a great vice when a horse does not go as well to one hand as to the other' (the Duke of Newcastle, 1658).

One of the first challenges we encounter when we begin to study this fundamental circular work is that it is full of paradoxes. Since the horse has four legs, if it were traveling on the circle over fresh-raked footing, we would see two concentric sets of tracks – one set left by the two legs on the left side of the horse, and the other left by the two legs on the right side of the horse. If we connected these hoof prints with a line we would see two concentric circles left on the ground. If we looked carefully at the tracks or pattern of the footfalls (let's say the horse is traveling to the left), they would look symmetrical. The left hind might step exactly on top of the track just imprinted on the ground by the left fore. (Forging happens when these feet do not miss each other.) If we went over to the outer set of tracks, we might see the right hind steps exactly on the track just made by the right forefoot. Depending on the horse and the size of the trot, the hind prints might go over or past the prints of the forefeet, or they might step short of the front prints, but it will usually be the same for both sides of the horse. In common dressage terminology, when a horse is moving in this way, with its hind feet in line with its forefeet, it is said to be straight. Straight whilst following a circle! This is even more of a paradox than it seems. Although the hoof prints appear symmetrical – the two inside legs doing the exact same thing as the two outside legs – they are not. A careful measurement of the distance between where the left (inside) hind strikes down from one step to the next, and a careful measurement of the distance between where the right (outside) hind strikes from one step to the next, will always show the outside measurement to be larger. To any engineer's mind this is rather obvious. Since the horse has four legs, and since the two forelegs and the two hind legs stand apart then, depending on the distance they are apart, the larger circumference of the circle of the outside tracks may add several inches to each stride of the outside legs. This is one of the most important fundamentals in the whole study of dressage. It impacts on almost all riding techniques in a positive or a negative way. This observation shows that the horse's body can lengthen on one side and shorten on the other. In riding, it is this ability to bend that allows the horse to remain perpendicular to the ground when circling. When its mass stays balanced over its feet it is safer to ride because it doesn't slip. This is especially true if the rider stays balanced above the horse and does not add to the problem by leaning. The horse is more nimble, can turn more quickly and tightly. (If you drive an automobile in a large, harrowed dressage arena and turn a small circle the rear tires cannot follow the front tires. The car, being made of steel, is unbendable and much less maneuverable than a horse.)

For hundreds of years (and to this day), riders have been constantly challenging this principle with experiments in bends to the outside (Photo 7). This has never worked. The principle of inside bend remains unshakeable (Photo 8) because of its simple but important physics: it remains one of the cornerstones of classical dressage. Almost all of the classical lateral exercises a rider/trainer uses in practice are aimed at perfecting this ability, and this work begins unmounted on the longe line.

When we start with the young horse, what if it doesn't track its hind feet in line with the tracks of the forefeet? What if it is not 'dressage straight' that is, matching the

curve, but is, instead, 'ship straight', metal-stiff, and swinging its haunches out? Or what if it is curved like a boomerang, constantly carrying its twisting haunches inside? Balance, repeated in so many forms, will become a dressage trainer's mantra.

The first balance required is the trainer's own mental balance. You must understand and get beyond strangling dual effects. You will quickly realize, for example, that although tightening the inside rein may give you more bend, it might also push the haunches out further and make the horse more crooked. You won't be able to adjust anything without a rippling effect. You will learn to be aware of and to control clusters of effects.

The bulk of the work starting now will be on the torso of the horse, the flexible, multi-dimensional cylinder of its backs, sides, and stomach. We will often use the neck and hind legs to get at the torso. Later, once our horse has had more training, when we apply the left leg we will learn to feel the energy go 'through' immediately, feeling a response on the right side of this cylinder. The ribs are flexible. We will learn to ride evaluating and responding to all these feelings at once. We will worry most when something goes into that cylinder on one side and does not come out. These are the ghosts of evasion that haunt a dressage rider more than any horror story. Nothing can

Photo 7. Bending to the outside forces the horse out of balance and to lean like a bicycle on the turn.

Photo 8. The principle of inside bend is unshakeable.

be attacked on one side only. Many problems will not have a single answer. The sooner the trainer gets more comfortable with thinking this way, the better. This is not easy to do.

When we adjust the side reins for bend, we can usually stand in front of the young horse without the influencing tension on the longe line (Photos 9 and 10). We can see the curve of the neck better from that angle. When we are going to the left, we can adjust the side rein until the neck is bent slightly to the left (Photos 11 and 12). If we feel uncomfortable because we are shortening and shortening but we still can't get bend and the overall length of the

Photo 9. The curve of the horse's spine must match the curve of the circle.

neck is compressing too much, then we let the outside rein out a little. One must get the submission to get a curve to the inside. Then we must get the same curve to the inside when we go in the opposite direction. Here, the trainer will run into the paradox of symmetry. It is important that the horse has as equal as possible a symmetrical curve to the inside in each direction. This does not mean that the side reins will be adjusted to symmetrical holes, from one side to the other. In fact, there is often quite a disparity

Photo 10. A common problem – the horse is bending right whilst traveling left. When this occurs, rather than shortening the left rein, you may have to let out the right. This happens constantly in riding: riders shorten on the left to correct the bend (so they now have two short reins) instead of allowing the outside to stretch and lengthen around.

Photo 11. When the horse is bent correctly to the inside it is 'dressage straight'; this bend allows the outside to extend correctly and the horse leaves two distinct sets of tracks.

Photo 12. When the horse does not extend on the outside or bend inside, it is forced to lean like a bicycle, moving here on one track. The horse is beyond 'ship straight' – it is actually bent to the outside. The result can be seen in the tracking and balance.

from left to right. Usually, the horse is only too happy to bend to the right and the side reins might only be a hole or two different in length. However, in order to get a bend to the left that matches the right, there may be many holes difference between the left and right side reins. The reason why the surcingle has multiple rings and the side reins have multiple holes is that every horse is different and even the same horse will move differently from left to right.

Once the horse has inside bend, we can check the tracking. When adjusting the side reins, always remember to give the horse a few circles to adjust its body. Sometimes, horses start out stiff in exactly the same position they were in previously, but then they feel the change and allow their bodies to fall into the correction. Let us suppose that both the horse's hind tracks are off to the outside of the front tracks. The trainer has to be flexible and creative. It is possible that there is still not enough bend to the inside and the horse is too straight through the body. It is traveling 'ship straight'. Therefore, it needs more bend. However, it is also possible that the inside rein is too tight and the horse has *too much bend* and the haunches are being forced out in a kind of leg-yielding position. The correction could be as simple as letting the inside rein out a little, or it might mean tightening the outside more to restrict bend, but also keeping the submission inside.

The young horse on the circle might be tracking fine on the outside legs, but consistently moving the inside hind leg over to the outside of its fore partner, resembling a mock shoulder-in. What is usually happening here is that the horse is dropping its inside hip. Instead of moving square with its hips parallel to the ground, which would demand good flexion of the inside (left) hind leg, the horse tips its pelvis. The inside hind leg swings over lazily, moving like a person with a cast on their knee. The outside (right) hip sways to the right and the whole pelvis buckles. You can try this yourself. Stand up. Swing your left leg over in front of your right leg; keeping your hips very relaxed. Feel your left hip drop as it follows your left leg down and over. Feel your right hip push over to the right. Now do it again, and this time keep your right hip firm. See how you will have to balance on that leg and how it will keep the whole pelvis from collapsing. The

pelvis stays level until the inside leg finishes its track and hits the ground. Both legs are now in a scissor of support. In the first case, your hips collapse as the leg moves under the center of gravity. It keeps you in balance without the expenditure of energy involved in raising and moving your center of gravity. In the second case, in order to stay in balance with straight hips, the center of gravity must be lifted and balanced over the right (stance) leg. Instead of trying not to disturb the center of gravity, or center of balance, the second way of moving becomes a practice or an exercise in deliberately adjusting balance, and building strength and dexterity in the muscles by doing so.

Usually with the horse that drops the hip to the left, for example, we add impulsion to compel that leg to do more work. If the leg continues to 'cheat', turn in the other direction, put that leg on the outside, making it drive the turn and work on it more until the action becomes more symmetrical.

This brings us to another very important principle connected with inside bend. If you have a boat with two motors on the stern and you wish to turn left, you will accelerate the right motor. If it were a rowboat, you would pull harder on the right oar. In the circling horse, the outside leg will do more work, thus using more force to drive the turn, which culminates in the slightly larger stride, bringing us full circle to our earlier discussion. Later, when we examine the lateral exercises we will explore this in much more detail.

It is impossible to cover every kind of problem or question that will occur in longeing. Even if it were possible, one probably shouldn't do it. Each of us has to learn for ourselves. It is not a matter of successive reinventions of the wheel. What we are trying to do is set up a system for approaching questions and problems – a way to think. That is precisely what the classical approach is all about: – learning how to think. Providing guidance so that trainers won't waste their time in fragmentation, yet offering a system that is open enough to include all the unique circumstances that arise from dealing with individuals. In the preface to Lt. Col. A.L. d'Endrödy's book *Give Your Horse a Chance*, William Steinkraus wrote:

It is ironic that so many of the people who have never studied the literature of riding…simply 'can't spare the time' to do so. That they should cherish time is reasonable enough, for, after all, time is life; but the only way in which we can truly save time lies in the borrowing from the experience (which is to say time) of others. Nothing is more wasteful than the tedious search for a solution to a problem which others have long since solved. [3]

What we are doing with all the specific adjustments in longeing is taking a more active approach to balance. Instead of letting the horse find a natural way to move we begin to deliberately correct fundamental aspects of balance. I once heard a professional baseball pitching coach say that more young pitchers were ruined in college than any other time. Through no one's fault, universities did not have the standard of coaches that were available to the pros, and yet the athletes were beginning to pitch the baseball at nearly professional speeds with professional forces. Small mistakes overlooked in the fundamentals early on could later have huge effects, prematurely injuring and wearing out shoulders, backs, and arms. Promising careers were cut short.

In the life of a horse being trained in dressage, the fundamentals of balance that begin in longeing can culminate in pirouettes, piaffe, levades, airs above the ground. These are ultimate proofs of balance. Even if a horse and rider do not reach the high school, we still have to prepare the horse, which has not necessarily evolved to be ridden, for the exercises of riding. If we do not, the partnership will start out of balance on every level.

Work in-Hand

The Giravolta

The in-hand work with our young, unbacked horse will be very elementary. However, as you can already see, the sophistication or degree of difficulty of an exercise does not necessarily have a correlation with its importance. After a few weeks or so of longeing, having finished working the horse in a particular direction, the trainer will coil the longe line and approach the head and shoulders of the horse.

Gathering up the lash of the longe whip so that it is not flapping about, the trainer strokes the young horse's sides, croup and haunches, until the horse stands quietly, comfortable with the touch. Then the trainer will tap, or push with the shaft of the whip, near the horse's barrel where the leg aids will be used, at the haunches and at the hock to get the horse to take some sideways steps. One should be careful that the horse doesn't rush in fear, stand still or (worse) push into the whip in defiance. One way or another the horse must learn to take measured, deliberate and fearless steps away from the pressure of the whip. The movement should circle around the trainer in a kind of turn on the forehand (Photo 13). The inside legs step forward and across the outside legs. The inside side rein may have to be tightened to keep the bend to the inside. The trainer may have to make arrets on the longe line to keep the horse from

Photo 13. Giravolta. Even with this good crossover, the hips remain parallel to the ground.

[3]Steinkraus, W., preface to d'Endrödy, A.L., *Give Your Horse a Chance* (J.A. Allen 1989).

charging past. The horse may be in a longe cavesson but, if it is strong, it may need to have the line attached to the inside bit ring, so that half-halts will encourage the softening submission to the inside rein. This will bend the horse to the inside while moving it toward the outside.

This work only needs to last for a couple of minutes in between rein changes. This simple exercise is amazing. Psychologically, it calms the horse down, insisting on controlled submission and the acceptance of the touch of the whip. Physically, it is very important as a precedent for the leg aids of the rider. When the horse is accustomed to moving away from the touch, it will be a tremendous help in straightening or 'standing up' the young horse in the first few rides, when it will fall in or out because of its greenness. As always, the work has to be practiced or both reins (Photo 14), until the horse does it with equal facility in both directions.

Photo 14. Giravolta to the left.

Trot to Walk and Trot to Halt Transitions

The next in-hand lesson will come in the last few weeks of longeing before we are preparing to mount the horse. It is usually reserved for later in the horse's training when we begin to prepare for piaffe, but I have found that, when done on an elementary level, it develops a greater level of comfort with the whole in-hand process. It can also be used more specifically to develop a safer degree of discipline with young horses that either are domineering and insensitive or too sensitive in the mouth. After longeing we trade the more cumbersome longe line for a shorter line made out of the same material, but only six or seven feet (approximately 2 meters) in length, called the short rein. We exchange the longe whip for a piaffe-type in-hand whip. This whip is longer than a riding whip (approximately six feet, or 1.8 meters). It has to be long enough so that the trainer, standing at the shoulder or girth of the horse, can comfortably reach the hocks or rear fetlocks. We take the young horse over to the wall and have it stand quietly. Then trot for a few meters and stop or walk, trying to make a downward transition before the horse gets strong. As in longeing, the horse should not be led off but gently and crisply driven off from the whip, the symbol of the driving aids. Most importantly, it must learn the downward transition, straight and accurate, neither going 'through' the trainer's arrets, nor being afraid of their touch. At first, the trainer combines the voice commands with the transitions, but later this will be weaned away.

A few such transitions daily have a great effect on the behavior of strong or dominant horses. Many young horses will have a tendency to come off the wall in a kind of shoulder-in position. The neck will be curved too much to the inside and the horse will push the shoulder off the wall into the trainer. The easiest correction is to shorten the outside rein, thus making the horse 'ship straight'. The second is that the trainer should stay closer to the horse and block the horse's escaping shoulders with his or her own body position, but not actually touching the horse. The horse should be straightened with half-halts. It is very important that the horse learns to respect this spatial control and does not charge into the trainer. Further to this, very often an inexperienced trainer will trot off with a leaning horse, the longe line in one hand, the other hand holding the whip toward the haunches, framing the horse between the driving and restraining aids. As the inexperienced trainer jogs along beside the horse, they will often unconsciously hold or push the horse over toward the wall with the whip hand. However, the horse should never learn to lean on the trainer/rider. Even light supporting pressure can have a dramatic effect on self-carriage, balance and especially crookedness – all of which will show up tenfold in the riding! The trainer should do everything possible to encourage the young horse to be responsible when free.

Once the young horse moves laterally away from the light whip aids, and once it can trot and halt or trot and walk, straight and in control, that is enough development of the in-hand work for now. We won't go further with such exercises at this stage, although their effects will be practiced, since we will be using them when riding.

Advanced Work In-hand

The piaffe, pesade and levade are discussed here in the context of in-hand work. We will consider these movements further in their ridden contexts in Chapters 7 and 8.

Collection and Introducing Piaffe

Although we may use the elementary in-hand work for remedial training or retraining horses, it is not otherwise revisited until the horse is being prepared to learn piaffe. By now the horse has made good progress in its training and is usually familiar with the full bridle. We bring the horse to the wall in both a cavesson and snaffle, in the snaffle alone, or on the snaffle of the full bridle. Since we are probably going to interrupt our riding with a light or short in-hand session, the side reins can be attached to the billets of the saddle. I have found that it is most useful to do this after a warm-up and not too late in the lesson, when the horse may be getting tired. At first we refamiliarize the horse with trot to halt transitions, and now we insist on engagement in the decelerating transition.

In most mechanical objects, deceleration forces the mass forward. If you touch the brakes of your car, the nose presses downward. Carelessly trained horses do the downward transitions in the same way – they brake with their forelegs and lean on the forehand. The classical system insists that the horse decelerates by engaging its hind legs, getting them under the mass and lifting or

carrying it as it slows down (Photo 15). This is not easy, and most smart or lazy horses will avoid this transition. But it is another cornerstone of dressage. In 1626, the Duke of Newcastle said that the whole objective of training the manège horse is to get the horse upon the haunches. Let me tell you the best way I know to do this. That is to trot and stop, and trot and stop. The horse has the amazing system of joints in the hindquarters that allow for flexion and great weight-carrying capacity. If the trainer allows the horse to lean on the reins when in-hand, there is no chance of developing balance to the rear when the horse is ridden.

The trainer should correct the hind legs with the whip if they are out behind for two reasons. The first is the obvious point of loading the haunches. The second is to begin teaching the horse to engage one leg or the other (Photo 16) further under the body by touching with the whip. This is preparation for dealing with any asymmetries in the horse's use of its legs. The horse has to learn to come *under* from the whip. If the horse *kicks up* in a bucking, hopping action, it will be learning to disengage the

Photo 15. Skeletal structure of hind limb superimposed to show the source of classical deceleration.

Photo 16. Teaching the horse to engage one limb or the other.

hindquarters, which is exactly the opposite of our intention. The trainer has to use the whip low at first. If it is used higher on the croup, the trainer can't be surprised later when the horse produces a stiff, croup-high piaffe. As the trot to halt and trot to walk transitions continue, the trainer's own movement will progressively slow down from trotting with the horse to walking, first with big steps, and then to shorter steps. All the while the horse must remain trotting.

Learning to progressively collect the trot more and more from our original ordinary transitions is very complex. To give this process of changing gaits one or two sentences really underplays its difficulty. The trainer will change from jogging facing forward, to turning the body at some point and walking sideways facing the horse. It can be one of the funnier sights in all of equitation to watch accomplished riders flounder around trying to learn these dance steps. It borders on cruelty if you don't tell them in advance to take off their spurs!

Over time, the horse learns to trot off energetically but in more and more collected steps, while the daily dose of transitions is strengthening the hind legs, abdomen and back. In this system the half steps and then piaffe steps will form from a very natural evolution of a continually shortening trot.

Another system is to acclimatize the horse to the whip and, from the walk, tap each leg alternately, quicker and

quicker until the hind legs are jumping off the ground with more suspension and coiling. This system needs a trainer with very good dexterity and skill. The timing is intricate and the necessary feel so exact that the horse's tail need to be tied up out of the way, with no boots or bandages on the hind legs. A trainer who doesn't have good feel can get the hindquarters bouncing up too high even though the cadence might be good.

Since, at some point, most horses have one lazier hind leg, or they swing out and can't always be corrected by positioning on the wall, I think most classical trainers use a combination of the two systems – transitions to build strength, the whip to correct a lazy leg. The goal is always to try to use the simplest system first, fine-tuning it with more sophisticated techniques.

As the unmounted piaffe begins to develop more and more, the trainer makes sure to practice it in both directions and gradually to set the piaffe a little more on the spot – yet always keeping it slightly moving forward, even if only a few inches (Photo 17). This will prevent it from

Photo 17. Piaffe in hand, always keeping it moving slightly forward.

being 'stuck to the ground'. Later, we will see how important it is to train-in this ability to move the piaffe forward in the in-hand work. Even if the trainer does not continue with the in-hand work to the levels of pesade, levade or the airs above the ground, I think it is crucial to understand the piaffe's historical relationship to these airs.

Disallowing these movements in competition has contributed to a general misunderstanding of the relationship of the jumps to the piaffe. I believe that this is one of the chief causes for the many fundamentally incorrect piaffes that we see today. I have described this problem as the difference between 'piaffe as preparation', and 'piaffe as culmination'. In the past, because of its collecting abilities, the piaffe (and also the terre-à-terre, a cantering preparation to jump) was used to prepare the horse for a jump take-off by getting the haunches to come under its weight, and to draw it further back onto the hindquarters. The forefeet are thereby freed to lift off the ground. This procedure is still used today at places like the Spanish Riding School and Saumur. If you go to watch the practice sessions at these schools, you will often see excited, engaged horses vigorously piaffing just before the set ups and leaps of the jumps. The jumps, especially the pesade and levade, put one hundred percent of the weight on the two hind legs of the horse. This is the ultimate in collection, the very logical end to the weight-shifting process that began with teaching the young horse the first transitions to get it off its forehand. If this process were truly understood it would be impossible to see horses performing at the highest levels and being rewarded when there is no weight shift or balancing going on. When the piaffe becomes the final aim or culmination of the training, there is an obvious danger that both horse and trainer may completely evade weight shift unless, like the ballet dancer, the classically motivated trainer never compromises the form for quantitative results. Piaffes that have perfect rhythm, mark time, crouch, but do not make a platform from which the horse could lift the forehand, are all seriously flawed because they miss the essence of collection. Furthermore, a trainer who deliberately alters a piaffe, knowing what it should be, is as fraudulent as a painter who steals a friend's ideas, or an engineer who builds an unsafe bridge to save money. This has no place in classical dressage.

Pesade and Levade

The pesade and levade (Photos 18 and 19) are similar airs. The horse collects itself and balances over the hind legs, standing motionless for several seconds until the trainer signals it to come down. The pesade is usually higher and straighter up than the levade – generally it is over the 45 degree angle to the ground. The levade is much closer to the ground and requires great strength. To me, it is the symbol of ultimate collection.

For these airs, the horse can be prepared in the same way as for piaffe. However, the trainer will sometimes use a longer line going over the saddle, hooked to the outside

Photo 18. Pesade – Mime, a Thoroughbred gelding.

Photo 19. A young Spanish stallion learning levade.

bit ring. There is no inside rein, but the trainer's body and whip are on the inside. This longer rein technique is employed along the wall at first. Because of the greater length of rein, and because the trainer can control both sides of the horse (albeit with different aids), this is the technique used for the higher jumps, such as the courbettes and capriole. This is a difficult technique and is usually introduced at first with an assistant (who does have a rein to the inside), until the horse is honestly in control when the trainer works alone.

In preparation for the pesade and levade, the trainer will ask for a good piaffe and then press the horse for yet a little more engagement. When this is forthcoming, the trainer takes a steady feel in an upward and slightly backward direction on the in-hand line (see Photo 19). (If the hand action is too staccato, it can be difficult to control the amount of lift of the forehand and the horse may go dangerously high. Furthermore, the trainer will not be able to help the horse to balance with a little guiding rein pressure.) At first, the horse may just break the diagonal rhythm and raise one knee higher than the

other. The trainer should then praise the horse and let it walk. It is better to proceed slowly so that horse initially folds one foreleg close to the body, then the other. This way, the trainer keeps the horse in balance, and the horse does not get too excited. Little by little, the trainer will interrupt the piaffe with light backward and slightly upward half-halts. Care must be taken in setting up the pesade or levade to avoid the horse's stepping backwards too much. Finally, exercising due discernment and depending on the strength of the horse, the trainer will ask for a lower and lower lifting of the forehand with a little longer period of balance. To stand a few inches away from a young horse, excited but in control, flexing its muscles and rocking back, is one of the greatest thrills in all of dressage training. However, trainers who try to show off and hold a levade just a little too long have not been made to understand what a privilege it is to be near such an animal.

Remedial and Rehabilitative Longeing

In the simplest terms, we would use longeing for remedial or rehabilitative work for three reasons. The first is as a diagnostic tool, because the trainer can stand back and observe the horse in a perfect circle in either direction. This is very useful in evaluating a problem and then later re-evaluating by way of comparison. The second reason is that the horse cannot be ridden. It has an injury, for example. The third reason is that the horse won't let itself be ridden. It has behavioral problems, which make it dangerous to ride.

In any other cases when the horse needed remedial or rehabilitative work we would try to correct it by riding, probably with some longeing as an auxiliary tool. However, in the saddle, a good rider has many more tools available: the whole body can be employed for perception and then correction.

When we use longeing more exclusively for rehabilitative or remedial work this usually falls into one of two categories: physical problems and psychological problems.

Physical Problems

Physical problems most often call for rehabilitative as distinct from remedial work. (You may have a good-natured horse that has been subjected to incorrect training, resulting in bad mechanics.)

A typical problem could be a horse that is rein-lame. These horses check out to have no really identifiable pathology or injury, yet they can intermittently move very unevenly, appearing to be lame. This is even more evident on a circle. The cause is that the horse is asymmetrical and very crooked. It often does not stretch when the stiff side is on the outside, or it twists, dropping one hip. Since tightness in the back just exacerbates the problem, correction without the weight of the rider can be useful. Even when the bulk of the correcting is performed under saddle, the trainer will still need to longe to evaluate progress.

If a horse has an injury and passes the acute stage it may need some additional rest, but sooner or later, unless it is going to be retired, it will need an exercise regime to build it back up. The trainer must be knowledgeable about the objectives and effects of the various exercises and will probably have to work in conjunction with veterinarians and the associated professions. (There are certain injuries which might need rehabilitation that does not involve any lateral strain. In such cases, the medical advice might be not to longe.) However, with some horses, long ridden walks across country, for example, might not be an option, since they would be too uncontrollable after a lay-off. There is always a need to balance therapies, and often the trainer who knows the horse best will have to design the work. Horses that have been taught to longe from the beginning are often more reliable and safer in the confines of the school, where the footing is usually excellent and uniform. There are many combinations of therapeutic exercise, and the options should be discussed as a team, in order to produce the best future for the horse.

Psychological Problems

These can include myriad behavioral problems, which require remedial rather than rehabilitative solutions. As I said, most of the time remedial work is best done while riding: that is where the root of the problem lies and a good rider has many more tools for sensing and correcting problems. However, in some cases, the horse's problem means (or is) that it is dangerous to ride. There are so many kinds of old remedies for rearing, bucking, shying or napping that they have filled books. However, over many years of retraining problem horses, it has been my experience that, if the professional or experienced rider corrects the problem, but the horse then returns to the former environment (for example, a timid rider, being generally spoilt, or bad stable staff), the problem will return very quickly. If this cycle is repeated a couple of times, the clever horse will differentiate between situations, making further professional corrections impossible for the simple reason that the horse won't misbehave with an experienced rider/handler. When horses learn to measure riders, the situation becomes unpleasant. They always seem to be testing riders out, and expend more energy trying not to work than working. Therefore, whenever a horse is being retrained and there is a good chance that it will return to the same, or a similar environment as before, the remedial training has to include its regular rider/handler, and not just the professional, or there is little chance of success.

Even though problems manifest themselves in many different ways – biting, kicking, shying, bucking and (perhaps worst of all) rearing – they usually begin from the same source: a lack of submission. Often subtly at first, a horse begins to dominate the rider/trainer in the cross-ties; starts crowding the groom; pins its ears back when being tacked up; pushes too boldly to the feed tub at meal times, and so on. In riding it's more of the same: leaning on the bit, stopping at will, ignoring the rider's leg aids. Depending on the personality of the horse, such behavior can remain at a slightly obnoxious level, or the problem may escalate very quickly. The root cause of the behavior was usually that the rider/trainer was too soft and/or inexperienced, or else a basically good-natured horse was incorrectly trained and bad mechanics developed.

In seeking to remedy bad behavior, longeing has the first, obvious, advantage of drastically reducing the physical risk to the rider/trainer. In taking away the fear of being thrown from a misbehaving horse, it immediately gives the rider/trainer a new confidence level.

Early in my career, I was taught that a problem had to

be fixed immediately and directly. A shying horse had to be ridden through the shying; a rearing horse corrected when it reared while being ridden. All problems were handled in the same way – elicit the behavior (provoke it if necessary) and then punish the horse, repeat, and then either the horse figures it out or the rider is incapacitated. Over the years, I realized this wasn't necessary at all. Problems of submission could be addressed almost anywhere and if they were corrected in one place the correction usually held good everywhere. The crux of this is that the problem can be addressed in the venue where the trainer has maximum advantage, and where risk to all parties involved is minimized. This is the beauty of longeing especially when (as just mentioned) it is necessary to involve a timid or inexperienced rider in the remedial work in order to have any real chance of permanent success.

It is, of course, best if the professional rider can work the problem horse first and then teach the less experienced rider the techniques. Regardless of who works the horse, the training must follow the same fundamental techniques employed in longeing the young horse, even if the time frame is more compressed. Introduction or re-introduction to the equipment in a patient but resolved manner; re-education to submission and bend; immediate obedience (going forward) to the long whip; immediate obedience to the half-halts and arrets to make downward transitions or halts; complete submission both right and left in the giravolta, and finally trot to halt transitions in hand. The trainer remains very close to the horse with the trainer, not the horse, in control of the space between them. If a horse will do all this, usually there won't be a riding problem. Note, however, that when retraining in this way, the trainer must be *very careful*, and determined, when nearing the source of the problem. This encompasses such matters as touching the hindquarters of kickers with the whip, and shortening the side reins on rearers.

It is important to go *slowly and thoroughly* through the complete retraining of the longeing and elementary work in-hand. By the time the problem of submission has become bad enough to warrant professional attention, it will almost certainly be coupled with some physical problem – a bent or 'frozen' (stiff, locked) neck, crooked body, etc. So, even if correction of the mental aspect proceeds quickly, it may take a few months to correct the attendant physical condition.

REARING

I have never had very much success trying to ride through rearing problems. Nor have I seen any other trainers consistently correct rearing through riding, especially when the horses were reunited with their original riders. I have seen many bizarre and violent practices, when the cure was at least as dangerous as the disease. Rearing almost always starts the same way – too much hand. Sometimes the rider feels justified because the horse keeps running off, but inevitably the horse runs into too much pressure on the bit, feels claustrophobic and stands up. Even if the rider could throw the reins away in time, it wouldn't solve the problem. The horse has to be systematically trained to accept contact and re-educated to bit pressure and its relationship to, and effect on, balance. If such horses are longed and progressively accustomed to feeling transitions controlled by the bit, with progressively shorter and shorter side reins, they are eventually rendered more 'through'. I have always ensured that these horses learn in-hand work and are completely comfortable with and accept obediently all half-halts and arrets. They have to be completely acclimatized to the compression that accompanies being 'through' and respond immediately to the requirement of going forward in a round shape. This can take months, but it has its reward and can often lead to a permanent solution. The horse will be taught to accept contact and not freeze against it.

BUCKING

Once ill-fitting equipment is ruled out as a cause, and the equipment is properly adjusted, horses that buck must be made to go forward immediately from the whip. The side reins should be raised and shortened so that the horse can't lower its head and neck. No matter how long it takes, the horse must accept stroking with the whip and then signals from the shaft and lash. Once the horse has really learnt to go forward and is submissive to the reins, it will be unable to drop its head and neck to buck. Furthermore, it will respond quickly to changes of tempo, which will allow the rider to obtain engagement and lowering of the hindquarters, which is the obvious antidote to bucking.

SHYING

One of the easiest ways of avoiding the horse learning how to run through the aids of the rider in response to a strange sight or sound, is to longe it near any problem areas. The inside bend produced by longeing reinforces the control, and the horse gets acclimatized to the source of potential upsets in a gradual way, without being forced to encounter its demons immediately and head-on.

The greatest usefulness of longeing lies in the safe way it works on a systemic level. It corrects problems at a root level, instead of addressing symptoms. Not only does it control the horse for dealing with problems of submission, but also the equipment can be adjusted to address the physical problems that develop from the submission problems. Longeing then can go on to reinforce the corrections.

The legacy of the old masters' constant experiments with and studies of this circular work was the understand-ing and enhancing of longitudinal and lateral balance. When either the forehand or the rear end of the horse is too high, it is a problem of longitudinal balance and control. If the horse misbehaves sideways there is a problem with inside bend and the classical symmetry in either direction.

It is easy to see why the techniques of longeing can take a lifetime to explore and master, yet how, even on a fundamental level, it has very important, positive effects on the whole of equitation.

Long-reining

As with longeing, complete books have been written about long-reining. It is an art form in itself, and takes dexterity and fitness on the part of the trainer. Working a horse whilst following on foot in deep sand is not technique to be thought of as a short cut. I personally do not use it very much for the primary reason that, because of the length of the reins, they are fairly heavy in weight

Photo 20. Long-reining.

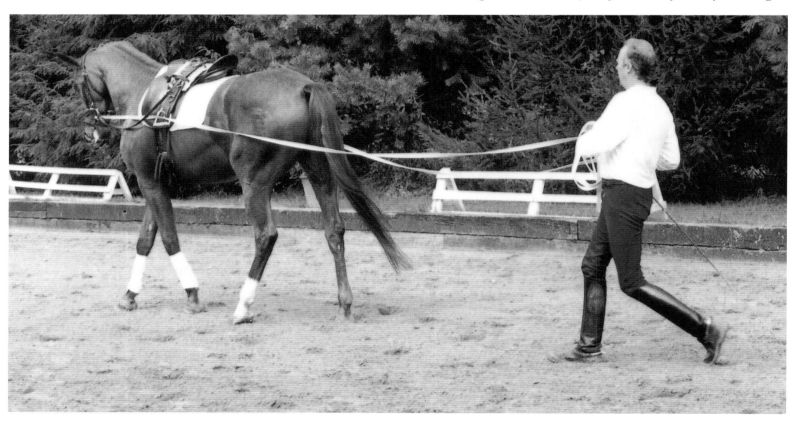

and draw, and lack delicacy of feel (that a normal rein might have). There is no question that, in the hands of some artists, there can be a beautiful finesse to this technique,[4] but in average use, they have this drawback.

The long reins are threaded through the lower rings of a longeing surcingle and clipped onto the snaffle rings of the bridle (see Photo 20). If they are run through the higher rings it is easy for them to slip on top of, or over, the croup of the horse while it is turning. If this happens, they obviously lose their channeling effect and confuse the horse. In the early stages, the trainer should be careful to stay far enough behind the horse to be safely out of the way of the hind feet, should the horse object to the feel of the reins or the urging of the whip.

The advantages of the double reins over the single longe line are threefold. First, the second (outside) rein can control escaping hindquarters and establish bend in a way that is impossible with one line. Second, the contact with the bridle (albeit heavier) is still the same in principle as the riding contact, with two reins having outside and inside effects. Third, because of this riding-type of contact, the trainer has access to limitless patterns and rein changes that are impossible on the longe.

These same advantages, however, are also disadvantages. Whereas the side reins and simple circle of longeing can develop a steadiness and light, balanced, seeking of contact, the long reins can be unsteady in balancing the inside and outside contact, and produce too much bend in the neck. Although they are useful in controlling the haunches on circles or in half-passes, or other lateral movements, at any time there is enough weight in the outside rein to displace the hindquarters, then there is automatically considerable weight drawing on the outside bit ring, to which the rein is attached. Furthermore, the trainer has to be careful at all times first, that the rein does not get caught under the tail and second, that the horse does not step over it and get the rein caught under its leg. Such things can be very upsetting to a horse.

Having said all this, I think that the greatest use of long reins is with problem horses. Horses that are over-sensitive to aids near the hindquarters can be guided and desensi-

tized by the reins draping along the flank and haunches. Horses that seem to longe well, but try to intimidate a rider when mounted, can be worked all around the arena and prepared for fairly advanced movements (Photo 21) within the structure of the double reins.

For the same reason that the weight of the long reins can provoke a horse into coming behind the bit, they are useful for those horses that lack submission and fight against actions of the bit. In general, long reins can be a useful step between longeing work and riding work, especially in remedial situations. To work a horse correctly, however, takes considerable practice and effort, and the practice time necessary can involve a lengthy digression from riding time.

Photo 21. Long-reining – half-pass right.

[4]see Karl, Philippe, *Long Reining* (A.C. Black 1992).

CHAPTER TWO
The Rider's Seat and Position – a Pure Form

Before we go over the academic and technical matters concerning the rider's seat, there is something that I feel needs to be addressed. Very often, when one studies the seat in riding, or balancing stances in the martial arts, or dance postures, a good master will give the student technical advice and corrections. But the student will also get a healthy dose of mystical talk. To students unused to this training, or those disinclined in that direction, this can sound like pseudo-religious or mysterious vagueness. It doesn't seem helpful and usually gets mocked and will quickly be dismissed. This is a very big mistake. There is a very important, highly practical reason why the best instruction has to be divided like this and why, if you want to be a good rider/trainer, you must be trained in the mystical and spiritual realm.

The seat of the rider has a dual purpose. In one way, it is a command center from which directions are issued to the horse. At the same time it is also a kind of information center – a place to collect data from the horse. The body of the rider feels things about the horse, or riding. It relays information to the rider's brain, which then issues orders back to the body as to how to react. The problem with the human brain is that it loves to impose order and under-standing. Often, where there *is* no order, that which the brain imposes is wrong. This is a common problem. People who have undergone amputations can suffer pain in the 'phantom limb'. At first, this phenomenon was dismissed as imagination. Later, physical causes such as inflamed neuromas at the site of the surgery were investi-gated, without great success. The most positive studies

pointed to a remapping of parts of the cortex of the brain.[1] It is almost as if the uninjured brain just keeps on doing its job of registering and sending sensations in a new area, to an area that has gone. The very real pain of amputees is only too vivid a proof as to how magnificently certain the brain is – even when it is evidently wrong – i.e. creat-ing/feeling pain from a non-existent limb.

Good pilots are trained to fly by instruments because what we *think* can be so inaccurate that under certain conditions it is dangerous. For instance, under certain conditions like darkness, or excessive cloud cover, it is impossible to know if a plane is flying upside down or right side up, or whether one is climbing or falling. In such circumstances, the pilot must fly by instruments. There have been a number of tragic accidents because the inter-pretation of circumstances by a pilot's brain was very wrong.

When a Chinese martial arts master says to a pupil 'You no believe, you no get' this cautionary advice is aimed at the development of the will, a kind of faith; that is, you do something without any logical reason, without the intel-lect of your brain backing you up. What is the point of all this anti-logic training, this doubting of the brain?

The point is to learn, over a long period and often with great effort and discipline, to circumvent the brain when necessary. You learn to perform when signals of fear insist that you run. You learn to be able to lean to the right when

[1]Ramachandran, V.S. & Blakeslee, S., *Phantoms in the Brain* (William Morrow & Co. 1998).

you are sure you should lean to the left, and to slow down when you are sure that you should speed up.

Somatics address the psycho-physical processes of assessing and reporting on sensation…Years of faulty alignment mean that our *idea* of what feels right can take precedence over our direct bodily sensation as to what feels right. To the average person this means that anatomically efficient posture no longer feels 'right' or 'comfortable', so often we reject it in favor of a collapsed slump. It is tempting to think that the body could be an authoritative touchstone if only we could just tap into it. And so we can. But first we have to unlearn the cultural conditioning that teaches us to ignore internal sensory experience in favor of abstract thought.[2]

The main thing you must learn early on is to suspend imposing your mind's cage-of-order on the seat. A good master will do whatever it takes to help you. If your mind is filled with targets, ambitions, fears, analysis, your attention gets captured by the magician that is your ego. You deprive the body of its great abilities of perception, intuition and connection. If you take up riding to conquer your fears, it is a real disservice to the horse. It may very well be that riding *will* conquer your fears, but that can't be your intention. Your intention has to be to want to ride well. If you take up riding to try to prove something to yourself or about yourself, it is a misuse of riding and the generosity of the horse. Again, it probably will prove many things to you, but if you limit your practice at the outset with so much intention, and so many goals, there will no room to learn anything new. Think how egotistical it is to set goals for something you know nothing about. Doesn't it seem ridiculous to aim your training before you have any? How do you know what riding is all about? Too many riders get obsessed with their feelings and goals instead of feeling the horse. If the orientation is wrong in the beginning it is impossible to get the right result later on. The seat becomes the opposite of being synchronized. It becomes one-sided and out of balance, with all of the information going one way. Too much attention to too many psychological considerations negate the use of the body. One of the greatest requirements and gifts of riding is how it must balance physical and mental intelligence. When one takes over, it blocks the other.

[2]Cranz, G., *The Chair* (Norton 1998).

The correct position on the horse is a very pure form for humans. It goes back thousands of years. It is crucial that the rider gets it right. The body will then become an instrument that lets the rider fly in the dark: it is *the* instrument. The rider develops faith that the body can be trusted when he is not sure in his brain. It will help the rider towards correct decisions. It will give him data to decide. When talking about the proper posture for zazen meditation, which is almost identical to the posture in riding, Shunryu Suzuki, a Zen master, said: 'These forms are not the means of obtaining the right state of mind. To take this position is itself to have the right state of mind. There is no need to obtain some special state of mind.'[3]

It is the same in the practice of dressage. The position is everything – it *is* dressage. Going to a show and winning a prize is not dressage – that is going to a show and winning a prize. Dressage is taking up the posture wherever you are. The posture, the position, will free you from the panicky searches in all the wrong directions. It will give you time to think with your whole body. As Pluvinel told the King of France in 1683: 'Thus, your Majesty can see quite clearly how useful this beautiful exercise is to the mind, since it instructs and accustoms it to perform with clarity and order all these functions amid noise, worry, agitation and the fear of constant danger.'[4]

So now, what is this posture, and how do we practice it?

East meets West

Almost three hundred years ago, the Duke of Newcastle wrote:

When he is once seated…he ought to sit upright upon the twist, and not upon the buttocks; though most people think they were made by nature to sit upon; however, it is not to be so on horseback. When he is thus placed upon his twist in the middle of the saddle, he ought to advance, as much as he can, towards the pommel, leaving a hand's breath between his backside and the arch of the saddle, holding his legs perpendicular as when he stands upon the ground, and his knees and thighs turned inwards toward the saddle keeping them as close as

[3]Suzuki, S., *Zen Mind, Beginner's Mind* (Weatherhill 1982).
[4]Pluvinel, Antoine de, Le Maneige Royal (J. A. Allen 1989).

if they were glued to the saddle; for a horseman has nothing else but this, together with the balance of his body, to keep himself on horseback. He ought to fix himself firm upon his stirrups with his heels a little lower than his toes, so that the ends of his toes may pass about an inch beyond the stirrup or somewhat more. He should keep his hams [calves] stiff having his legs neither too near, nor too far distance from the horse; that is to say they should not touch the horse's sides, because of the aids which shall afterwards be explained....The rider's breast ought to be in some measure advanced, his countenance pleasant and gay, but without a laugh, pointing directly between the horse's ears as he moves forward. I don't mean that he should fix himself stiff like a post or that he should sit upon a horse like a statue, but on the contrary, he should be in a free and easy position, as it is expressed in dancing with a free air. Therefore, I would have a Gentleman appear on horseback without stiffness or formality, which rather favours of the scholar than the master; and I could never observe such formality without concerting the rider to look awkward and silly. A good seat is of such importance, as you will see hereafter, that the regular movement of a horse entirely depends upon it, moreover I dare venture to affirm, that he who does not sit genteelly upon a horse, will never be a good horseman.[5]

Aside from some minor adjustments of this position, such as a more bend in the knee, the timelessness of the major descriptive features of Newcastle's seat is amazing: the stance-like position balanced over the feet; the turned-in thigh and fixed knee; a draped calf, deliberately not fixed to the horse's side but even kept off until needed for aids; a muscularly toned, but not stiff posture. All these attributes measure up to current biomechanical and ergonomic findings.

Is this so amazing? Or do the fundamental requirements of bipedal balance (and health) create a universal form that transcends specific activities. How else can one explain the almost identical postural advice in martial arts, dancing and sport?

The rider's position has evolved under two inseparable sets of pressures. The motivating factor of the first set is to establish a rider's posture on the horse from which the *rider can efficiently effect the action of riding*. The motivating factor of the second set is that the rider should be positioned on the horse is such a way that (if not ethically, then at least practically), the *horse can efficiently effect the action of being ridden*. The horse's *form and that of the rider*, meld to produce a new form that moves differently than either being by

itself. This new form has distinct biomechanical, dynamic, and physical properties. And, amazing as this physical shift is, there is an equally radical psychological shift of perspective, when both beings connect.

It turns out that, in order to accommodate the sometimes strong forces inherent in the athletic exercises of dressage most efficiently, the rider's ideal position must be in optimal balance. It must also be able to utilize strength effectively to maintain or re-establish balance, for relatively long periods. Let us see how good riders, in the classical stance-like position of dressage, are in an optimal posture to constantly adjust and change the weight-bearing from seat to legs, and legs to seat with infinite gradations.

When we talk about balance, it is in relation to the force of gravity, and although gravity is frequently viewed as a negative force, its effects are completely engineered into the bodies of humans and horses. Bones and connective tissue lever and cantilever in a complex manner, like tents or geodesic domes. They hold form because of the tension produced by gravity. Without it, they would lose their stability. Yet humans and horses have some important fundamental differences in their engineering. The skeletons of humans, unlike horses, are largely composed of ball and socket joints, which are unable to lock against the effects of gravity. Unless standing upright, the human must sit or lie on something, which takes over the job of supporting these joints. The human body must make constant adjustments to remain upright: the center of gravity cannot move very far forward or backward without the human feet having to be repositioned beneath the bodyweight. Horses, by comparison, have joints which can lock so effectively that the horse can even sleep standing up. Of course, since it is a quadruped, it has a much greater range in which to shift its weight without moving its feet.

Good riders retain their sensibility to balance when they mount. They don't rest as when sitting or lying down supported by something else. To me, this is the essence of Newcastle's advice: '...he ought to sit upon the twist, and not upon the buttocks; though most people think they were made by nature to sit upon...it is not to be so on horseback.' The best riders do not succumb to the support of the saddle for position. Their position is autonomous. It makes their balance superior. This is the secret. The old masters knew it. *Take your balance with you.*

[5]Newcastle, William Cavendish, Duke of, *A General System of Horsemanship* (Winchester Press 1970).

Humans have evolved to be masters of the vertical balance because of their bipedal make up, yet what is the first thing riders do? Sit in the 'chair' of the saddle and ask it to do all the work. Now, of course, good saddles can greatly help in balance, but I have been constantly amazed as to how good riders have the same position whatever saddle they are in.

The force of gravity can have unhealthy effects when the body gets out of a balanced position. In riding there is double jeopardy because, not only is the rider adversely affected, but also so is the horse. Two-legged men have exploited the four-legged horse for mundane purposes for thousands of years because of the horse's superior movement. However, for nearly as long, certain artists have proclaimed the necessity for an ethical riding system, which exalts the horse, and all of Nature. The first group, often searching for physical gold, missed the real gold found by the second group. Like the alchemists of the past, their real prize was in the freedom from the limits of perception; the opening of the mind, not the manufacturing of a metal.

One has to wonder whether the reason why there are so many postural disciplines: martial arts, certain sports, yoga, dancing, meditations, etc., is that they have evolved as healthy corrections for otherwise deteriorating posture and health. I have called the riding position a pure form because, as we shall see, experts from other fields look upon it as a model way to be in balance:

Many experts consider horseback riding healthy because the legs drop away from the spine while the pelvis is widened…Mandal as well as other physicians, physical therapists, and Alexander teachers recommend the saddle as therapy for some back problems…because the angle between the spine and the legs in perching is similar to horseback riding, several experts recommend it as a reasonable facsimile. (In Denmark) Dr. Mandal wants seats in schools that put children's legs into the same relationship to the spine as when mounted on a horse. He reasoned that since sitting is hard on the back and standing hard on the legs, the compromise position of perching averages the strain of the two extremes.[6]

In fact, as we have said, this stance-like position is the key to the balance in the classical seat, which has been known for a long time.

[6]Cranz, G., *The Chair* (Norton 1998).

When we look at the form of an ant or a wasp and see the slenderest connections at the abdomen and neck, we can easily imagine these same, seemingly frail, connections in the human body. In fact, these are the two sites where the human rider is most likely to fall out of balance and bend to the force of gravity. Sato Tsuji has written about this very clearly from a Japanese perspective in his book, *The Teaching of the Human Body*:

The most important, the strongest and also the most sensitive part of the body and hence the body-soul unity is called the Kyusho. It lies in the whole of the trunk below the level of the navel. This region is called the koshi…If the koshi is not filled with force, the body no longer contains a center of strength in itself and will be drawn downwards by a force exterior to itself, i.e., by the gravitational pull of the earth.

To fill the koshi with strength means also to tense the abdominal muscles a little. If one tenses the abdominal muscles in the right way, there appears as a result of this tension a point of concentration below the navel. This point is the center of man as a human body unity. It is called the *tanden*. The art of activating it is to release the strength of all the other parts of the body and concentrate it there. [7]

Tanden and hara are extremely important concepts in any body balance in the East and are especially crucial in the actions of martial arts. (Hara is a broader term than tanden, and refers to the vital center of man, both physically and psychologically.) Hans Joachim Stein, a German who lives, teaches and studies in Japan, has written a wonderful book about Kyudo – Japanese archery. He writes:

The subtle element of chi [life-force energy] can be consciously directed as required to any of the psychic energy centers and to any part of the body…making it possible to sense the circulation of breath as a kind of current of heat. One will also be able to focus on any chosen psychic center, directing breath to it so as to accumulate psychic subtle energy there and channel it onwards.

The highest of these centers, called chakras in yoga and tantrism lies behind the forehead exactly between the eyebrows. It is where Indian women placed their caste mark. The lowest of these chakras is to be found at the bottom of the spine. The center situated about 3 cm below the navel is of prime importance in Japanese archery. Taoism calls this center chi-hai, the ocean of breath. Japanese Zen has the same expression, ki-kai, but today it tends to use the more popular term, tanden.[8]

[7]Tsuji, S., *The Teaching of the Human Body* quoted in Durkheim, K.G., *Hara the Vital Centre of Man* (George, Allen & Unwin 1962)
[8]Stein, H., *Kyudo, the Art of Japanese Archery* (Element Books 1988).

The importance of the koshi and tanden in the context of riding posture is shown in Photos 22 and 23. However, if you have not taken martial arts instruction it might be useful to get an idea of the feel of the tanden before we examine in more detail how it influences the rider's seat. There are two simple methods of doing this. The first is to lie flat on your back on a firm surface. Concentrate weight or force, muscular tension in your legs. Then release that force and even lift your legs slightly. Concentrate on the area below your navel – there is the tanden. Another way is simply to exhale. When you feel there is no more air in your lungs, cough gently a couple of times until you feel a tensing below the navel – there is the tanden.

In Western literature the only place where I have come across volumes of mystical, scientific, analytical writings that compare in volume, depth and quality to the Eastern writings on tanden and hara are the writings about the rider's seat. There have been arguments and agreements as to nuances and applications but, on one point, there is unanimity. As Egon von Neindorff said: 'The seat is the alpha and omega in riding'. On this, all horsemen agree.

The neck is the second vulnerable area for the human being and human balance. I have always found it irritating when a therapist tells someone, 'You hold tension in your neck. Relax.' The slender human neck houses a spinal cord, which is a life connection to the brain. Neck injuries are very serious affairs. Therefore, it is completely natural for a fearful or anxious person to pull their shoulders up and squash their head close to their body like a turtle. This instinct protects the vulnerable neck connection between the head and torso. The problem is, protecting the neck in this way on a continuous basis can lead to many other problems. The neck needs to be made strong in other ways.

Because through wrong posture the upper body must, as it were, sit on a crumpled lower body, the muscles of the chest, shoulders, neck, face and head, become cramped and it is only a makeshift remedy to loosen the cramp by kneading or massage. To obviate the source of this cramp completely one must straighten the spine and adopt the right posture... [9]

[So, in many disciplines, instead of shortening the cervical vertebrae in a slump for protection, students are trained to

[9]Tsuji, S., *The Teaching of the Human Body* quoted in Durkheim, K.G., *Hara the Vital Centre of Man* (George, Allen & Unwin 1962)

Photo 22. East meets West. Abdominals prevent hyper-flexed back; firm knee and thigh stop forward pull – 'filling the koshi with strength'.

Photo 23. Firmness in the rider's body blocks the horse from pulling on the reins. In dressage, no one pulls – neither horse nor rider. (There is a big difference between the rider pulling the reins, and stopping the horse from pulling.)

be straight and made strong by pulling the chin in slightly with the ears over the shoulders. The neck becomes stronger, the spinal cord safer, straighter. Massage is no longer necessary. The kink is permanently corrected. Let us go back to Dr. Cranz on the evils of chair sitting.]

When a person leans backward into the chair back, that initiates both a backward and downward force. The downward force pushes the bottom of the pelvis forward. Eventually the sitter finds himself sitting on his tailbone out at the edge of the chair with the spine as a whole transformed to a C-shape slouch. Sound familiar? We've all been there. This particular slump proves to be uncomfortable in several ways: congestion is created in the lungs and in the guts, the ribs fold down over the diaphragm toward the belly; strain is created in the lower back.[10]

I believe this is one of the reasons why breathing exercises are often such an integral part of meditation training. (I am including here active meditations such as different martial arts and riding.) In one respect, if you 'fix' the pieces of the body, the lungs, for instance, will be free to do their work. On the other hand, if the person were to breathe correctly, good posture would necessarily result, because one cannot possibly breathe deeply and steadily in a crumpled and tense body. Of course, the best path is a blend.

I have said before, it is difficult to write about breathing because it is so important that a few words trivialize it. As humans, we can live without food or water for days, but without air it is a matter of a very few minutes. Breathing is connected to psychological states. Its rhythms are tied to calm and anxious mental states. So much so, that some psychologists can help train elite athletes not to lose their tempers, for example, by keeping track of heart rates (with the use of a heart monitor) and controlling the heart through breathing. In the knowledge that, when the heart rate gets to a certain point, the individual is very vulnerable to losing emotional control, the person is trained to become aware of their state, use it as an alarm, and get it back under control before psychological trouble ensues.

Posture affects breathing, breathing affects posture. Mental and emotional states affect breathing, breathing affects mental and emotional states. Once again, we see these processes going in both directions. The process that fuels the temper can control the temper. The point is, as I have said, that one must learn, over a long period and often with the greatest of effort and discipline, to circumvent the brain when necessary.

In the ancient practice of tantric yoga, masterful yogis learned to send energy back and forth along the seven chakras of the spine. In China, acupuncturists mapped

nerve meridians and found stimulation had magical restorative powers to a body, by getting energy to flow into fixated and injured bodies and tissues, thus rebalancing the body by restoring harmony to the nerves flowing off the spine. Chiropractors realign the spinal vertebrae: the patient gets dramatic relief.

All over the world, for thousands of years, people rode horses. An almost magical form developed which, by necessity, took into account all the influences of gravity. A posture developed and, at its core, was balance. A form at first trained by the violent forces of an athletic horse, then perfected in a ritualization of this violence called dressage. Great martial artists often copied this near-perfect balanced form and called it the 'horse stance'. This pure form was so healthy that it became a great therapy for severely injured and handicapped people. When this physical form was coupled with a psychological form it was nothing short of an elixir.

Perhaps nothing defines dressage more than a rider's quest to learn and perfect his or her form. And nothing will determine one's effectiveness in riding so much as how far one gets in mastering this form. Almost everything in dressage, all the exercises and the challenges, aim at developing the rider's balance and the horse's balance — and therefore, the position. So what are the features of this pure form?

The Seat

The pelvis of the rider supports the lower portion of the spine and rests on the legs, which attach to the pelvis at the hips. Just to the inside of the hips are the ischia, the rocker-like seat bones on which the rider sits. The center of gravity of the rider's head will be positioned directly over the heads of the thigh bones, which attach to the pelvis, forming the hip joint. A line connecting the hips bisects the center of gravity of the whole body. This is not the line connecting the ilium (the big part of the pelvis that sticks out on either side, close to the belt line), which is in line with the navel. The center of gravity is lower: it is the tanden. When standing upright the thigh bones (femurs) are aligned vertically, perpendicular to the ground. The hip angle is at its most open. As the thighs

---

[10]Cranz, G., *The Chair* (Norton 1998).

and spine are, relatively, in a straight line forming an angle of 180 degrees, one hundred percent of the person's weight is on their feet. If a person sits on a conventional chair, the knees come up; the thighs are now horizontal, or parallel to the ground. The thighs and spine form an angle of ninety degrees. Almost one hundred percent of the person's weight is on their seat.

In riding or perching (as when a person sits on a stool, not to be confused with a 'perching seat', which is synonymous with a 'fork seat' – a fault in riding), the thigh and spine form an angle of approximately 125 degrees. In such a position, the rider's weight should be distributed through the skeletal structures of the ischia, not through the flesh of the buttocks. Especially on a firm surface, like a saddle, the pelvis will widen to give maximum support to the spine. However, sitting on the buttocks will constrict the spread of the pelvis and curve the spine. The approximate distribution of weight on a stool might be sixty percent on the seat bones and forty percent distributed through the legs. One of the most important elements of the classical seat is that *when very good riders are positioned this way, they exploit the ability to redistribute weight instantly without moving. They can take weight off the seat bones and put it in the thighs, knees and legs if they feel a horse needs help in the back, or for better balance in more violent actions. They can take weight off the legs and settle it more on the back to move the back of a well-trained horse or to inject impulsion through a projection of the center of gravity.* The knees are at the bottom of the thigh and must be fixed to the saddle. As part of the thigh, the knees are one of the principle components in giving the rider this ability to distribute weight more evenly around the whole back and sides of the horse.

Just as a good saddle adheres at the maximum points of contact to dissipate shock, so the rider's seat avoids pressure points. If the thighs and knees come off the saddle, or if the feet are not directly under the hips, then the force of gravity will concentrate the entire weight of the rider, as if seated in a chair, in a few square inches on a small and vulnerable spot on the horse's back. The best saddle in the world won't cure this. Just as important, the knees must be turned inward so that the adducting muscles are developed. Every writer from Newcastle to Podhajsky has insisted that the hips be opened and the buttocks softened. When the buttocks clench, the hips and the

thighs turn outward, and the pelvis can't widen (see Figure 1). The rider's seat will be concussive and shallow – 'on top of' the horse instead of around the back of the horse.

Unfortunately there are still those who teach that clenching the buttocks and curling the spine under is a legitimate driving aid. Furthermore, that using the adductors and closing the thigh and knee will lift the seat bones out of the saddle. In fact, it is when the buttocks are tightened (as when gripping with the calf and contracting the overall leg length) that the seat bones lift off the saddle. The rider's weight becomes dense and dead.

To get a feel of this, sit in the saddle, and relax. With the feet out of the stirrups, you can feel your seat bones. The heels are kept under the hips. Sit up straight, take a good contact with your thighs (turned in from the hips), and press the knees together as if you were trying to break a balloon. Let the calves come off the horse. Make sure that the buttocks stay soft. Feel whether the seat bones actually break their contact with the saddle, or whether they lighten. Then, clench the buttocks and grip with the calves. Where do the seat bones go? When the rider rolls back onto the flesh, contracting the buttocks (Figure 2), the connection to the back of the horse is shrunken and lost. The sacrum and pelvis are pushing forward, thus taking out the natural curve in the spine. The body then slumps and the whole spine is unstable on a narrow base, making balancing very difficult. Any fluid projection of the center of gravity is impossible. The subtle weight aids that will later guide the piaffe and passage and the illusive transition between the two is impossible.

The Zen master Taisen Deshimaru, in talking about the posture of zazen, said: 'In the lotus position, the feet pressing against the thighs activate major acupuncture points corresponding to the meridians of the liver, gall bladder, and kidneys. The samurai of old automatically stimulated these centers by the pressure of their thighs against the flanks of their horse…'[11] (I think it is very interesting that the late Nuno Oliviera used to say that he rode with his kidneys…)

The buttocks should always remain 'doughy' as Seunig said, with the thighs remaining firm and in good tone,

[11]Deshimaru, T., *The Zen Way to the Martial Arts* (Arkana 1991).

Figure 1. When the buttocks clench, the hips and thighs turn outward, so the pelvis cannot widen.

Figure 2. The 'C-'shaped slump.

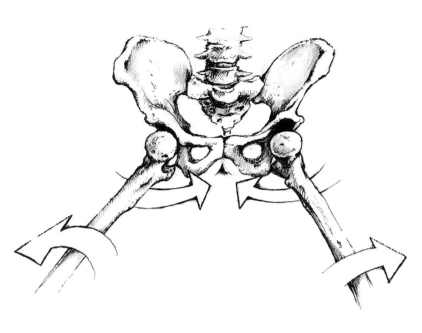

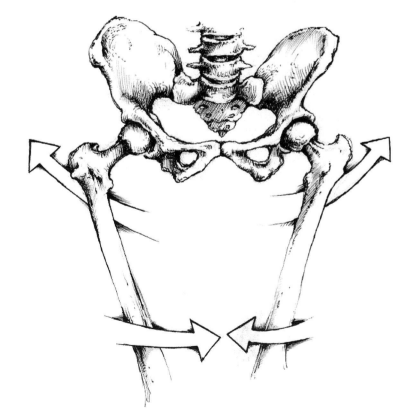

always ready to redistribute weight at a split-second's notice. This is one of the keys to understanding the power of a good seat. Horses respond to weight shift better than signals from a pricking spur or a convulsively tightened calf, or pulling on the bit. Not only is it more ethical, it is much more effective for keeping balance, since it is a more continuous and subtle connection. The spine of the rider relates to the spine of the horse. Furthermore, the horse will tell the rider many things through its back and, like the rider, it will communicate through weight shift. If the horse is sore in a foot or a leg, or if it uncomfortable or nervous, it will shift its weight. A good rider must be able to send signals to the horse and read all of the horse's signals at the same time.

Regarding signals, strong lower leg aids should be used only as punishment. Riders have to learn that there is no relationship between the strength of leg aids and the quality of impulsion. I have always felt that no rider's education can be completed without riding many mares.

As a rule, a mare will not tolerate crude and sustained leg aids and must be ridden with good balance. There is a very important relationship between the center of gravity, the tanden, the seat of the rider, and the center of gravity and balance of the horse. To demonstrate this, all the novice rider has to be shown is how, by posting more strongly in the rising trot, carrying the hips forward in the upstroke, even a young, untrained horse will follow this leading weight and increase the length of stride without the rider having to use any lower leg aids. Gripping with the calves will often slow a horse down and restrict any lateral bend, because a sensitive horse will tighten in the ribs – just as you or I might tighten and hold our breath, if someone teasingly squeezes us in a powerful hug.

Above the seat bones, the abdominal and back muscles surround the spine (see Figure 3). We have already talked about the vulnerability in this area and the attention and strength, both physical and psychological, needed to keep this area straight, thus making the whole body powerful. There is a saying among some Alexander teachers that the abdomen is not a joint. This is a wonderful piece of advice for riders. Many riders collapse here. 'Tummy trot' is an old phrase, which refers to a rider who absorbs the up and down action of the trot by letting go in the abdomen. This fault often coincides with the fault of head bobbing, because the same upper body weakness shows up in the loose neck. When the wave initiated in the seat whips up the rider's spine, it ends up snapping the head. American cowboys ride bucking broncos and violent bulls. They stay on these animals by letting go in the abdomen and absorbing tremendous force in the seat by letting it whip through their upper bodies. This is an effective style for following the action of the animal wherever it wants to go, but it is basically an antagonistic ride. It cannot lead or direct the animal in a harmonic way. In dressage, the principal sets of aids are the weight aids, which are primarily governed by the rider's center of gravity, or seat. (When I refer to 'seat' from now on, the reader should remember that, classically, this word is almost synonymous with the Eastern concept of tanden.) In order to direct the horse, the rider's back must be firm, to help give authority to the motions of the hips. It is this quiet, invisible style that is the benchmark of our art.

If the rider is not permitted to absorb the concussive forces of riding by loosening the stomach and/or relaxing the neck, then another method must be taught. The brain will not allow itself to undergo constant jarring. It will tell the body to let go somewhere else, even though, in letting go, the rider loses control. This is where the entire leg position is so crucial. The femur is the largest bone in the human body; the thighs are the largest muscles. The length from the hip to the heel is a major portion of the rider's overall body length. Here is where the rider has the means to be trained to absorb shock and adjust balance. This is one of the reasons why dressage riders have been traditionally trained without stirrups on the longe. Absolving the rider of the duties of steering and controlling the gaits of the horse allows the rider to focus all the attention, physically and psychologically, on the seat. Over months and months, the rider will master exercises to improve balance and establish a secure base on the horse. The master trainer is relentless in correcting the smallest flaws in position. The student rider must be diligent and patient. The rider's body is often unable to understand all the theoretical nuances, nevertheless it gets formed just as the young horse gets formed on the longe line. That form, if it is correct, will serve the rider for their entire life. If it is not correct, it will haunt the rider the rest of their life.

Richard Wätjen, who has been considered to have had a sublime position once said, 'No fault in rider position was ever corrected by suppleness. Suppleness is the result of riding in the correct position for years.'[12] This is an excellent statement. Riders need to come to riding with the idea of an alert body capable of efficient toning, not slumped or relaxed. There is a great quotation from the brilliant and legendary French music teacher, Nadia Boulanger. An advanced student came in one day and began to present a new composition that he thought was free-flowing and rangy. A little way into it, she stopped him with a stern look. 'Let me tell you something', she said, 'Loose is not beautiful. Loose is loose.' The Zen master, Shunryu Suzuki told his students, 'It is easy to have calmness in inactivity, it is hard to have calmness in activity, but calmness in activity is true calmness.'

The torso of the rider approaches straightness. The shoulders are back and down. Not stiff, as in a military

[12]Wätjen, R., *Dressage Riding* (J.A. Allen 1958).

Figure 3. Key musculature of the rider.

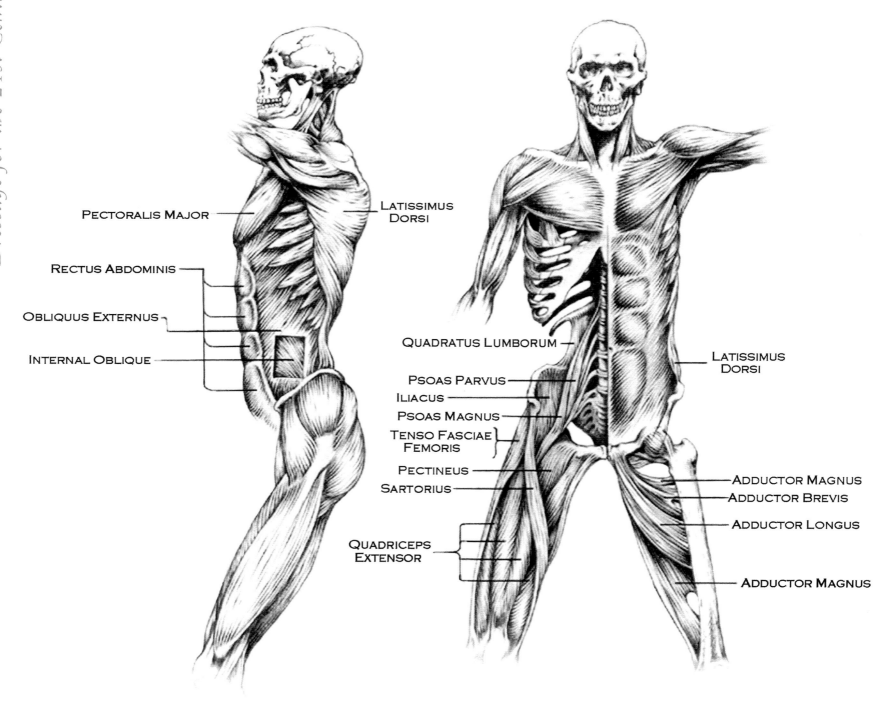

PECTORALIS MAJOR

LATISSIMUS DORSI

RECTUS ABDOMINIS

OBLIQUUS EXTERNUS

INTERNAL OBLIQUE

QUADRATUS LUMBORUM

LATISSIMUS DORSI

PSOAS PARVUS

ILIACUS

PSOAS MAGNUS

TENSO FASCIAE FEMORIS

PECTINEUS

SARTORIUS

ADDUCTOR MAGNUS

ADDUCTOR BREVIS

ADDUCTOR LONGUS

QUADRICEPS EXTENSOR

ADDUCTOR MAGNUS

salute but soft, as if shaking off a shawl – although strong enough to be capable of staying in that position (see Figure 4). If the rider reaches out too far for contact, eliminating the break at the elbows and rounding the shoulders as if offering a tray of hors d'oeuvres, any pull from the horse will tip the rider over. If you sank a pole into the ground, tied a rope to the top and stood a few feet away, it would be much easier to pull the pole over from there than if you tied the rope lower down the pole, or sank half the pole into the ground. If the rider keeps a break in the elbows and keeps the hands nearer to the center of gravity, keeps the shoulders back and firms the lattisimus dorsi muscles (which run all the way down the back), this has the first effect of lowering the rope down the pole. If the rider couples this upper body position with a strong, turned-in legs and low heels, with the knees in firm contact, this mirrors the effect of burying half our pole in the ground. The combined effect is that the rider's

Figure 4. Good riding posture.

body becomes a long lever, incredibly strong. If the horse tries to pull on the reins, it instantly realizes that this is futile (see Photos 22 and 23, page 39). Once the rider learns this position of supreme strength, only purposeful action in the hips is allowed. By this, I mean no more sloppy motions. Aids must become clean and definite, but not hard. As the exercises develop, the rider will learn to direct with the hips with more and more finesse. Suppleness will result, as Wätjen said.

One of the great thrills of my life has been to watch some great riders working away from exhibitions in their practice. Over the years, my eye had to get more and more sophisticated to see what they did with their seats. In the beginning, it often seemed as if there was nothing to see but the horse changing under them. I am sure this is the inspiration Holzing and Decarpentry had also experienced and wanted to stress when they wrote Article 401 of the FEI rules for competition dressage, which says: 'The horse gives the impression of doing on his own accord what is required of him'.

The rider's neck should be extended, with the chin slightly tucked in. Like the horse, the rider must also be put 'on the bit', thus giving strength and length to the neck, and being careful not to push the head forward and lead with it. The head has to be centered over the pelvis, with the ears in line with the shoulders and hip sockets.

From the knee down, the leg drapes. How much of this part of the leg is in contact with the horse depends on the height of the rider and the size and shape of the horse. A short rider on a large horse may have most of the calf in contact, while a tall rider on a small horse may have most of the calf past the belly of the horse. It is purely a matter of the conformation of the individuals. (Bear in mind that the upper part of the leg position is more universal.) The foot should be parallel to the barrel of the horse. Most important of all, it must be directly under the rider's hip.

There is a simple exercise I use with riders who sit too far back (whether beginners or advanced), who have lost their sense of balance. This is to have the rider in the posting trot, imagining four cavelletti on the ground. At a point called out by the instructor, the rider stands up or holds the posting motion like a jumping position for four strides or so. (If the rider cannot clear the pommel of the saddle, the stirrups are too long). Riders who don't have their legs under their seat fall back almost immediately. Some can hang on for a couple of steps, then they will also fall back. Others stick their rear ends out backwards and, sensing intuitively that the center of gravity has been pushed even further back, they dive forward with their heads and upper bodies and usually push their feet out in front. These riders hyper-flex the small of the back, and instead of opening the hip angle and stretching out the bodyline, they close it. Well-balanced riders will have no trouble standing on their legs, since they have been keeping their torso and hips connected in one piece. The whole upper body rises straight up towards or even over the pommel. The knee angle opens. The hip angle opens until the rider appears to be almost standing in a crouch, with all the joints elastically absorbing the impact of the rise and fall of the horse.

This is a great exercise for building leg strength, testing balance and opening and stretching the hips of stiff riders. I often use it to warm up middle-aged riders before the sitting trot. It gets the hips open without the concussion of sitting. A test in this exercise is to watch the rider's head while they are in the posting trot. If the head remains on the same horizontal plane, then the rider is throwing the hips back and forth, breaking at the waist. The back has to remain straight as the hip angle opens closer to the 180 degrees of standing. The rider's head should rise and fall in an exact ratio to the rise and fall of the center of gravity. Besides the gymnastic values of this exercise, it establishes beyond doubt for the rider that they are capable of generating force and impulsion with the seat, a projection of the center of gravity or center of balance. It will be more difficult to learn to do this in the sitting trot, but at least the rider will have felt the sensation and the power accessible in the seat.

The parallel foot is an extension of the turned-in hip. I have seen riders struggle and struggle, torturing their ankles to twist their foot position because the rest of their entire leg is turned out. Good foot position is a product of good hip and thigh position. When the leg rotates in, then, like a heel strike in a karate kick, the toes move out of the way as the leg seeks maximum extension. The heel is, of course, down. It must be down to use the calf muscle with different degrees of tension. If the rider points the toe, or pulls the heel up, the calf will be in complete contraction. Do this, and try to adjust your calf: you see,

it is impossible. Only with the toes up does the rider have degrees of control of the calf. In many cases when riding, merely brushing the horse with a firm calf is enough of a leg aid. There is no elegance in riding with stirrup leathers too long and the toes pointing down. The lower leg aids get wooden, only moving the horse from the bones of the tibia and fibula, or the steel of the spurs, instead of through finer gradations or degrees of muscle tone.

Although work on position was traditionally developed on the longe, it cannot reach its completion until the rider takes up the reins and makes contact with the horse's mouth. The rider must learn a feel that, as the great Guérinière taught, is light, definite and elastic. As the doors of position begin to open, new levels of perception occur. However, it is often unclear to riders what they are supposed to do with this position they are mastering.

The international models presented over the years tend to move in two directions when asking the rider to use the seat, engage the back, and so on, to direct the horse. One model (Figure 5) proposes that the rider try to eliminate the curve in the lower back by pushing the coccyx down, forward and under, tipping the pelvis. As the rider rocks further backward on the seat bones and buttocks (ischia), the pubis rises up, abdominal muscles collapse, and the buttocks clench as the spine shifts toward a 'C'-shaped slump (as illustrated in Figure 2), or a roached back. Since the pelvis is connected to the femur and thigh, when there is a vigorous attempt to use the upper body, abdomen and hips in this way, the rider's leg will often have the tendency to move forward. The rider may fight this kind of recoil by gripping with the calf, or letting it go.

Although almost no dressage book promotes the chair seat (Figure 6) as the correct seat, plenty of instructors routinely teach this kind of seat. (There have been, in recent history, some very charismatic riders/trainers who have ridden with this seat, thus encouraging, by example, worldwide imitation.) It is often explained as a driving seat, or a restraining aid, or as an interpretation of bracing the back. In fact, like a badly fitting saddle that throws a rider backwards, this seat tends to concentrate the weight of the rider over the weakest point of the horse's back and stiffen the horse in the ribs.

In order to put breath behind their voices, singers must expand and loosen the ribs, especially those in the back. I

Figure 5. Skeletal basis of the 'C'-shaped slump (see also Figure 2.).

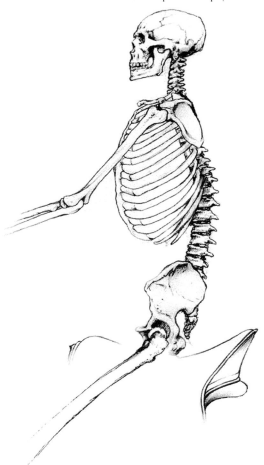

Figure 6. The chair seat.

am totally convinced that this same constriction, a protective stiffening of the ribcage in the horse, is one of the most harmful effects of a bad seat. It doesn't take much imagination to see how far-reaching this kind of constriction is to breathing, and also to all the core organs located inside the ribcage. Depending on how badly the legs have shifted from under the rider's center of gravity, almost all of the rider's weight will be concentrated on a few square inches, right on top of the spine and ribs of the horse. Even when the upper body of these riders appears to be straight, the heaviness of their seats is reflected in unengaged hindquarters and hollowed backs.

In the other direction there is a position (Figure 7) in which the rider again sits on the seat bones but this time exaggerates the curve of the back. The coccyx rises up and, as the rider rocks forward on the seat bones, the pubis goes down towards the pommel. The rider thrusts the chest forward, usually jamming the shoulders back. Once again, because of the connection of the thigh bone (femur) to the pelvis, this exaggerated action above the seat bones forces a reciprocal action of the legs below, as the rider grips with the legs (if strong enough) to keep them from swinging backward. Often, though, the lower leg is way behind the hip, and thus is too far back. This seat often has been described as the 'crotch' or 'fork' seat, for obvious reasons.

When very good riders are observed, it is seen that there is, in fact, not much movement away from the ideal stance-like position (Figure 8) – a position which is described fairly clearly in many books. There is a very real and important reason for this, and it is not aesthetics. Although we often use skeletal illustrations to demonstrate riding position (because they are easy to manipulate, visualize and understand), a good seat and proper use of the back is a matter of very complex, symphonic, changing use of musculature (see

Figure 9). The reason why little movement is observed in the skeletons of very good riders is simply that little movement is necessary. Correct muscular control can maintain the rider's body in a position from which the rider can talk to and listen to the horse at the same time.

Alternatively, this muscular control can, as necessary, steel the body rigid as a pole, or soften it to soothing relaxation without any apparent outward difference. Remember when you were a child and your Uncle Freddy told you to lie on your back on the floor. He told you to make yourself stiff as a board and he lifted you from the back of your neck and shoulders. He tipped you up as if you were a long piece of firewood. Can you remember

Figure 7. Skeletal arrangement in the fork seat.

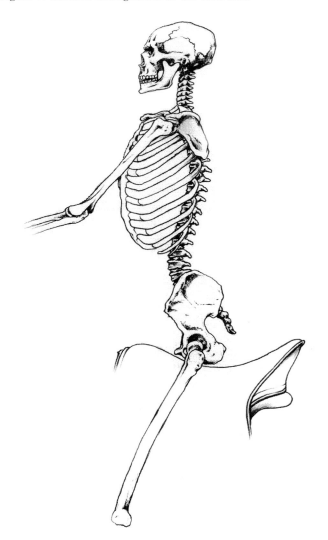

how impressed you were with your magical strength? How easy it seemed for him to tip you up on your heels? Then he said 'OK, same thing, but relax'. You looked the same on the floor but when he went to lift you, your neck gave in and your head bent forward. Your stomach collapsed. He could hardly move you unless he grabbed you under your arms and lifted with all his strength. The temporary rigidity of the first example turned your body into a lever. This is similar to the process that happens in a good rider.

When this lever is connected to the reins, which are connected to the bit and the horse's tender mouth, the rider, using the propriocentric feeling we discussed earlier in breaking the young horse, can feel and then apply leverage to the horse to adjust its balance. Instead of the rider doing the tipping, leaning this way or that, the horse is trained to tip, not from the hand, but from the body of the rider.

It is, for example, entirely possible to take a very strong rider and mount him on a small horse. This strong-legged rider can hold himself into and on the saddle, which is fixed to the horse by a girth. He would be holding the reins, which fasten to the bit. Now no one who has been around horses and riding should have any doubt that such a rider could sit this little horse down on its tail without leaning back very much. For a horse to resist these forces, it would be like you trying to stand still if someone sitting on your shoulders decided to lean stiffly one way.

However, even where this kind of leverage is possible, it is not practical or ethical. Practically, it would be poor training judgment, because the cure is worse than the disease. Such a violent action to lighten the forehand would risk serious injury. Ethically, it is cruel and abusive treatment of an animal. When the Duke of Newcastle said over three hundred years ago that the whole object of dressage was to get the horse upon his haunches, he did not mean by any means possible and without a reliable way of repeating the exercise. Leaning onto the tailbone to pull the curve out of one's back and putting a worse (reverse) curve in, or jerking your shoulders back to hyper-arch the small of your back, are both overkill.

In training human athletes, including riders, to control their lower back curves by developing increased abdominal strength, trainers, doctors and therapists have recently taken a unanimous dislike to the straight-legged sit-up exercise. This exercise, a sit-up with the legs straight and

Figures 8. and 9. Skeletal basis of the good seat...and the external effect.

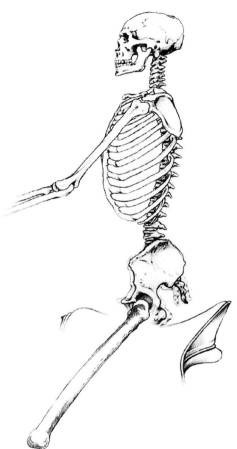

flat on the floor, is a psoas-dominated exercise (see Figure 3). The psoas muscles are attached, via several of the lowest vertebrae, through the pelvis to the front of the legs. This exercise tends to pull an arch into the lower back. (Go ahead – try one!) This arch causes pressure on the vertebrae which, if severe enough, can lead to disc degeneration.

Strong abdominal muscles can counteract this arching, but the abdominals will tire first, putting risk on the back if the exercise continues after the abdominals become fatigued. Sit-ups with the knees bent and only raising the upper body 30 degrees or so from the floor are better for the abdominals and safer for the back. Strong abdominals can prevent too much arching in riding as well.

The complicated muscles of the legs must secure the lower part of this great pelvic hinge or else applying leverage to the horse will be like trying to move a stone with a pry bar that is broken in the middle.

My contention is not only that too much movement in the saddle unnecessary, but it can also be counterproductive. To take the pry bar analogy a bit further, if the rider leans too far back over the weakest part of the horse's back and tries to use leverage, it will be like trying to move a stone this way. Imagine that we place our bar under the edge of a big stone, then we find a smaller stone to set behind the bar to use as a fulcrum. Now we pull our bar backward. The end of the bar is under the big stone, and we are pulling it over the small stone. Unfortunately, the small stone is on soft ground. We pull harder. The big stone is unmovable. The bar is unbendable. But the small stone is being squashed into the ground. The strong rider does the same thing to the horse. Attempting to raise the heavy front end, the rider tries to pry it up by pulling on the reins and leaning back. This only ends up squashing the soft back of the horse down further and further, which forces the hind legs out more and more behind the center of gravity, thus freezing the lumbo-sacral joint.

Both horse and rider must have strong and connected backs, with energy flowing up and down a healthy spine. Leverage cannot work if the horse's back is hollowed, or squashed down. The horse's spine must elongate, connect and have energy flowing straight through. The horse's neck must be in extension. The horse must be connected through the back to the haunches. This then forms its own lever so that the haunches, not the back, sink. The hind legs can come under the body to relieve and lighten the forehand. This is the only possible way. This is why the term 'lightness in the forehand' doesn't necessarily mean lightness in the reins. It is easy to get lightness in the reins – just use a severe bit and the horse won't touch it. However, to have lightness in the shoulders, you need to feel the bit as Guérinière said, 'light, definite and elastic'. The training necessary to strengthen the back and to get the hindquarters to redistribute weight will take a long time. This is the true essence of collection.

This rebalancing leverage starts in the simplest manner with basic transitions and halts, then proceeds to half-halts and more complex exercises. First, the horse is trained to not pull and lean forward and down in transitions. Essentially, the rider tries to keep the balance from falling more onto the forehand. Then the transitions are practiced in a more horizontal balance, a more equal distribution of weight over four legs. Finally, with collection, the horse actually begins to shift more weight onto the hind legs. The reins connect the horse's mouth to the rider's body, which is connected to the horse's body. The firmness of the rider's body blocks the horse from leaning on the reins (see Photos 22 and 23, page 39). There is a big difference between pulling back on the reins to make a transition, and setting the body, with hands connecting into the back, and legs connecting to the pelvis, by which action the hip hinge is stopped. In both cases, the rider will feel weight in the reins but in the first case the rider is pulling, while in the second case, the horse is pulling. Once the horse runs into the fixity of the well-balanced rider, and finds no weakness, the horse will begin balancing itself. On the other hand, if the rider pulls on the reins, then just as when tapping the brakes in a vehicle, the mass will tip forward. The horse will decelerate by bracing with the forelegs

instead of stepping under with the hind legs. No vehicle is constructed like the horse, which almost defies physics by decelerating while tipping back. This is a remarkable phenomenon (see Photo 15, page 26). It is not easy, in fact it is very difficult to do, and that is one of the reasons why true collection is very rare. True collection must be set in place by the proper fundamentals in the earliest transitions.

Later, though the rider never pulling but often stopping the horse from pulling, there is mutual respect. The rider augments the connections of hands to back and seat, and will use combinations of driving aids and restraining aids to suggest tipping the balance back. This is the fundamental purpose behind all the longitudinal exercises of classic dressage. So, then, the difference between an uncontrolled rear and a levade might be eight years of training.

Riders and horses tend to fall into two general groups when learning about leverage. In the first, there are the riders who are afraid to hold the reins and feel the horse's mouth. These riders can never really collect their horses because they cannot create leverage. Likewise, horses that are afraid of the bit, or have no respect for it, cannot be collected or connected and made reliably 'through'. They duck behind the bit or hollow above it, or freeze against it, breaking off any possible connection to the hind legs by these actions of the neck and back.

In the second group are riders who constantly pull straight back on the reins, which actually disrupts good contact, or else they pull to one side and the other. The horse's neck either becomes weakened and looser, much like a wire that is bent too many times, or else it becomes 'frozen' – stiffened and isolated away from the back and hindquarters. Riders in this group grapple more and more in frustration as the horse's neck becomes either weaker and looser, or stronger and stiffer. Either way, the condition of the neck becomes increasingly instrumental in blocking the flow of energy to and from the hind legs. Horses associated with this group can be great pullers, since they have been taught (if even by accident) to use their necks to avoid rein connections going through to the hind legs.

Once the rider understands the principles behind leverage, many riding concepts and master's statements will make more sense. When Guérinière insists on light, definite, elastic contact with the horse's mouth, we know that without that kind of contact there will be no way to train the horse to lever its balance toward the rear. When he goes on to say:

…an error which is fallen into all too easily is to put beginners on jumpers, before they have learned to maintain balance at the trot by strengthening the thighs, in order to hold their seat in the saddle. Those who aspire too quickly to jumping take the habit of holding their seat with the calves and heels, and upon leaving the riding school never fail with their supposed skill to be embarrassed when riding young horses…[13]

we know that the quality of equilibrium in the saddle will require serious training of the upper leg. It is clear what the great master thinks of calf grip! When the Duke of Newcastle says: 'there are three parts of the rider's body, two of which are moveable and one which is not. The immovable one is from the rider's waist to his knees', we see that the rider's back, abdominal and leg muscles must act harmoniously to create firmness at moments when leverage is required, thereby controlling the rider's pelvic hinge. Without these systems working together, one could never hope to collect the horse. When Seunig spends practically a whole page on the importance of the inward-turned thigh and the fixity of the knee, we know that, without a base in the legs, the lever of the body would be hopelessly too short to get the job done.

The rider's body is trained to go in and out of lever mode by muscular control. Timing is everything. Too much tension could frighten a horse. Nevertheless, it would be foolish to say that strength is not a factor. It is, of course – but not *brute* strength. It is the strength of the dancer. There are photographic proofs of riders in the greatest moment of thrust in a capriole, where their seat is off the saddle. All that is holding them in position is their thighs and knees, with the strength of steel. A split second later the legs, still in position, are soft. The seat is settled and deep again. In the highest level of dressage riding, this kind of strength and split-second timing are necessary. Even those who are never going to ride a capriole must learn this kind of leg position, strength and dexterity within their own level. To patronizingly invent a new way to sit on a horse to avoid this discipline is not dressage.

After years of training and repetition, the horse and rider

are sensitive to each other's muscular pulses. For the rider, there is no need for thrusting gestures of the pelvis. The physical training of the dressage rider is athletic but suggestive, not forced. Although the practice of dressage is beautiful to watch, in a real sense, it is not for watching. It is for doing. If it is proceeding correctly, it is too subtle for the observer to see anything change on a given day. Usually, it is just practice. The rider seems to be in a same position day after day but the horse is being magically sculpted.

In fact, there is a physical melding; rider and horse do gradually become one. There is also a psychological melding, which is too often glossed over. Riders become fitted with a 'twin' that gives them literally superhuman strength and speed. This can entail a strange shift in perception. An insecure person's ego can rage, indulging in this newfound power. In such cases, let the world beware! However, if the lessons of the seat go correctly, this should not happen. The shift of perception should have cleared that base human egotistical stranglehold, so that what comes about is a conversation with the horse. When they undertake the study of dressage and position, I don't think many riders realize what is about to unfold – or what they are going to have to face.

It is easy to be corrupted by the power that the horse avails to the rider. It is hard to overstate what a gift the horse gives: this chance to enter back into direct communication with Nature, from which we humans seem more and more estranged. Like the yoga master, the horse starts teaching feelings from the lowest chakra in the seat, and proceeds through a whole process of education. Finally, the horse might be teaching really big feelings, like empathy and compassion. How many horses have died for men? And how many men have ever died for a horse?

The lessons of the seat say that communication can't always go one way. The process needs to be more reciprocal before we can fit back into the real world. When you meet a good horse, you meet nothing less than a great Zen master. If you want the lessons, they are there: reduction of ego, practical balance, to be more comfortable without judgment, to be more responsible for your actions. Remember, when you are learning the lessons of the seat, that you are not only listening to your instructor; you are also getting help on how to listen to your horse. I can tell you personally, you won't believe what the horses are going to tell you!

[13]De la Guérinière, F.R., *School of Horsemanship* (J.A. Allen 1994).

CHAPTER THREE
Straight, Forward Riding

Gustav Steinbrecht was a brilliant German horseman. His book *The Gymnasium of the Horse* is considered to be a German riding bible. He handles all complicated subjects with clear authority. Of all the subjects he has covered, if you were to ask what was his most famous quotation, it would certainly be: 'Ride your horse forward and make him straight.'[1] If people miss this message, it is usually because they mix it up with another very similar quotation from the equally famous French horseman, Alexis François L'Hotte. L'Hotte was an amazing horseman. He has a piece of advice on piaffe and passage that to me is so perfectly written, so crystalline, and so important that later in this book I quote it verbatim. However, if you were to ask knowledgeable riders what might L'Hotte's epitaph be, it would not be his words on piaffe or passage. Without a doubt, it would be his saying: 'Calm, forward, straight'.[2]

Two of the greatest horsemen who ever lived, from two great equestrian nations, gave the same advice. Not to ride the piaffe in one way or another because it is the key to this or that, not some key providing the answer to flying changes. No, ride your horse forward, keep him calm, and make him straight.

Why is straightness such a big deal? And how is it that these riders came to give the same advice?

On the simplest level, horses do not bend the same in both directions. This difference might not be obvious when the horse moves on a straight line, but especially in young horses, it is noticeable when the horse circles. The horse will turn, bend, circle, more easily in one direction than the other. When turning into or toward the stiff side the horse will lean, move sideways off course, block the rein, and in general, fight or struggle with the rider's attempts to straighten it. This stiffness will affect the stride and can make horses appear to be unsound. To this day, few veterinarians understand that this is not pathology, but a natural phenomenon.

In order to illustrate the interaction between the 'stiff' and 'soft' sides, let us imagine that a rider gets on a horse that is fitted with an invisible side rein; one that bends the horse slightly to the right. Turning softly to the right might be no problem. However, on trying to turn left, the rider finds the horse resistant. That side feels stiff and the horse does not want to bend to the left. The rider does not understand why and assumes the horse to be disobedient to the left leg aids. In fact, the horse cannot bend left because it is trapped by the invisible rein on the opposite side. In the simplest sense, a lot of horses come with natural asymmetries like this. A horse that bends reluctantly to the 'stiff' side might in fact be blocked by a restriction on the other side.

After one trains a lot of horses, one begins to realize that specific movements are not really the most difficult part of the training. Some horses need different approaches, but the shoulder-in comes without too much difficulty. For some, flying changes might be trouble;

[1]Steinbrecht, G., *The Gymnasium of the Horse* (Xenophon Press 1995).
[2]L'Hotte, A-F., *Questions Equestres*, (tr. H. Nelson), in Nelson, H., *Alexis-François L'Hotte The Quest for Lightness in Equitation* (J.A. Allen 1997).

others might find them easy. Piaffe and passage are enhanced by strength and practice. However, *all* horses have trouble with crookedness, and this lack of straightness will impact on every one of the movements and, in fact, on everything the rider tries to do. This lack of symmetry can be very complicated. It is so pervasive that, unless it is addressed, not one movement can be considered correctly trained, by classical standards. The rider/trainer realizes the effects of straightness, or crookedness, early on, and recognizes that this problem must start to be addressed early in the training. In any case, it cannot be ignored, and it is very difficult to correct. The two great trainers mentioned earlier knew it, and they tried to teach us.

Where does the crookedness come from? Over the centuries there have been many theories, none of which has ever been proven. I think the most logical answer probably lies in the split brain of mammals. The two hemispheres control different activities, and there is a kind of polarity or 'sidedness', if you will, built in. So much so, that if a creature has an injury on one side of the brain, the result might affect only one side of the body. A common example would be when a human being suffers a stroke. The person can be left paralyzed on one side of the body only, while the other seems unaffected. There is an obvious 'sidedness' present in human beings who are right- or left-handed. Maybe it goes even deeper than that. All biological materials – peptides, DNA, etc. – seem to be 'handed', that is, either oriented clockwise or counterclockwise in their structure, as in the helix of DNA. Maybe 'sidedness' in horses goes deeper than the split brain. Perhaps it is on some molecular level, which is at the core of Nature itself.

Addressing this issue in the horse also goes to the core of the training of the rider, who will come to the practice with 'handedness' and asymmetries of their own. Although straightness presents a difficult technical problem, it also presents an important spiritual and philosophical test. As part of the induction of a new rider/trainer, the teacher must train the student to look deeper, with more sophistication, past the flashy tricks to a fundamental way of going. The advice of Steinbrecht and L'Hotte is simple but, as so often in life, the simple things become the most difficult to do. The classical eye cannot be fooled by the glitter of fancy movements. It always knows how to see deeper, to the fundamental way of going. Thus the quest for straightness becomes a challenge of physical engineering; of understanding and acquiring symmetry and physical balance, but also a spiritual challenge of understanding and acquiring mental balance. Balancing the horse becomes nothing short of an exercise in the symmetry of life: balance in everything we do. The new rider is educated to build the strength of character needed to do what is best for the horse, not necessarily what is best for the rider. (Ultimately, what is best for the horse *will* be best for the rider.) Classical dressage is elitist. Not because of prerequisites of social class, but because few will have the strength to live up to its credos. And one of the most important of these is straightness.

The best riders have always judged the newcomers by their abilities to work in partnership with – even to exalt – Nature. So, in correcting asymmetry, the aim is not to improve upon Nature, but to achieve its highest potential, and to use all of the horse's and rider's talents. It does not matter at all how talented, or not, each individual is. What matters is that, whatever the raw material one is presented with, one tries and leaves no ability wasted, living life to the fullest.

It is an odd thing to be trained by classicists. Once the hook is set you are caught for life. You find yourself, years after the masters have gone, at some party where people are marveling at the newest dressage sensation. They look at you and say 'isn't he (she) wonderful?' In your mind, you curse your old teachers. How they ruined it for you! You want to have fun with the glitterati. You fumble to be polite, for respect was also part of your training. You, by now, have been made legitimately humble by the strict lessons of certain horses! Yet inside, you know that, beyond that rider's handmade saddle, beyond the golden brow-band, the tailored coat and the custom beaver hat, no it is not wonderful. The horse is not straight!

The First Free Steps

In the first stages of riding a young horse, it is helpful if someone can longe the rider. At each end of the session during the last, preparatory, weeks of longeing, the rider should lean on the saddle, take off the surcingle, pull down the stirrups, step into the stirrup, and stand up. In this way, the horse is gradually accustomed to being ridden. For the first few attempts at mounting, it is much easier if the inside stirrup leather is over-lengthened. The rider might not be able to swing a leg over the saddle, but can stand with most of the weight on one side of the horse and lean over the saddle. Some horses that are skittish seem to mind this less than having a tall presence looming above them. With these more sensitive horses, an assistant can move the young horse just a few steps on a small circle while the rider is standing on one side, leaning over the saddle. With both people on the same side of the horse, if it becomes upset or anxious, the rider can step off to the ground with the horse turning around both people, instead of running over one or the other.

Once the horse feels the weight of the rider and accepts how the rider's weight shifts as the horse moves off in its initial steps, it should be no problem to shorten the inside leather, mount conventionally and sit up on the young horse. The side reins will have been removed for the riding, since, as they cannot be adjusted quickly to change direction, they can be dangerous on a free horse. The young horse is still retained by the umbilical cord of the familiar longe line. If the horse is kept on a familiar routine, it will be psychologically reassured by the familiar patterns and all should go smoothly. If it does not, proceed slowly: perhaps just stand still mounted for a few more sessions, or stay leaning over the saddle a little longer. It will work. As soon as the rider feels a certain amount of trust on the part of the horse, the longe line will be unfastened and the rider can go large, gaining support from the school walls.

Contact and Impulsion

The two biggest challenges that face the rider immediately are contact and impulsion. Contact with the reins will make a finite chute, and impulsion will drive the horse into it. It is very important that the rider's hands are steady and mimic the side reins. If the rider tries to be too kind, or coaxes the horse forward by loosening the reins instead of driving it forward, the work of the preceding months spent in positioning the young horse to be on the bit can be ruined, both in terms of longitudinal submission and the acceptance of lateral boundaries. Remember, by the end of the longeing, the horse was circling with a light tether. There were no walls to hold the horse obediently on a perfect circle. The side reins made lateral boundaries and, because the horse respected the driving aids, it stayed in between them.

Not long before writing this, I was longeing a young horse in its early training. It had not yet been backed. Inadvertently, I did not notice the longe line snap was getting old and the pin was stuck open. About halfway through the longeing session, the line fell off and lay in the sand like a perfect radius. The young horse kept trotting. Out of curiosity, I kept going. The horse trotted perfect circle after perfect circle. When I asked it to canter, it did, then went back to trot, and so forth. I was rather amazed, especially because this had not been an easy horse to train. Obviously, though, it had learned better than I had thought. It kept on its circular track, guided only by the chute of the side reins, in which it was kept by impulsion. Horses are very smart. If they find they can pull on the rider's hands and go where they please, they will. So, instead of accepting contact and guidance, it becomes something of a challenge for them to take over and go where they want to.

Obviously, changing rein as in a figure of eight will present the biggest test of steadiness and acceptance of the bit. Up until now, during longeing, we could not have these instantaneous changes of direction. One has to remember that 'on the bit' is not a concept for the horse in its second year of training – it is for now: it is for the beginning. There is a small window of opportunity in which to gain and keep the same submission and respect for the bridle that was obtained while longeing. The rider has to be tactful yet firm. At this stage, timing is everything. If the rider gets through the next few months, the horse can remain light in the bridle, with respect for the bit, for the rest of its life. If the rider misses this opportunity and lets the horse learn that there is a difference between being longed and being ridden, the horse can develop mouth problems that never seem to go away. Such horses constantly challenge the rider's hand. To this end, for the life of me, I cannot figure out why amateurs think that the breaking of the young horse is something they should do, especially if they have no experience! If there are financial limitations, make cut backs later on, but try to have the best trainer possible prepare the young horse. It is important. For the mistakes made can be permanent.

Engagement and Impulsion

The only way to keep the hand steady and the horse seeking the bit is to push the horse toward it with good forward impulsion. By definition, forward riding ensures vigorous engagement of the hind legs. This activity is nothing less than pure exercise, that will eventually build the strength necessary for the carrying power of collection. Engagement can be a confusing concept because some people use the term synonymously with collection. This is incorrect. A racehorse can have tremendous engagement, but show no collection. Engagement has to refer primarily to the reaching under of the hind legs. All young horses need to engage their hind limbs actively in order to build the strength necessary for collection. Attempts to load the hind limbs without a proper forward stage of riding could easily cause the horse to develop evasions, since the horse would not yet be strong enough to collect correctly. A prematurely shortened step that is spasmodic in its rhythm, shallow in the flexion of the hock, hip, stifle, etc., or stiffly bouncy in the croup, can never be confused with true collection. True collection takes time, and has the great, elastic muscular control of a trained dancer.

There is another system of working young horses, which involves a lot of lateral work at walk. This seems to be the antithesis of calm, forward, straight. This is more complex system, which has more of a French tradition – although probably one of its greatest proponents was the Portuguese classicist, Nuno Oliveira. Oliveira would walk young horses in the beginning of their lessons in shoulder-in, haunches-in and half-pass, constantly bending, turning and weaving. He had great equestrian tact and feel and, as the horse worked, he carefully isolated one hind leg and then the other, and taught it to respond quickly. He would engage the left hind in a travers to the right, making it step

up under the horse's center of gravity. Then after a few steps, he would switch to travers in the other direction, or to shoulder-in. The result was that Oliveira's horses were very quietly trained to be very responsive with their hind legs, one at a time. Later, when he straightened his horses and proceeded to piaffe, it seemed that the horses continued to become more and more engaged, collecting mysteriously from invisible aids. Where was this power coming from? It came from a very, very focused training for immediate engagement, one leg at a time, the moment he asked.

Many imitators of Oliveira simply saw the serene, majestic walking and copied the sideways passes. But they did so without the lightning response and engagement that Oliveira was training into his horses. The results from these imitators was the opposite – the horses disengaged by stepping sideways, always more like leg-yielding than accessing the eventual powers of collection. Whereas Oliveira always seems to be getting one hind leg or the other to step up under the mass of the horse, his imitators were weakly letting their horses step over past the center of gravity, or just letting them step lazily halfway under. While Oliveira's horses progressively gained more and more power in response to his aids, his imitators' horses went flatter and flatter, weaker and weaker. The fact that so very few people ever replicated Oliveira's results is testament to the difficulty of this system. It requires great feel to know if the horse is engaging so early in its career – especially at the walk, and even more so when one leg is isolated at a time. There are some very important lessons here, but they are for later – certainly not now in the straight, forward stage of riding.

It is virtually impossible to talk about forward riding without exploring the equestrian concept of impulsion, in particular, impulsion's connection to speed. Alois Podhajsky once said, 'Impulsion is not the wind blowing through your hair'. What he meant, of course, was that impulsion is not necessarily created just by going faster. I think that, in a converse way, discussing speed can illuminate the qualities of movement sought after in dressage. When a racehorse is at maximum speed, the gallop is a four-beat gait. The essence of this is an attempt to spread the action of the legs out evenly, like spokes of a wheel, for a continuous, smooth transference of power. Long moments of suspension would actually slow the horse down. A second interesting aspect of the racehorse's stride is the initial acceleration. In order to accelerate as fast as possible, the horse will take very short, rapid, strong steps to overcome inertia, and will then gradually lengthen the stride to maintain momentum. When, in dressage, forward-moving horses are discussed, neither of these aspects of stride is desirable. Raw speed changes the emotion and the physical stride too much, and, in dressage, hurried steps are almost always a fault (except temporarily, when trying to liven up a sluggish horse).

The propulsion that is sought in dressage, which we call impulsion, has certain special qualities; namely, well-engaged legs with long, unhurried strokes that should result in clear moments of suspension. At this stage in the training, the object is to develop working gaits. The horse should have good engagement, not collection. It should gain enough power from flexing its limbs during their stance phases to follow their moments of suspension with fluid, not stiff, advancement. It should have steady rhythm within the stride, when a series of strides are strung together. (For example, a horse that is sore on one foot will not have an even rhythm of footfalls within each stride, whether it is in the walk, the trot or the canter. *The rhythm of the stride will be uneven.* If a horse is sound, and steps evenly in the individual stride, but it fluctuates by going slower or faster over a series of individual strides, then *that horse is not rhythmic in the gait.*)

The young horse will be impulsive if it also keeps its strides well pulsed with energy (not with the adrenalin of a racehorse – remember, this is calm, forward riding). This energy must pass through a swinging, toned – but never a tensed – back, which is responsible for the transmission of power both in acceleration and deceleration. The rider has to remember that the suspension phases of the trot and canter are part of the stride sequence and must be clear and present, and that they can be proof of prior coiling of the limb. If there is too little impulsion, the suspension phase may float, with the horse hovering lazily over the ground. If there is too much impulsion, the horse could start to hurry to get its feet back on the ground, and push the stride like a racehorse, thus reducing the suspension phase and increasing the speed. (These concepts of

tempo, rhythm, engagement and impulsion will be discussed in more detail in Chapter 4).

The problem with all this talk of forward riding is that, in the early days, the young horse doesn't understand the leg aids. This is where the whip work and voice commands of longeing and the in-hand work will pay off. The horse understands that the whip means forward and that it can also mean to move sideways. Therefore, in these first days, the voice, the click of the tongue and the whip will initiate forward movement. The leg aids coincide until they are firmly rooted by association. At that point the rider weans the horse away from the whip, voice aids, in favor of commands from the leg.

Concurrently, the rider introduces the weight aids and the effects of the center of gravity through the balance of the seat, not in the form of the full contact seat of a conditioned dressage horse, but in the form of the rising trot. Transitions down to the walk and halt must be practiced at this point, more for safety than anything else. We don't want to interrupt this tentative early work too often, but we do use the walk for rest, while still trying to keep the horse on the bit.

I also think it important to introduce some simple leg-yielding exercises, mainly at the trot, but if the horse gets too excited when trotting, we can use these at the walk. If we don't want to develop an insensitive mouth from too much 'steering', we need to train the horse quickly to be guided by our legs. Leg-yielding off a turn down the center or three-quarter line, with an easy sideways traverse (Photo 24) will come naturally to the young horse, especially if it has been prepared by the in-hand work. Once the horse begins to understand the leg aids, so much so that the rider can bend the ribcage, if you will, and push the horse forward and sideways, this is the beginning of one of the foremost important tools for starting to correct crookedness. When the rider signals with the left rein to initiate a circle to the left, and the horse grabs the rein or stiffens, the rider uses the left leg on the barrel of the horse, thus bending the body. This is an attempt to stop the horse resisting and blocking. The rider then rides firmly forward. If, instead, the rider pulls harder on the inside rein, the risk is that the horse will just bend the neck and the rider will inadvertently be teaching disconnection or worse, crookedness. As the horse

Photo 24. When a young horse has been prepared with in-hand work, leg-yielding off a turn with an easy traverse will come naturally.

gets better at answering the leg aids, the rider will have a tool to combat the leaning that most young horses will do, in one direction or the other. If (perhaps better, when) the horse learns to yield to the leg so well that it starts to anticipate and just falls or run sideways, then the rider should go back to a circle or the wall, and ride vigorously forward to re-engage the outside lateral of the horse, which will then drive the turn. A rider who understands the mechanics of turning (as discussed in Chapter 1) will remember not to initiate turns with the outside rein.

Turns are signaled with the inside rein. They are supported and made 'dressage straight' with the outside rein and outside leg (which can be positioned slightly back.) Even a little too much outside rein remaining on for too long, or a rein that is too heavy, can destroy the extension of the outside of the horse, thus compelling the horse either to swing its haunches out, or to tip over like a rigid-framed bicycle. (See Photos 7–12, Chapter 1.)

Canter

During this time, in the context of straight, forward riding, the young horse must be trained to the canter strike-off. If the proper preparatory work has been done, longeing the horse should have included hundreds of canter transitions. So, if the trainer returns to a circle and uses the voice, the strike-off should be successful. Once again, the leg and rein aids will initially be used in association with the voice and whip until the tactile aids alone will initiate a correct strike-off into either canter lead.

The canter is a three-beat gait. The right lead canter, for example, is initiated by the left hind leg, followed by the right hind and left fore hitting the ground simultaneously for the second beat, and finally the single right fore. This is followed by a moment of suspension, after which the sequence repeats (see Photos 25–28). The traditional rider's aids (for right canter) are as follows. The rider's left leg moves a few inches further back than the right leg, which is directly under the rider's hip, near the girth. By moving back, the outside leg (in this case the left), makes the obvious signal to the horse's outside hind to start the canter sequence. Simultaneously, the rider's inside (right) hip advances, in a way similar to a cross-country skier advancing the right hip when bringing the right ski forward: the rider's right leg should exert equal, simultaneous, pressure to the left. The upper body is kept steady and does not twist. The rider pushes the center of gravity forward and projects energy from the tanden (see page 38). The right rein may signal to the horse to flex slightly to the inside and the contact should remain definite. The young horse must learn to come under the rider's weight at the time of strike-off by engaging its hind legs under the center of gravity, and

Photo 25. First beat of right canter: left hind on the ground.

Photo 27. Third beat of right canter – the right fore (leading leg) grounded by itself.

Photo 26. In the second beat of right canter the right hind and left fore strike the ground simultaneously.

Photo 28. The moment of suspension before the canter sequence repeats.

not to throw its head and neck up in an attempt to shift the weight back. It is very important to make these initial strike-offs as straight as possible by using *both* legs and by not using the outside leg too strongly, since this will push the hindquarters sideways.

Let me give you an example of a very common advanced problem that begins at this very early stage. Later, in the Campaign School, the horse will have been trained in shoulder-in, haunches-in, renvers, and half-pass. If you will, all of these exercises are purposely-crooked exercises. The horse will move its hindquarters at the slightest hint of unilateral leg pressure. Eventually, it becomes time to teach the tempi flying changes. But this particular horse was trained to strike-off into the canter from the signal of the outside leg. As the rider changes from one strong outside leg aid to the other, he can't understand why the changes are not straight! Therefore, the rider must take care not only to keep the leg pressure more even, but also to accustom the horse to follow the rider's hip and center of gravity, or weight aids, for direction. In the canter strike-off, both legs create impetus while a slight, asymmetrical shift of weight signals the lead. The rider, again like the skier, brings the right hip (in this example) forward, without twisting the upper body, and the horse learns to bring its right hip forward also. So, although the canter is signaled in part by the rider's outside leg, it is really a complex gesture, which must also be directed by the inside leg and by the rider's hips, which feel as though they pull the hind legs under, the inside hip being just enough in advance to govern the lead. In order to get good quality flying changes later on, these initial strike-offs must be straight, powerful and governed by the rider's weight, not by excessive lower leg aids.

The classical system is old, carefully knitted and built on a very logical progression. The earlier lessons establish certain principles, and repetition reinforces these principles. New lessons are associated with the old, and the complexity develops much like a symphony, with constantly recurring themes embellished in virtuoso specialties. As obvious and redundant as some of this early advice seems, the rider must not be fooled into thinking that it is unimportant. Anyone who does, will have to fix it later. Here are a couple of examples to emphasize this point: the first, a practical extension of the matter under discussion, the second, a more symbolic extension of the overall philosophy.

Although the voice and whip may initiate the first canter strike-offs in the young horse, the rider almost subliminally attaches the more subtle tactile aids, in this case, the slight weight shift and direction of the hip forward, not to the side. If the action is repeated precisely, an association develops between the rider's hip and the horse's. The rider, knowing where the lesson is heading (and that one-time flying changes may not be far in the future), emphasizes its importance and reduces the other signals. In the end, straight one-time flying changes will only be possible if the subtle hip-to-hip relationship is begun now.

Anyone fortunate enough to see the solo ride at the Spanish Riding School, or anyone looking at an old engraving of the same, would notice the rider holding the curb rein in only one hand. The other hand holds the whip upright. The quiet rider guides the horse with draped legs. It is all highly symbolic. The one hand holding the reins symbolizes that the reins are unimportant for control. The whip is turned upright – the rider doesn't need it anymore. This most advanced pairing of horse and rider, demonstrating exercises more difficult than the Olympic Grand Prix test, communicate only through the rich language of the seat. The rider has to bring that sensibility early to the canter work. From whip and voice, to leg and hand, to seat. This refrain will be repeated over and over again if one stays in the practice of dressage.

Counter-canter – Work on the Wall

Once the canter strike-offs and canter itself are fairly well established, segments of the counter-canter may begin. If it understood that the counter-canter was devised to straighten horses that cantered with their haunches in, the riding is self-explanatory. Historically, if the young horse cantered with haunches in to the right, for example, the old masters continued cantering on the right lead but going to the left against the wall of the school. The wall prevented the haunches from moving in and eventually the canter was straightened. This would also work for crooked shoulders. The point is that the counter-canter is a straightening device. When a rider is seen counter-cantering with pronounced bend, the observer knows that the rider has not understood the exercise. Only when the canter is made absolutely straight can the flying changes be considered.

Since I mentioned the tradition of using the wall to help school horses, there is something I want to mention. I have often seen ambitious trainers insist that their young horses and inexperienced riders work off the wall or on the quarter line for long periods. The theory behind this is that the horse and rider need to learn to be autonomously straight. I think this is true for more highly trained horses and riders, but particularly for young horses, it is a pitfall. If the young horse is ridden off the wall, the rider has to hold it more with the legs and other aids. The result can be that the young horse is always 'ping-ponging' between the rider's aids. Furthermore, the horse gets used to being guided by heavier aids. On the other hand, the horse that is guided by the barrier of the wall gains psychological security and is given a perfectly engineered straight edge, which enables the rider to use fewer and lighter aids for guidance. Once the horse is thus accustomed to moving forward and straight, when it *is* worked off the wall, the result can be a much lighter and more responsive horse.

Transitions

When the horse truly understands forward engagement and has an athletic swing in its back; when the signals from the rider's legs and seat generate calm impulsion; when the wave of energy goes all the way up to the bit and does not get absorbed in a pillowy back or a soft, collapsing neck; when that wave is not blocked by a stiffened or crooked neck, then the horse, for the most part, is confidently on the bit.

It is then time to begin to train 'throughness' from the reins to the hind legs via the same corridor of the neck and the back. This time the transitions are not just for safety –

they become an important factor in longitudinal balance. Now is the time to start breaking up the long segments of forward riding with transitions between sitting trot and walk. When this work is kept in short intervals, say twenty strides of sitting trot, five or six strides of walk, the horse's back will become conditioned with less risk of fatigue, because of the breaks. Perhaps more importantly, this is the beginning of the first serious lessons of the complete circuit of 'throughness'.

In the beginning, the chief aim in the transitions is not to let the horse decelerate by leaning into the reins and braking the forward momentum with stiffening forelegs. That is why, at first, we use trot to walk transitions instead of trot to halt. If the horse is kept moving forward through these first downward transitions, it is easier to ensure that the hind legs are staying engaged and are playing an active role in the rebalancing during deceleration. It isn't important to load the hind legs at this point; it is only necessary to keep the horse balanced over all four legs. As that balance becomes established, then it is time to begin the trot to halts. It was the Duke of Newcastle who emphasized how important the halt transitions were in teaching the horse collection. In these transitions the position of the rider is crucial. All these downward transitions are signaled with a passive hand, but are pressed into deceleration with a firm body. The rider's hands feel connected to the waist and hips (rather than the shoulders) as the latissimus muscles of the back become firm and the thighs close (see The Rider's Position page 45). During the transition, two important things happen. In readiness for the first, the rider's body is prepared as a lever at the same time or slightly before the hands signal. If the horse doesn't pull, nothing changes. The rider's thighs control the rider's weight, ensure that the seat is soft and thus encourage the horse's back to come up, so that the haunches can engage and the hind limbs can carry the weight. If the horse pulls and tries to lean onto the forehand, the rider's body is unyielding, so the horse has no option but to relent and try to rebalance another way – the correct way (see Photos 22 and 23, page 39). The second thing that happens is subtler, and is another of those associative connections that the horse learns. Just as the young horse learned progressively to follow the rider's hips into forward or sideways motion, canter strike-off or leg-yielding, it now learns to stop its hips as the rider's hips stop. When the rider's thighs close and the back and abdomen firm up, they can lock the hip hinge, as it were, and the horse feels this arrest of motion and learns to copy it.

These are some of the most important introductory lessons in balance and its association with the rider's seat. On the other hand, a rider who simply goes around pulling on the reins to stop the horse, thinking this is successful because the stops are sharp and square, cannot be surprised if later the horse resists all attempts at collection. This horse has, in fact, been taught to make transitions on the forehand, and then becomes practiced in perfecting them. In teaching correct transitions, the sensibility has to be that these are the beginning of piaffe. Remember, everything in classical riding is layering.

Deep Work

When the horse is respectful of the bit and contact and becomes relatively steady, it is time to teach it long and low work. At first, this is done at the end of the lesson. The horse is allowed to chew the reins out of the rider's hands and stretch downward (Photo 29). When the young horse is trustworthy, and will not buck, then the deep work can be used at the beginning of the lesson as part of the warm-up regime.

There are many trainers who do not use or believe in long and low or deep work. This seems more than anything to reflect a general past bias in the West toward muscular development rather than exercises of the tendons and ligaments. In many sports and some arts, we Westerners have sought to develop physically powerful athletes, and the gains in muscle mass and strength have often been at the expense of flexibility. I say 'past bias' because I think that most open-minded trainers have realized that a lot of injuries are attributable to this system of training. Most athletes today are well aware of the importance of stretching in general, and in fact emphasize it in training regimes, especially in warm-ups. This principle is no different for the equine performer.

There is no question that the best lifting of the back comes with the complementary abdominal contractions that one sees in high collection (see Photos 30, 31). The

Photo 29. At the end of the lesson the horse is allowed to chew the reins out of the rider's hands and stretch forward and down.

Photo 30. The rider suggests stretching...the horse seeks the level it's capable of.

Photo 31. This horse is ordinarily croup-high and long in the back, but in the supreme collection of the canter pirouette the back has been made practically level.

Figure 10. The problem with long and low or deep work like this is that the nuchal system can be slack and the horse may be ewe-necked in spite of being low.

problem is, the young horse isn't capable of this kind of collection and older veterans may need an easier warm-up before they step into such physically demanding exercise. The deep work can begin to condition the back muscles. It could never be used as a substitute for or to supplant training in collection because in this work the muscles are stretched whereas, in collection, they will be contracted. This exercise, however, can be useful to prepare the muscles for the collected work.

In deep work, there are two principle schools of thought. Both require active forward movement from behind. As the hind legs and haunches come under, they lift the back like a see-saw over the fulcrum of the lumbo-sacral joint. The differences lie in the position of the head and neck (see Figure 10). In one school, it is sufficient to have the horse's head low, with the neck stretched. The nose of the horse may be pointed out. The fundamental requirement is that the neck be lower than the withers, so that it satisfies a second see-saw effect in front. When the neck goes down, the back behind the fulcrum of the withers goes up. The problem with deep work in this system is that it is possible for the horse to stretch without stretching along the crest of the neck. The nuchal system can be slack and the horse may be ewe-necked in spite of being low.

In the second school of thought, the horse need not be so low in the neck (but it can be). However, the horse should have more flexion (Figure 11, Photo 32), the nose must be in, and the horse's head can even be slightly behind the vertical. If you want to get a feel for the difference, sit in a chair at your desk or table, and lean forward slowly. Touch the flat surface in front of you with your chin. Next, lean forward slowly again, and touch the table with your forehead. In touching with your chin, you can feel how straight your neck can be – even hollow – down to your back. However, when you touch with your forehead, you can feel the stretch, the pull or curl, all through the neck into your back.

When we work the horse in this second deep-work system, the crested neck ensures the stretching of the great nuchal ligament system along the top line. When the horse is slightly flexed at the poll, this lever action adds a little more pull to this ligament system. Remember, *slightly flexed*. The important thing is that the horse stretches out into an arch. Then, even when the neck is low, it still maintains an arch. It is this arch which stretches the top line of the neck into the withers and pulls the back up behind them. When this nuchal system is stretched, it acts like a spring and with each step an elastic ripple can be felt through the back. (If

Figure 11. Work like this stretches the nuchal system, which arches and lifts the back.

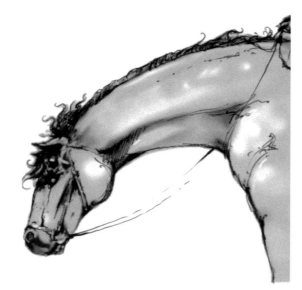

Photo 32. Deep work in correct form (see also Figure 11).

you want to feel the see-saw effect or demonstrate it, stand in front of a mounted horse and place your hands gently behind its ears. In a soft, playful way, pull the head and neck down and let it go, then pull it down again. If you are gentle, the horse won't mind, and the rider on top will bounce up every time you lower the head. If the horse is quiet, you can bounce your friend until he or she feels how the back and neck are connected over the withers.)

It is my opinion that the horse does need to be flexed at the poll to get the best effect of the elastic stretching. Sometimes the horse may be behind the vertical in the deep work. Yet, when the haunches engage for collection, the forehand raises the same arched neck, which will now assume the correct position of poll-high and nose not behind the vertical.

I think it is very important that deep work should be done on as light a rein as possible, for two reasons. The first is that, with the lightest of reins, the horse cannot seek support from the rider's hands. This will build big, elastic gaits while emphasizing self-carriage, even in this long and low position. This, by the way, addresses the biggest criticism of long and low work, which is that it makes horses heavy on the forehand. This need not be so. Although the balance may shift as opposed to collection, it is not necessary for the horse to become heavy. With a little practice, the horse develops psychologically as well as physically, and will stay responsible for its balance with complete freedom of the reins in all gaits. Thus not only does self-carriage improve, but also self-confidence.

The second, and perhaps most important reason to ride this exercise with the lightest of reins, is that, in this way, the rider *will not force the horse into overbending or over-flexing*, which can physically tear tissue and eventually has the opposite effect of stiffening a horse rather than freeing it up. With light reins, the rider can only *suggest* stretching and arching (see Photo 30, page 62). The horse will seek a level it is capable of which over time, of course, should improve and deepen. When this kind of work is juxtaposed eventually with collection, it virtually eliminates sore backs by making them strong and elastic.

Quite recently, in some competitive dressage training stables, a new kind of 'deep work' has surfaced (Figure 12).

This new work is neither long nor low, forward nor down. Whenever the horse comes behind the vertical, the neck is being shortened, as in Photo 33. Only when the neck is in extension in deep work will it keep its connection so that the body is in one piece and 'throughness' is established:

Figure 12. This kind of 'deep work' is neither long nor low. It is not a physiological exercise, but a psychological one aimed at complete submission.

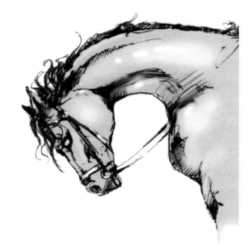

Photo 33. Hand riding like this causes all kinds of distortions in the neck.

the horse does not absorb the rein aids in the neck.

I have found no logical, positive physical explanation for this new type of work. Horses trained in this system often exhibit a similar flaw of being unable to sink sufficiently in the haunches in highest collection – piaffe, for example. This is not a coincidence. Excessive lowering of the head can stiffen the back. What seems, at first, to be roundness, turns into a lock, which seizes the lumbo-sacral area and prevents a coiling under of the pelvis.

I have, however, found a psychological explanation. All this holding the head and neck down for thirty minutes at a time demands submission. In many show horses today, complete submission means no mistakes. This work has turned into a kind of Greco-Roman wrestling, where one party must be pinned down and then surrender to the conqueror. This kind of dominance posturing is the same thing one sees in the disciplining of puppies. (Certain trainers flip the dogs on their backs and hold them there, as another older or dominant dog would do in a fight until they surrender.) I am not suggesting that horses are angels and never need firm correction, but if you base a system of training on domination, it can never reach the realm of art.

There is one place where I have seen this kind of obsession on neck lowering and, oddly enough, it is in Spanish bullfighting where picas are placed in the trapezius area directly in front of the bull's withers for the sole purpose of weakening the neck muscles. The bull then cannot raise its head and horns, which could otherwise be very dangerous for the matador. In a converse way, the more riders keep their horses' heads down, the more they weaken the same muscles of the neck, and the more manageable they make their horses. We know how the bull ends up – it is the goal of the horse trainers that is confusing.

If one took a jumping lesson anywhere in the world, from either a very bad teacher or a very good one, the instructor would jump up and down if one got behind the motion and yanked on the reins when the horse was trying to bascule and reach into a round-backed, arching jump. Yet instructors in dressage are routinely teaching this very thing – to grab the reins and stop the horse from its attempt to bascule, and to pull its neck in. The results of such coarse riding are instantly evident in jumping – a hollow back, head thrown up, pulled rails behind, etc. The results in dressage, albeit just as damaging, are ignored or, worse, rewarded. Cramped necks and hollow backs are common, but true collection will be a function of true engagement, which in turn is a function of true extension of the top line. This means that a horse must be encouraged to seek the rider's hands, and its hind legs must carry and push up into a higher bascule. The rider must not pull the horse back onto the hind legs.

Deep work (Figure 13) is, then, primarily a careful stretching regime, which stresses long movement. It can develop self-confidence and self-carriage when it is done with vigorous movement behind, but with a free rein. It is a healthy counterbalance to the physical demands of collection, and ensures that the horse is kept truly elastic.

Figure 13. Good deep work – or long and low, or forward and down – can embody the old concept of 'the ring of muscle'.

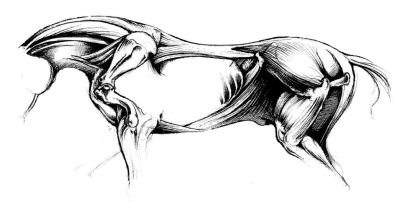

Descente de Main

Warp is a twisting often caused by shrinkage or uneven shortening. Although we will talk more about warp in the next section of this chapter, we should realize that one of the cures for a warped neck would be longitudinal straightness and lengthening of the neck itself. Yet this brings us to consider one of those many paradoxes in riding, the movement or application called descente de main. This is described by General Decarpentry as: 'A relaxing of the pressure of the fingers on the reins which are allowed to slide and gradually lengthen, whilst the horse having first been balanced and placed so that he

achieved perfect poise, rigorously keep this poise, *without modifying his attitude in any way.*'[3] Decarpentry goes on to say that this is basically the classical description. However, during the nineteenth century at Saumur, the great French equestrian establishment, under the influence of Count de Montigny and Commandant Dutilh, descente de main came to mean a totally different gesture. 'An almost completely opposite one, in which the horse, on feeling the same relaxation of the rider's fingers, seeks his bit and lengthens his neck as the reins become looser.'[4]

Now this brings up a very interesting proposition, because the horse can't do both. How is it supposed to differentiate between a release of the reins, which means 'seek my hands, go long and low, extend your neck', or a release of the reins which means 'stay on the bit, keep your balance, don't follow my hand or fill up the loose rein'. This is not an obscure problem because, at the time I am writing this, there are competition dressage tests which ask for these exact same, apparently contradictory, movements! Decarpentry reconciles the apparently irreconcilable by bringing in the subject of leg aids, arguing that, if certain leg aids are used, descente de main is achieved, while others should be used to produce descente d'encolure or, in our case, long and low.

If I can beg to differ with the great General, I feel that different leg aids are not the answer. The whole reason I mentioned this topic is because, to me, the correct answer is a perfectly logical extension of the classical theory, and everything we have been talking about up until now. The way the horse differentiates between these two seemingly contradictory sets of orders, is by feeling the rider's balance. If the rider maintains position as a 'lever' and guides the horse with the seat, then softening the reins as in the second part of the half-halt, or as in descente de main, will be only a momentary test of how self-sustaining this balance is. If, on the other hand, the rider softens the rein and leans forward with the back and seat, the horse immediately recognizes and follows the shift of balance out further toward the front. There are so many times in daily training when the horse

[3]Decarpentry, General, *Academic Equitation* (J.A. Allen 1971).
[4]*Ibid.*

is not correct in the neck (warp is one example), that result in a hollowing or stiff back. Therefore the rider needs to have the ability to adjust the longitudinal shape to get the horse to stretch out evenly in both reins, and free and swing its back.

So, what are we really talking about? Sophisticated French exercises? Descente de main? Descente d'encolure? Or is it, in fact, that very difficult but also simple matter of making the horse straight? Once again, reins continue to be receptors, perceptors, while the actual balancing will be done first in the body of the rider (who must be in good classical position), and then in the body of the horse.

Difficulties in Achieving Straightness – the 'S' Curves

As we have discussed in longeing, the classical ideal of straightness in riding does not really mean 'ship straight' although, historically, there have been attempts to train horses to remain 'ship straight' even in turns, etc. In classical dressage, the hind foot on each side of the horse will follow the track of the forefoot on the same side. Regardless of whether the hind feet track up, under-track or over-track, the important point is that the feet be in *line.* In this straight, forward, segment of the horse's and rider's education, this requirement holds true through the straight lines, all curves and all circles (see Photo 11, page 22). Since the bulk of classical dressage has always been practiced in a rectangular space, the practitioner is obviously constantly turning and changing patterns.

In classical dressage, straightness is, in a real sense, symmetry. We are looking for an exact correspondence of form on opposite sides of a dividing line, namely the spine. All exercises must appear symmetrical. The right rein work must be a mirror image of the left, *even though it is quite possible that they will never feel perfectly symmetrical, nor will there be symmetrical effort to produce a symmetrical appearance.* Such a beautiful balance would be the ideal.

It is hard to say why symmetry is such an important requirement of classical art, and why it is a big part of the definition and appeal in the idea of beauty. Certainly, it has a heavy basis in its connection to health and well-

being. (This is particularly important in performance arts.) In Nature, gross asymmetry is morbidly pathological. If a tree grows too close to a building, so that only one side gets light, it grows in one direction. Eventually, with too much foliage and weight on one side, it becomes extremely vulnerable. A heavy snowfall and a strong wind topple or crack the tree, and it dies. A caribou with lameness acquires an asymmetrical gait, making it slower than its herd mates and thus vulnerable to predation. The pursuit of symmetry is the pursuit of life, and in art the glorification, ornamentation and embellishment of symmetry is really homage to balance as health. The reverence attributed to ideal balance, and the effort expended in its production, are highly pragmatic in essence. The better the balance, the better the quality and length of life. This is also genetically desirable, because the longer the organism lives, the more time there is to pass on those particular genes, and so on down successive generations.

What has all this to do with dressage, and the straight, forward stage of riding? Everything! This is what Steinbrecht and L'Hotte were trying to tell us! It is the foundation stone of classical dressage, both physically and philosophically. Later, in the Campaign School, part of the training will be in the lateral work, which will become the pinnacle of these explorations of symmetry. But these are impossible without a correct foundation of straight, forward riding.

I think that the easiest way to approach the difficulties associated with straightness is to think of the problems in terms of the spine as opposed to the muscles, which are far more complex. The evasions and problems in the horse tend to occur when the spine starts recurving toward an 'S' shape as opposed to a more simple 'C' shapes. However, before one can design exercises to correct asymmetries, one has to define or diagnose them.

The most common root cause of crookedness is that the horse is stiff in the ribcage. To locate that particular stiffness, the horse is ridden down the centerline in a leg-yield. This is performed, for example, coming down the long wall on the left rein, then down the centerline. If that turn is too sharp, continue over a little to the three-quarter line. As the horse is turned, it is bent to the left. The rider applies the inside (left) leg to signal to the horse to bend and bring its left hind leg up, under and sideways, and to move the horse over. More importantly, the rider's leg must be directly under the hip, so that the rider does not lose balance in attempting to 'talk' to the horse through the leg. It is also important that the rider does not lean or shift weight in the required direction, nor uses the reins to step the horse over. This is a very simple test: yielding to the leg, not yielding to the weight aids or the hands, which will come later. The horse should give in the ribs, curve evenly through the body (see Photo 24, page 58) and sidestep to the right.

Next, the exercise is performed in the opposite direction. After a few attempts, it should be clear which side is the stiffer. On the stiff side, the horse will not yield to the leg, or worse still, it will push back against the leg. It will feel heavy in that rein: it won't bend or soften to a signal or arret from that rein. If the proper in-hand work has been done, the horse will be familiar with moving away from the whip and thus curving its body. The horse must now move over from the leg. If the rider is 'stuck' and the horse is getting angry or belligerent, the rider should dismount and refresh the lesson in-hand, being firm, but not hysterical. The horse may be either mentally resistant or physically stiff. After remounting, it may be useful to change the rein and ride the movement on the softer side, which can help break down the resistance, before going back to the problem side.

This simple lesson may take minutes, or it may take days if the horse is in rehabilitation, but the problem must be solved. Once the asymmetry has been identified, the rider will exercise the horse more on the difficult side until greater symmetry is achieved. In our example of leg-yielding, the yielding in both directions should look like mirror images. Of course, the goal is for all work, right and left, to be mirrored. This may take years. Also, it should be borne in mind that, even when a symmetrical appearance is achieved, this would probably not represent a symmetrical effort on the part of horse or rider. It will still usually take more effort to get the residually stiffer side to match the movement of the softer side. However, very soon, the rider will run right into one of the most difficult problems in dressage. The physically demanding side, the stiff side, may turn out to be the less difficult side! The natural stiffness will

actually help keep the pieces of the horse's body – and the rider's own, for that matter – in place.

Unfortunately, the rider does not always seem to know just exactly on which side the difficulty lies. The softer side can become very sneaky, very liquid, and subtle. The two sides are like two very different twin children: one is obstreperous and difficult, but you are always aware of this; the other is a silent child, who broods, and you are never quite sure what is going on. Each has its own challenges. You, as the parent, have to raise them both. *From the beginning, the rider must learn there is never a problem on one side in dressage. If the horse is too heavy on the left, it is almost certainly too light on the right.* The rider must always address the dual nature of a riding problem. One cannot obsess on the stiff or heavy side, just

Figure 14. The horse should maintain an even curve – a shallow 'C' shape.

because it is so obvious. The horse can set itself against the rider, and then repetitions can become counterproductive.

One common evasion of straightness is when, on the arc of a circle, the horse does not maintain an even curve, or shallow 'C' (as in Figure 14), but bulges and pushes through the outside shoulder, thereby forming an 'S' shape (Figure 15). The physics here are usually something like

Figure 15. When the horse bulges through the left shoulder, tightening the left rein is not the answer – that would produce the form of crookedness shown in Figure 16. Instead, the rider must ride out straight, getting the horse's outside (left) leg to drive the outside around, then guide with the outside rein.

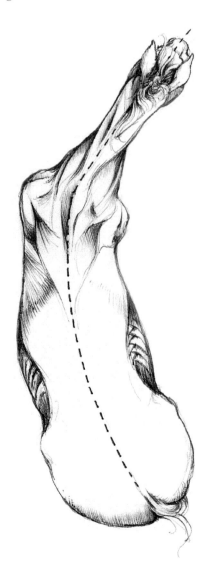

this. A speed skater sets their skate off to the side to push off the slippery surface to start a race. When they push, the body goes forward but it also goes inefficiently sideways. The other leg reaches out, blocks the sideways energy and pushes it back. As quickly as possible, the skater gets the energy going forward without all the sideways waste. If one of the skater's legs were significantly weaker or lazy, the line of travel would develop a drift (the skater would be leg-yielding.) If one wants to go straight, both legs (as motors) must push equally. If a body is going around a turn, the outside leg must push more. Simple physics.

When the rider uses only the outside rein to trap the horse's errant shoulder and bring it back in line for a nice curve, the rider is very often putting a handbrake on the outside hind leg. If the rein aid remains on continuously or too strongly, this is the set up for big fundamental problems. Forwardness will be destroyed, and the calmness is very likely to be disturbed. The horse is forced either to tip over like a bicycle, or to swing the haunches out with the stiffened body (see Photos 7 and 12, pages 20 and 22).

The correction has to be more like that of the speed skater on a curve. We want impulsion and power, and this strength must be developed early in the horse's training. Thus, on a turn or circle, there needs to be more push from the outside hind leg, and less from the inside hind leg. Any outside rein correction to realign the shoulders must be made quickly, and must then be softened to allow that side to extend. The rider must avoid hanging on to that rein. If the horse insists on leaning, turn in figures of eight to disrupt it from locking up. Once the horse is negotiating circles correctly, tracking straight and seeking the reins, driving the turns with the outside leg and reaching through the outside and therefore softening that side, you have accomplished something very beautiful!

There is another 'S' curve type of evasion that can be more difficult to see and feel, but it is rather poisonous. That is when there is an 'S' curve in the neck (Figure 16). Even for the experienced rider, this can be hard to see. In order to check it, the horse must be braided so that the rider has a clear view of the horse's neck muscles. The horse's head will seem to be in the correct position, i.e., positioned to the right on a right curve. In fact, the cervical

Figure 16. Riders who use too much outside rein contract the neck and impede the whole of the outside – to them, the horse seems bent to the right, but it is too short in the neck and the bend is not true ('wave neck').

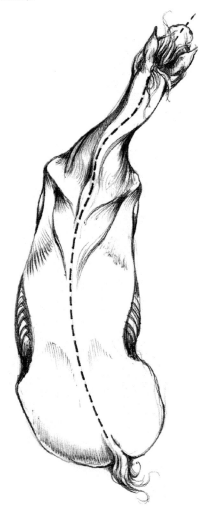

spine is warped, but the thickness of muscle can hide it. In reality, the muscle is also warped and, with the braids, the rider can see this more easily from astride. The horse may be stiff on the right rein, but in fact the base of the neck is bulging to the left.

A lot of things can cause this evasion, but often it is a bit or mouth problem. The hind legs and ribcage can be fine. I think of this problem as warp, and all warp as shrinkage, so the correction has to be to get the neck stretched out. In the situation illustrated, the rider may feel that there is a right rein problem, when in fact the left side of the neck is rigidly braced. A rider who is absolutely

stuck for a solution should go to the long and low work and release the tension. However, the dilemma here is that a clever horse will see the release as a reward, so it is preferable if the rider can loosen the reins and ride more forward on the bit. If it proves really necessary to let the neck go 'deeper', the rider should make sure that the impulsion is kept up, so that the horse will have to keep working its hind legs and won't perceive the change of shape as a rest.

The final 'S' curve I want to address is more longitudinal than lateral. It happens when the rider brings the horse's neck up too high and depresses the horse's back, as in Figure 17. In this kind of reverse leverage, the back can become so hollow that the hips of the horse tip, thus raising the tail, which is the opposite of engagement. The conformation of certain horses predisposes them to this problem. If a horse has a high-set neck (which is ordinarily more desirable than a low-set neck), but this is coupled with a long back and flat croup, the horse might

Figure 17. Longitudinal 'S' curve – sea serpent shape.

not be the best candidate to specialize in dressage. But horses such as this *need* dressage. Their dressage exercises should be aimed at making them strong and connected by riding them forward, keeping the neck and back in one piece.

When addressing crookedness, the rider has to remember that it is a little like fitting braces on a child's teeth. When a good orthodontist fits the braces, he addresses and stops crookedness on the first day. A good rider does the same: from day one, the crookedness will get no worse. However, from then on, the progress is deliberately slow. The orthodontist is shaping the teeth with guiding pressures, gradually, until one day they can come off and the child's teeth are straight. The rider must do the same. The resistances that arise from crookedness cannot be regarded as disobedience. Crookedness is natural; straightness is extraordinary. From this day on, the crookedness will get no worse.

CHAPTER FOUR
The Campaign School — Exercises of the Walk

At the stage of training known classically as the Campaign School, the practice has two essential aims. First, it may be found that, despite the fundamental importance of straightness, it cannot be achieved by just riding straight. Correcting natural crookedness or faults of conformation will require more sophisticated and specific exercises. Moreover, the Campaign School is not just about physical development: it also addresses psychological development. Horses with generous natures very often overcome their physical faults of conformation. Too often, this is without the help and knowledge of the rider. There has always been an argument in some sectors of society that the bigger the impediments, the more character will flourish; that only the strong survive. In equestrian circles, the adjunct to this is – so go full steam ahead in the training! However, good riders and trainers always seem to know better.

All rider and trainers are familiar with the term 'overfacing'. It is really a horse trainer's word. Even a trainer who does not live by it, has an awareness that somewhere there is a line. It is as concrete as the rail height of a jump, and as ephemeral as a certain number of piaffe steps. This is the line, which, if crossed during training, can do irreparable damage to the spirit of the horse. The spirit, mind you. Not legs, or bones, but spirit. We have all been taught this. We all know it, even when we choose to ignore it. This should always be in the mind of the trainer, as the work becomes more difficult. To challenge and train the mental strengths, to tend to the spirit of the horse, the work must never crush the horse. Also, although the horse must be stressed with challenge, there must be time for recovery. In the hands of a perceptive and compassionate trainer, the horse can be stressed repeatedly with challenges, which will build greater and greater aptitudes.

The Campaign School is a committed embarkation upon a special kind of practice. It does this primarily by being dedicated to the learning and mastering of a second stage of exercises, which is comparable to the ballet dancer's class or practice. There are symmetrical exercises performed on one side of the body, then the other. In ballet, these are done at the barre, a horizontal rail fixed to the wall, and at center, the free space in the middle of the studio where the dancer works unsupported by the wall. In part, the exercises of the Campaign School have a very pragmatic, technical, physical goal. However, just as in ballet, there is a second part to these same, pragmatic exercises, as they evolve stylistically in combinations toward little dances, which can be woven into art.

In the previous chapter I mentioned that, in this one, there would be more detail defining tempo, engagement, cadence, and impulsion. However, we need to acknowledge that precise, meaningful definitions present some serious difficulties. Engagement, for example, can mean the traveling under of the hind limbs. Two horses can engage an equal amount and can therefore share a quantitative comparison. However, one of these horses may yank the limb forward in a stilted, jerking fashion, while the other glides it smoothly into the same position. Obviously, there are vast qualitative differences in technique. (This is the area in which dressage as a sport has some serious problems. This is not a condemnation of sport, but a clarification of the classical principles in practice, so they may continue to survive.)

For a moment, let me refer back you to the Introduction, to where the composer Phillip Glass has his enlightening lesson with the legendary music teacher, Nadia Boulanger. After two years, Glass realizes that Ms. Boulanger has been trying to teach him the differences between technique and style. 'The style of Mozart is a special case of style. Your ear can pick up a certain composer's predilection to resolve a technical problem in a highly personalized way. All within the rules.'

When two horses engage to similar extent, and one has a very poor technique, it seems easy to make a comparison and judgment. However, when a 'Mozart' and a 'Bach' both engage in front of the trainer, the ranking becomes totally subjective. The styles of both Mozart and Bach are specialized styles. Both are within the rules. To rank them is to miss the point. In the classical rider's education, the master takes great care to train the student so well technically that the rider can recognize these differences, but simultaneously the rider is trained to expand the mind so as to *enjoy* the differences. One of the great, appealing factors of the quadrille and the pas de deux is the tension that is created between individuals (in some cases, master, riders and horses), and the harmonic totality of the whole picture. It is not how physically close the riders and horses are to one another, it is how psychically close the riders are in their philosophy about riding. There is a palpable tension evident in the differences of individuals who compromise or fit together; who form an ensemble for a larger picture. The spectators, whether they realize it or not, are compelled to enlarge their vision from the base measurements of quantity, to the subtleties of quality. (In talking about pirouettes, George Balanchine, the famous ballet master, once said that two, maybe three were permissible, 'but that after that, the audience starts to count.' One gets the idea.)

This said, I should emphasize that classical riding education does stress fundamental technique. As Phillip Glass says, 'You cannot have style without technique. It is your platform for choices'. Also, it develops the student's faculties to discern what is aesthetically excellent or appropriate. The classical master also teaches 'taste'.

Symmetry and its lofty relationship to art have practical roots. Gross asymmetry has morbid aspects: balance is healthy. Taste also has a very technical aspect. It is not silly, elitist or esoteric knowledge. Students well trained in the subtleties of fundamentals, with solid, healthy, symmetrical technique develop the ability to recognize and enjoy differences – and are less presumptuous. Good education in taste pushes the individual out of insecure, parochial protectionism toward more universal appreciation. In a contemporary and relevant way, the classical master shows the student the historical lesson of Pignatelli's school, which is that the roots of dressage are universal.

In true practice of dressage, the greatest value of that practice is the effect on the body and mind of the participant. There may be secondary and tertiary values of inspiration and education for observers, but it is the individual practitioner who must be trained first.

There are no famous books which tell people how to *observe* dressage. All the important books were written by practitioners for practitioners. If one is undertaking the practice of dressage to show off, then the teachers are failing. Today, too many teachers who know better are failing their students because of ego – of both student and coach. This is not classical dressage. Classical dressage is not riding in a three-cornered hat or a costume. It is defined by the quality of practice. It must be correct inside.

Some Dressage Concepts

In the previous chapter, we looked briefly at rhythm, specifically how it could fluctuate within a single stride (arrhythmic stride) or within a series of strides, slowing down or speeding up within the (arrhythmic) gait. In discussing engagement, we decided not to confuse it with collection or other concepts, but to leave it simply as the traveling under of the hind limbs. A sickle-hocked horse may have lots of engagement; a racehorse may have extreme engagement, yet neither form may be desirable in the horse intended primarily for dressage. The young horse being aimed at dressage needs time being ridden forward correctly, so that it gains simple, energetic engagement and learns to flex and swing the limbs efficiently while gaining strength for the later work.

Let us now examine those other concepts that are fundamentals of dressage: impulsion, tempo and cadence.

Impulsion

If impulsion is not the wind blowing through your hair, then what is it?

Physics uses terms like impulse, impelling force, thrust, momentum, body mass, and linear velocity, but these will not necessarily explain impulsion in dressage terms. For example, what kind of thrust? In dressage impulsion is power, but power regulated.

If one were to go to a human athletics meeting and watch a sprint race, and then go and watch the high jump, one would notice obvious differences. The sprinter, like the racehorse, will want the legs firing in the fastest possible succession. The mass cannot be pushed forward while the legs are floating in the air. For the most rapid acceleration one leg drives and, the split-second that this finishes, the other drives. (Racehorses get so excited initially that, in the early moments of acceleration, both hind legs drive at the same time.) The high jumper, on the other hand, bounds gracefully up toward the bar on a beautiful, arcing line. As the jump get closer, each successive stride bounds the athlete's mass more and more vertical, while also regulating and sustaining, but building to a crescendo of timing.

It might be assumed, then, that in dressage, the horse should show maximum suspension, with little speed. This, however, is a misapprehension. Suspension is easy to see, and people are often seduced by it. In fact an inflexible, stiff recoiling of the legs, like a child's pogo stick, can create suspension. A horse showing the fault of the hovering trot moves like this. It bounds stiffly off tendon and ligament systems instead of flexible muscle. The quality of the stride is really determined by the quality of flexion and extension of the hind limb joints. Strong, controlled, elastic muscle and joint movement is the long-term goal of training. Any suspension must be the product of the preceding flexion and extensions.

There is an old famous dressage anecdote. A man comes to the Spanish Riding School to observe. The chief rider is riding his horse in piaffe. The observer says 'how wonderful!' He recognizes the movement as being the same as he saw recently at the circus. The chief rider, indignant that the observer has missed the quality of the movement, asks an assistant for half a glass of water. He places the glass on the horse's rump and executes a piaffe with such depth and elasticity and balance that there is not enough harsh thrust to upset the water in the glass. He asks the man if his friend at the circus could do that.

Now I hope my friends at the circus will not be upset by such a story. It just illustrates the great difference in the kinds of thrust. In classical dressage, impulsion refers to this controlled quality of thrust. Not the stiff, rocketing extension of the hind limbs, which jars the mass of the horse up and down like a golf ball on a concrete floor.

Tempo

Tempo is the number of strides in a given length of time. For example, an average horse, at the trot, should be somewhere near one hundred and sixty steps (diagonal beats) per minute. However, in dressage, a raw number of strides per element of time is not really the most important part of the concept. (Although, of course, if a horse's tempo is laboriously slow or significantly too fast, this has to be corrected for aesthetic, harmonic reasons, and because it can affect the mood of the horse, lulling it into laziness or exciting it into nervousness and ruining the work.) Where tempo is particularly important is as a proof of collection and extension. If a horse maintains the same tempo whether it shortens or lengthens its stride, this proves that the horse is athletically adjusting its body and the length of stride. These adjustments include the suspension phase and the trajectory of the limbs during that suspension phase. If the tempo slows down during collection, this is evidence that the horse takes a shorter stride by virtue of adjusting and weakening the power. Likewise, if the tempo speeds up when lengthening, this again signals more an adjustment of power and speed, rather than athletic elasticity.

Cadence

Cadence refers to the beat in the rhythm and flow of the stride. Two horses might have the same tempo, and even the same rhythm, yet one horse has a more pronounced beat. Stronger cadence is often a result of more amplification in the stride. It is almost as if, because the horse sends itself up further in the air, it returns to the ground with more force. Yet cadence also encompasses an element of purity of gait. In the trot, for example, some horses' diagonal pairings will be so perfectly in accord that the two legs strike the ground absolutely in unison, creating a pure single note of sound (Photo 59, page 111). In other horses, one leg may strike the ground a split second before its diagonal partner, the result being a fuzzier, muffled beat. Since it announces energy and purity, cadence is always desirable.

The Hard Work Begins

People always ask, if they have a young horse, whether it can go all the way (to Grand Prix). They wonder about the potential. Any experienced trainer (who is not trying to make a sale) knows that early evaluation is impossible. Conformation alone cannot guarantee it. Pedigree alone cannot guarantee it. Attitude alone cannot guarantee it. Many factors are involved. However, once the young horse and its rider reach the stage of collection, the trainer begins to have an inkling as to the upper level potential. This time is exciting. The rider and trainer have waited, and the horse has been patiently prepared for a year or more. Things will start to reveal themselves. With the introduction of collection comes the introduction of some more stressful work – mentally and physically. Rather than give some validation of what a horse and rider can do in the future, this period is sometimes more revealing of what they cannot or will not be able to do, or might not be able to do for now. If one cannot get past this phase, one cannot advance.

Very often, during this phase, the horse realizes that everything is becoming harder work, and looks for a way out. A rider/trainer who has a horse that is willing to try to do everything is very lucky. In most cases, the horse needs

mentoring, pushing (or holding back if it tries to run away from the rider's aids), praise and discipline, further physical development and also development of the mind. It is a case of progressive challenges, with time for recovery, then more challenges. These challenges can take many forms.

Evasion

Evasion is when the horse performs the exercise, but incorrectly. Either the horse or rider does not understand how to do the exercise, or one or the other cannot physically do it correctly because of lack of conditioning. When the problem is simple ignorance, the answer lies in repetition – try and try again. Not necessarily trying harder, but trying smarter. The trainer must have a good knowledge of the objectives of the exercise and experience in executing it. Repetition is a two-edged sword. When, in the majority of cases, an exercise is repeated incorrectly, it is the incorrectness that is getting ingrained in the muscular and mental memory.

The rider has to be careful not to get fragmented by evasions (see Introduction page 5). When one loses track of the fundamentals, all kinds of little feelings seem overimportant. It is not that they are in one's imagination: they are very real, but often they are actually unimportant. Obsessing on them can keep one from finding a cohesive answer to a problem. When things start to go wrong, one has to analyze where they are going wrong, and not just guess. The classical exercises will be shown to be great diagnostic tools as well as cures. Riders say the same thing: 'I don't have much experience in this new movement. How do I know if it's right or wrong?' The rider has to study, to read, to view films, to ask questions, to observe. The whole point is *learning*, not imitating without understanding. And what is even worse is to succumb to peer pressure, and the like, when one knows that something is incorrect, and is in direct conflict with several masters. This can become a way of life that is the antithesis of the classical lessons.

The second biggest cause of evasion is improper conditioning. The exercise is performed incorrectly by the horse or rider (or both) because they are physically not yet flexible enough, or strong enough, to do it correctly. Better physical conditioning is an obvious result of time and repetition. Both horse and rider will get stronger.

I would like to develop this theme a little, in a philosophical vein. In terms of what might be referred to as talent – that is, natural ability – there is nothing wrong with running into the limitations of one's talent. In fact, there is something noble and inspiring about seeing a horse or a human use up all their skill in a dignified way, even if they don't get exactly where they wanted to go. This is the essence of the Zen master's advice to the archer: don't worry about hitting the bull's eye. Get the attitude right; the form right. Get the dignity right. Today, the sight of gloating, giggling winners and depressed losers has demeaned the whole idea of sport, which was to build character, and to train dignity.

When I wrote *Riding Towards the Light*, I described a scene which many people still mention to me, where I was judging a handicapped rider show. A rider really struggled through what would have been a very simple test for an able-bodied rider. She completed it, and when she finished, she rode out of the arena and dismounted. I could still see her, and I noticed that she looked wobbly. Some aides ran to catch her. She either passed out, or almost did, from the exhaustion of the effort. I was so completed overawed by the living example of the mandate to live every day as if it were your last; to do things with all of your effort, that for me, to put numbers on her performance was the most ludicrous idea anyone could have thought up! To this day, it is easy to recall the scene in my mind. I don't think that rider could ever possibly realize how she inspired me, and continues to do so to this day.

In classical riding there is a long and simple tradition, that is very hard to live up to. Every day one must try one's best. There are no excuses. Every movement, every exercise, should be ridden with importance and dignity as if it were one's last. One of them will be.

Resistance

Resistance is really different from evasion. In resistance, the horse tries not to do the exercise. Of course, there can be a fine line between evasion and resistance, but to me it is a clear line, and it might take some experience to discern it. But a good trainer has to know it.

Resistance is usually a matter of dominance. In some of the clearest cases, a horse knows an exercise very well, but begins to defy the rider. The horse challenges the rider's authority, sometimes passively, sometimes very aggressively. Whereas evasions can be corrected with patience, in cases of resistance, dominance has to be addressed more immediately and with little tolerance. (This does not mean sadism.) The world could not exist without authority and obedience. We yield to commands all the time, when they are in our self-interest. For example, if a complete stranger were about to step into the path of a moving car, the observer would yell for them to stop. Not only would the pedestrian obey, they would also be grateful. When the horse can be shown a reason to obey, or when the horse has an established relationship with a trainer, then obeying the trainer is usually good for the horse. It does not become party to a 'power trip' on the part of the trainer. The horse obeys because it respects the trainer, not because it hates or fears the trainer. When a horse is trained by fear, then someday the horse fears something more than the trainer, and the trainer is finished. There is no further constructive relationship.

In the section on Psychological Problems in Chapter 1, I mentioned that, at the start of my career, I was taught that all riding problems had to be solved by riding. When I encountered a resistance like rearing, I realized that it was (and is) very dangerous to ride through it. In dealing with such resistances I learned, through experience, that it is often only necessary to re-establish respect. The particular resistance is often irrelevant. The rider has to regain control and *make the horse do something* – stand still, back up, whatever. The actual command is not all that important – the point is to get the horse to obey. However, make the command sensible so that you have the best chance of success. Better yet, if this psychological control can be coupled with physical control, obeying the trainer will make more sense to the horse. If, for example, a horse that rears is retrained with in-hand exercises, instead of trying to ride through the problem, this is a much safer and more productive way to get the training back on track.

In many cases, dealing with evasions and resistances

should be likened to human physical therapies. If one were to visit any hospital, in some severe cases, the therapy witnessed would seem tortuous. However, the therapist is well trained and is always governed by the goal of improving the patient's condition. Progress, or lack of it, is closely monitored. A medical team constantly supports the therapist. Good trainers of horses operate in the same way. Just as a therapy is tailored to an individual patient, so the training of the horse must fit that individual horse. The trainer consults with veterinarians and associated professionals, farriers, management staff, etc., to make sure that the training is improving the horse's well being, condition and abilities, and is not breaking the horse down in some way. Good trainers train healthy, long-lived horses.

Frustration

There is a familiar cliché scene in films. A detective walks into a store. Something seems suspicious. He makes his way to the counter. The cashier stands there. He asks if everything is all right. The cashier carefully replies that it is. But an armed robber is hiding under the counter: she does what he has instructed her to do. The detective senses apprehension in the cashier, but doesn't know why. His intuition tells him to wait. He makes a little small talk. Her words suggest that he should leave. He stalls a little longer, his eyes, ears, all his senses scan the store. Finally the robber has to move slightly, and his shoe taps the counter. That is all it takes. To the detective, the whole situation is revealed. He finds a way to save the cashier.

If anyone is trying intensely to do something that is difficult, frustration is inevitable. It is easy to avoid frustration — never try anything that is really hard to do. But if one wants to experience life on a complete level, frustration will have to be dealt with. In all my experience, by far the greatest cause – and cure – of disabling frustration is communication. Unfortunately, this is not the communication of intellectuals in a Parisian café. It is more like the communication in the film scene. One person says 'go', but their eyes say 'stop and help me'. They are told, at gunpoint, to relax, but their body language is unmistakable. Their words don't mean what they say. After some scrutiny, a situation becomes totally different.

For the student, the instructor can seem arbitrary, inept, deceptive, and contradictory from day to day. In Chapter 2, we discussed the necessity of learning to resist the brain's logical impositions of order. There is a paradox here: the good student must learn to try to 'hear the cashier'. The student must learn to suspend what seems to be the simplest, most absolute truth. One of the reasons why a good instructor teaches and infuses this cautious suspicion into the student, is an awareness that the instructor's own words may fail the student at times. To succeed, to learn what the instructor is trying to say behind the sometimes-confusing words, the student will need to learn how to hear like the detective in the shop.

In the learning/teaching situation, every person of integrity tries to be honest. But when uncharted waters are entered, who knows what things mean? I remember vividly the day when I first sat on a saddle with no stirrups in the trot. I was convinced that this was not possible to do, and that somehow I had been lied to. But how could I prove it to be a lie, until I learned as much about it as I could? The student and the master have to keep talking. The conversation does not always have to be profound, but there must be a ritual door between them as in Zen studies, where the student routinely must meet and ask questions of the master who guides their practice. If the riding student wishes one day to become an instructor, then it is even more essential that student and master be forced to vocalize their feelings. The masters have to learn and practice how to clarify and elucidate and listen like the detective to their students, and the students must do the same with their teachers. All good teachers are always students first.

There are no rules to this communication: it will be different for everyone. I think it is most important to use the best words possible, but to realize the limitations of words and their inevitable distinction from the world of action. This process will need constant effort. Sometimes a problem is rehashed a thousand times, and on the one, thousandth, time, there is enlightenment.

When teaching, I have always found it amazing how the same phrase can have such different effects in different situations. A certain phrase will crystallize action for one student and mean nothing to another. The only answer I have found to this is to keep talking, even if this is no more than the stalling inanities of the detective until an important clue reveals itself. Then, at that moment, the instructor has to be immediate and accurate in validating the action. If the instructor is inaccurate at this point, this can be the cause of a lot more frustration and confusion. Take for example, a rider and horse both learning the flying changes.

In the beginning, the change might be indistinct because the rider does not realize the horse has changed correctly and thus keeps on asking. This can frustrate the horse. If the change is consistently late behind and the rider is unaware of this, it can develop into a bad habit, which will be hard to correct. In such cases, the instructor's words must set up a course of action and then provide validation of that action. Furthermore, by asking the right questions, the instructor can test that the student is not being 'talked' into feeling something that is not actually being felt.

If the communication between human beings is a source of frustration when both speak the same language, think of the possibilities for confusion when the horse and rider must learn a whole new tactile language. Imagine if someone had lost their hearing, and was trying to learn to sign, but people were giving the student the wrong signs – and some were even punishing the student for not understanding the erroneous language. This is the life of many horses. It is no wonder that many horses rebel, or even shut down. If the horse is going to be reprimanded for disobeying an instruction, the rider/trainer has first to be sure that the horse understands the language. Now, once more, the beautiful, layered construction of the classical system can be seen. All the time spent on practicing position comes out now. The position is the rider's voice, the tactile grammar. The way that the aids are used will determine whether the syntax is understandable to the horse. The better this communication, the easier and better the horse is trained.

The best teachers do not try to give the student every answer to every problem they can think of. The best teachers know that they cannot entirely determine the course of events even on a good day, let alone on the days when things do not go as planned. The horse, it must be remembered, has a life and understanding of its own. The best teachers learn to be flexible. Nuno Oliveira once said

'I am a man with much discipline but no order'. Thus the rider/trainer must learn a way to think and a way to look at things that will make sense to the horse. Through constant practice, a superior awareness develops, and from that awareness different courses of action open up. This awareness does not always follow the rules of logic. It is rarely arrived at purely from intellectual analysis. It is usually best when it is a multi-sensory effort.

I often think that, because all riders are different and all horses are different, in a sense all problems are slightly different. This can make the rider feel alone – as if no one else has faced the particular predicament. However, any rider/trainer who takes up the practice of classical dressage, and plays by the rules is, as it were, 'admitted to the club' and is consequentially not alone. This is because, in seeking help from the words of the past masters, such an individual automatically becomes part of a great tradition Any rider who reads these masters is their student. So even if things seem bleak, the classical student must take courage from the fact that many eminent figures have traveled similar paths, and have left guidelines specifically for this situation. It is the nature of one's study to face the challenges by oneself, knowing that one is part of a great tradition, and from that tradition, help is available.

So there is a trade-off: the rider/trainer must conduct him or herself in the traditional way. It must be as if Pluvinel were observing the situation, or as if there was a lesson booked with Guérinière next Wednesday. When all practice is carried out with this kind of respect and attention, then all becomes imbued with importance. The highs and the lows level out: the rider/trainer begins to realize what a privilege it is just to practice dressage every day.

The Exercises of the Campaign School

It is at this point in the training program that the rider may introduce the young horse to spurs, almost always starting with a short, blunt (mild) pair. The whole idea behind the use of spurs is that they add to sophistication of touch. They are not reductions down to a level of crudity, but rather the opposite. Just as they point towards a more refined response from the horse, so they also require that the rider refine the leg aids and develop the subtlety to use the spurs correctly. With some sensitive horses they may hardly be needed, and it will be a matter for the trainer's discretion exactly when to introduce them. However, at the later high school level, they will be mandatory. A horse that is afraid of the rider's leg cannot be considered classically trained.

In a broad generalization, the exercises of the Campaign School can be divided into two groups. There are those exercises which occur in a longitudinal field, and those which occur in a lateral field. The chief goal of these exercises is to develop a strong, elastic, connected horse. Exercises of bend – the lateral exercises – will promote suppleness and can work toward conquering one-sidedness and the natural asymmetries that occur in horses. The exercises of the straight horse – the longitudinal exercises – develop the horse's elastic ability to change its weight distribution from a horizontal balance over four legs to one a little more loaded evenly on both hind legs.

'Throughness' will develop from these exercises. When this condition exists, the rein action is able to pass through an elastic but strong neck and a supple back into the hind legs. Similarly, the action of the hind legs will be transmitted smoothly through an elastic, swinging back to a lightly held bit. This can only occur when the horse's neck is arched, the spine is in extension, and the ribcage is flexible. The neck carries the head up. The nose is not cramped into the chest, behind the vertical, or made so rubbery that the rein aid is absorbed in a neck 'disconnected' from the body. When the horse is trained and ridden 'over the top', so to speak, the whole top line becomes one piece – strong but elastic. The horse is therefore 'connected'.

In the previous chapter, I mentioned how, in the old Spanish bullfights, picadors speared the bull near the base of the neck, near where the trapezius muscles of the horse are, that is, in front of and behind the withers. Their object was to tire the bull's neck so that it could not raise its head and horns, and would therefore not be too dangerous for the oncoming matador.

When a horse is ridden too low for too long, the same muscles that make the bull proud and deadly get weakened in the noble horse. It has already been acknowl-edged that, just by raising or lowering its head, the horse can change 4 or 5 percent of its bodyweight, either onto its forelegs or towards its hind legs. But 'throughness' and collection will deal with much greater percentages than this. However, as I have mentioned several times, in riding – the actual act of riding – things can be more complicated than they seem.

I would like to offer the rider three points for consideration. They are not in any specific order and, in fact, what makes real collection difficult is that all three must occur simultaneously and yet, in some ways, they are somewhat contradictory.

First, in dressage, the horse is not 'dressed' in order to be slain. The neck is never to be weakened as a means of submission. Like a hunting falcon, the horse must be controlled by training in such a way that, in its best work, it is practically free from restraints. The horse's body must be in the best condition that husbandry will allow – the best food, the best care, the best exercise. When the neck muscles hold the horse's head up, the trapezius, among others, will tie into the area of the back close to where the saddle sits. This will make the most flexible part of the spine more solid. It is the preparation of a strong lever, if you will.

The second consideration is that, although the tone must continue through the back toward the lumbo-sacral joint, which might be termed the hinge of the hindquarters, the back must remain flexible. If the back is stretched to the point of stiffness, either hollowed out or humped up, it will freeze the action of that hinge. In a good piaffe, a good pirouette, or a good levade, the horse will firm up that hinge in tremendous engagement. But it cannot stay that way for long, so the good rider relieves it and changes the exercise. Bad riders seem unaware of the changes in a horse's back or, because of faulty position, cannot change their own seat to do anything about it. No matter what exercises are being presented, when the rider is that ignorant, or the seat is that faulty, the riding is at a novice level.

A third consideration is that, although the rider's eyes are forward, as are their hands and feet, the best riders develop an almost psychic, obsessive instinct as to what is behind them – namely, what are the hind legs doing. This has parallels with the many stories of real martial artists, who are deep in meditation when some young student tries to sneak up behind them to land a blow – but the master is already aware of the student when he enters the garden gate, much less the room.

So it becomes a rider's lifelong job to juggle these tasks, blending firmness, softness and power in the classical 'uphill' frame. If this is accomplished, the horse will be 'through' and that quality will allow the rider to truly collect and extend. If it is not accomplished, all attempts at such work will be a parody.

The Walk and the Universal Theory of Collection and Extension

With the advent of dressage competitions, a lot of attention has been focused on the tracking of the horse's feet at the walk. The FEI regulations imply that collection and extension of the walk can be partially assessed by the tracking of the horse's feet: not quite tracking up with its hind feet into the prints of the forefeet in collection, and over-tracking 'clearly in front of the forefeet' in extension. In fairness to these rules, they do imply that tracking is only one part of the overall requirements of lengthening and shortening the stride. However, some trainers and judges have unfortunately focused on tracking to the exclusion of other, more important, factors, such as the true overall lengthening of the stride, which is harder to see.

In the late 1990s, data for a study on stride length was gathered from just six Warmblood horses. The study stated that the stride length depended on the diagonal distance (the distance between the diagonal pair of limbs when they are on the ground), and the over-tracking distance (the distance between the imprint of the front hoof and the subsequent imprint of the hind foot on the same side). It also concluded that only a small fraction of the increase in stride length results from a longer diagonal distance. *However, the vast majority of the increase in stride length is a result of more over-tracking.*

But if over-tracking in the suspension phase is going to be a key identifying characteristic of collection and exten-sion, what is to happen with the walk, which has no moment of suspension? The study cited that little extension or collection can occur without over-tracking, or under-tracking respectively, and that over-tracking is the result of greater suspension. If we accept this description, then collection and extension will be different for every gait – there will be no universal principles. I believe, however, that classical principles describe collection and extension. It is not gait specific.

In my own measurements over a period of twenty-five years, I have found over-tracking *not* to be an accurate gauge of overall stride lengthening. I have included a recent random sample of eleven horses. These ranged in size from 16.0h to 17.0h, and included Thoroughbreds, Andalusians, Oldenbergs, Dutch Warmblood, and Canadian Sporthorses. I found these particular samplings to be relatively typical of what I have seen over the years. In this sample, the horse with the greatest over-track did not have the longest extended walk, nor the greatest range of increase from collected to extended walk. The horse that, by far, showed the greatest extended walk, and the greatest range from collected to extended walk, did not have the greatest over-tracking. The horse with the short-est over-tracking was not nearly the shortest in overall stride length, nor in the increase from collected to extended walk. One horse increased its stride length by eleven inches (28 cm), with no over-tracking whatsoever.

Almost all horses will over-track to extend the walk, but the amount by which they do so is mainly a matter of conformation. A horse that sickle-hocked (that is, the hind cannons angle forward), will often step way under the body and show large ranges of over-tracking, which do not appreciably change the overall length of the stride as compared to another horse. The flexion of the horse's hips, the length of its back, pelvis, cannons, etc., and especially their relationship to each other, will all affect over-tracking.

It is quite possible for two horses (as measured previ-ously in 1995) to lengthen their respective strides by fourteen inches (35 cm), collection to extension. Even though both these horses had a collected and an extended walk of exactly the same length (and in this case, both horses were 17.0h Thoroughbreds), one over-tracked by twelve inches (30 cm) in the extended walk, and the other hardly over-tracked at all. How is this possible? *Over-tracking is a visual description of the relationship between at least two legs.* The classical idea of collection and extension is based on what each leg does individually, not what it does in relation to another. *Regardless of the gait, each leg has a stance time and a swing time and acts individually.* In that sense, every step in every gait will show suspension. Thus the walk also has a suspension phase, but it has to do with individual leg suspension, which is the key to lengthening and shortening. The key is not the suspension between strides. Any collection or extension will require a symphonic adjustment of all four legs. (Their relationship to each other individually is another subject.) This individual suspension will be created by the individual flexion and extension of each leg, and the trajectory of this suspension will be controlled by the aids of the rider. If the tempo remains the same, in collected or extended gaits, the power might be nearly the same. A cannon, if you will, is loaded with a constant amount of gunpowder. The trajectory of the cannon ball, and the overall distance from the cannon at which it comes to earth, are determined by the slant of the cannon barrel. With the cannon pointed up, the trajectory is higher, but the overall distance is shorter. Lower the barrel and the trajectory is lower but longer. In a similar way, the rider controls the trajectory of each of the horse's feet through complex aids, including the bridle, as discussed in the latter part of Chapter 2.

If the rider holds the mass of the horse over the coiled leg and it fires upward, it pushes the mass up into a higher arc. In some movements, like the canter pirouette, each limb will have great individual differences in trajectory, all within one stride. The pivoting inside hind will be moving nearly straight up and down. The other hind will also move up and down but additionally, it will have to move to the side. The trajectory of its flight will be a longer, flatter 'U' shape. The next foot to move, a forefoot, will also move up and down but it will have to cover a much greater distance sideways than the preceding hind foot, so its flight path will be an even longer 'U' shape. The final, leading foreleg travels the longest distance. Thus the movement of each leg is all very different, yet all are symphonically coordinated – not as pairs, mind you, but as four individuals. Although the relationship between the different pairs of legs is intriguing and revealing for differ-

ent reasons, it cannot be considered the primary describing factor – and certainly not the cause – of collection or extension. This is especially true in any turning movements, which will be naturally asymmetrical.

If one is to think of the stride length as being created by adjusting the suspension phase (swing time) of each leg separately, it is easier to understand how some trots are not pure in their diagonal relationships; how pirouettes work; how walks can extend without over-tracking, and so on. Instead of thinking that 'the increase in stride length is a result of more over-tracking', which suggests that this relationship of two legs is the cause and chief identifier of stride length, it would be better to think of each individual limb by itself. Each has its own swing time, or suspension time. This is more important than where it lands in relation to its neighbor. *The increase in stride length is not a result of over-tracking. Rather, over-tracking can be one result of an increased stride by each leg.* The key distance to be measured is not 'the distance between the imprint of the front hoof and the subsequent imprint of the hind foot on the same side', but the distance from the imprint of the hind hoof to the next imprint of the hind hoof on the same side; or the distance from front hoof to front hoof again. If this principle is adopted, *it will be seen to be consistent with the universal theory of collection and extension, which applies equally to all gaits and all horses (regardless of whether or not they possess the conformation which enhances over-tracking).* When, for example, the left hind leg flexes with controlled power and then extends with controlled power, finally gliding through the air in a graceful arc, that is what is important – not where it lands in relation to the forefoot. That flexion and extension will apply to every step in every gait.

This classical theory of collection and extension will clarify suspension phases as in the passage, which does not fit into the over-tracking theory. It will explain dissociating diagonals, and canter pirouettes in which all four legs act differently. It will also make people judge stride length more correctly. *The only absolutely positive way to know if a horse lengthens its stride in comparison with other horses, is to measure the stride, not the over-tracking.* Furthermore, regardless of the regulatory factors of a specific horse's conformation, the classical consensus has always placed more importance on the *relationship* between various walks than on the size, or scope, or features, of a specific horse's walk. The *range of difference* between the collected, medium, and extended walks, is a product of training: the size of a horse's natural walk is genetic (see Figures 18, 19, 20).

How does the trainer develop the eye to make correct judgments? Looking at films is too remote. Since so much important information is gleaned from the tracks made by horses' feet, perhaps now is a good time to look at some ways of learning this skill. To get a rough feel for stride length, the trainer should block out a space, for instance, in the dressage arena, along the long wall, where it is fairly easy to use two of the marker letters. The trainer stands far enough back to watch the horse pass through the predetermined space, and counts strides. Riders and trainers of jumpers do this all the time, at the canter in particular. ('The in-and-out is a long three or a short four', for example.) The dressage trainer must learn to get a feel such as this for all three gaits and, in time, in free spaces such as the long diagonal. To begin with, however, it is a mistake to make the distance too large, or the eye will get lost. Instead, keep the eye focused on the wall, or on real, or imaginary markers. Rather than following the horse, let the peripheral vision keep track of the horse's movement.

When watching the horse's legs to see tracking patterns, the observer should focus on one foot, for example the right fore. To train the eye, this foot must be observed as it strikes the ground a number of times. After a few strides, the observer's eye should freeze on the track left on the ground. The eye must not follow the leg or hoof. If the attention is focused on the track left on the ground, a split second later the hind foot on that side will come toward it, and then land very near it. The focus must be kept on that forefoot track. The observer must walk quickly up to that track, and when right on top of it, will be able to see whether the hind foot tracked short of it or over it, or if the hind foot steps to the inside or outside of

Figures 18–20. Collected, medium and extended walk. As the trapezius and the muscles of the neck relax, the weight falls forward. The rider allows the whole frame to open up without running. (This horse has a naturally huge walk stride).

I think that the length of the femur is the key to engagement or length of travel. It appears that, while the pelvis may be short, if the femur is short, there is little scope.

Figure 18.
Collected walk.

Figure 19.
Medium walk.

Figure 20.
Extended walk.

the print. If the footing is soft enough, the observer will be able to discern which print is deeper; which has more force. It takes a little practice, but soon the observer can do it repeatedly, even from a distance – when longeing, for example.

All this talk concerning equine biomechanics might lead one to think that assessing the walk is entirely a matter for tape measures. However, when one reads the remarks and directives on the grace of the rider by Pluvinel, Guérinière, or the Duke of Newcastle, one realizes that it is impossible to assess any movement on the basis of the horse alone. The aesthetics of the rider and horse as a team are inseparable. A pas de deux in ballet with the finest female dancer and a clumsy male would be unthinkable. By definition, it is about what they do together. So it is in dressage. Dressage is not just what the horse does. To assess the walk without considering how it is being ridden is, in classical terms, impossible. If someone says 'high quality walk', and one thinks of the horse stepping in a preconceived way then, if the aim is to practice classical dressage, one's thinking must be adjusted. As Guérinière put it:

Grace is so great an adornment for a rider, and at the same time so important a means to the knowledge of all that which is necessary for persons aspiring to become riders, that such persons should willingly spend the time required to obtain that quality at the outset of their endeavours....Given that this accomplishment has been neglected and that nonchalance jointed to a certain laxity has displaced the efforts made in the past to acquire and maintain that attractive seat which so charms the spectator and brings out the beauty of a handsome horse, it gives no cause for surprise to note that the art of horsemanship has lost a measure of its former brilliance. [1]

Gait Variants in Walk

Ordinary Walk to Collected Walk

From the ordinary walk (Photo 34), which is a horse's natural walk on the bit, the rider collects the walk. In the collected walk (Photo 35), the rider is in as perfect a position as possible. The rider gently takes up more

[1]De la Guérinière, F.R., *School of Horsemanship* (J.A. Allen 1994).

Photo 34. Ordinary walk.

Photo 35. Collected walk.

contact with the reins. The connection to the back and the seat is emphasized (refer to text on leverage, pages 48–51 in Chapter 2). The rider's hips subtly keep the horse from losing any power or slowing down the tempo while the step is shortened. The legs are ready to reinforce the seat aids if the horse stiffens even slightly in the mouth or the neck. The rider's back is poised and the center of gravity is directly over the legs. Because of this gathering up with no reduction of power, the step of the horse changes and its overall shape changes. The step becomes higher and might *seem* slower because of the higher arc in the suspension phase. The shape seems rounder, not *because* the overall length of frame has been reduced, but because of *how* it has been reduced. If it were reduced and the horse was hollow in the back, any compression would become grotesque, with the tail pointed up, and the cervical vertebrae strained upwards in a 'U' shape. However, when the horse is already on the bit and engaged in the ordinary walk, a compression of this round form is made even rounder, into a shape which more closely resembles a 'C' (see Figure 21). The compression of the horse's power is palpable. An observer could easily imagine the horse stepping into a cadenced piaffe.

Figure 21. The 'C'-shaped horse. The compression of the horse's power is palpable.

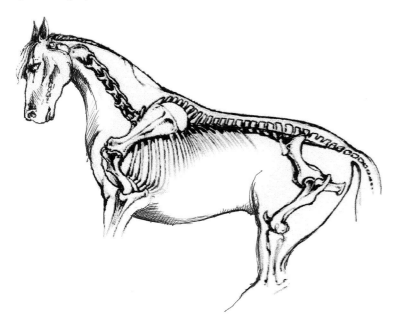

Medium Walk

In the medium walk, the rider releases some of the stored power (see Figures 18 and 19, page 83). The reins advance, but this time it is not a check to see if the horse will remain in balance as in descente de main. Also, there is some release of the rider's own back, so the arresting lever is softened and the rider's center of gravity imperceptibly advances a fraction. The horse feels the weight shift and follows it forward. Once again the legs are ready to reinforce the weight aids, but now they must be careful – too strong and the driving aids could combine to tip the horse too much onto the shoulders. The step of the horse immediately seems less formal as it opens up. This is very much like the way marchers on parade change a little after they pass the reviewing stand.

Extended Walk

In the extended walk the lengthening process reaches its physical limit (see Figure 20, page 83). For every horse, it is different. It does not matter how big the walk actually is. It matters only that each horse and rider reaches it. The challenge of the extended walk is to maintain balance and tempo while the frame of the horse opens up (Photo 36). The reins offer a space for the horse to fill up. The neck must remain up, reaching out, not down; otherwise, the extended walk would turn into a kind of walk on a free rein. The balance would fall too far onto the forelegs and the hind legs would push the weight rather than carrying it.

Walk on a Free Rein

Here, the horse walks at a comfortable tempo. No overt attempt is made to balance the horse. Of course, neither is the horse allowed to misbehave. The back is allowed and encouraged to stretch and swing, and the neck levers down. The hind legs take large but comfortable steps. Free walk should give the feeling of satisfaction, contentment, but also the deliberation of 'going home'.

Photo 36. Extending the walk.

Walk as Rest

The walk is often used to punctuate training. There is the physical punctuation as in any transition between gaits – trot to walk, canter to walk. Here the emphasis is on the gymnastic value of the exercise. There is also emotional punctuation – few quicker bursts of medium trot to awaken a sleepy horse might be one. More than in any other gait, the horse must be relaxed to walk purely. Thus the walk, when strategically placed between other work, will reveal if the rider is making the horse too nervous in its other gaits. The walk can also calm a horse down if it is strategically employed.

Diagonal Walk; Pacing

The walk is a four-beat lateral gait. The limbs advance first on one side of the horse's body and then the other. For example, right hind, then right fore, followed by left hind, and finally left fore, in repeated sequence. Whether the walk is collected or extended, this distinct pattern should stay intact. The horse's body should be free from tension but the gait should appear to have purpose. It should be

going somewhere, not loitering. The neck should be arched in extension, allowing the back to swing, and the hind legs should move freely forward. The poll should be at the high point for the most part, with the whole top line connected.

It is easy to push the walk from a four-beat rhythm to a two-beat rhythm. If the two beats are of the diagonal or contra-lateral pair of legs, the gait will resemble a jog trot, or a trot with basically no suspension. Some old masters would deliberately practice this gait (called the diagonal walk) as a precursor to piaffe. If, in the two-beat walk, the two beats are ipsilaterally coupled (that is, the legs on the same side have the same stance and swing time), then the gait becomes a pace. Old masters also experimented with and trained ambling (as portrayed in the paintings of Eisenberg, mentioned earlier), and exhibited more variations of the walk. However, a modern consensus has evolved which agrees to keep the walk as natural as possible in its four-beat rhythm but, as with the other gaits, to demonstrate collection and extension within the gait.

Lateral Work at the Walk

Virtually all of the lateral exercises used in the trot and canter can also be used at the walk. Each of these exercises will be explained more specifically in the next section on the trot. Very often, however, the lateral exercises will be introduced at the walk so as to limit the confusion and excitement that can occur when trying to teach a new movement with full impulsion. It is easier to first slow down and show the horse the aids at the walk, then increase the impulsion so that the exercise has its real gymnastic value.

Walk Pirouette; the Passade

Faults in the pirouette are difficult to correct, so the movement must be taught carefully and slowly. Probably the easiest method is to go down the long wall in travers (haunches-in), which is explained fully in the next chapter. Near the corner, the horse is collected a little, and while keeping the haunches in, the rider asks the horse to step

Figure 22. Passade.

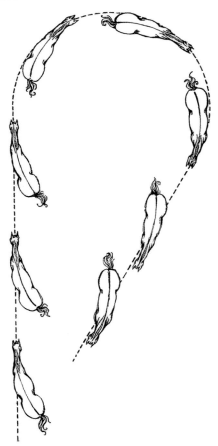

into a small circle (Figure 22). The haunches are held in around the half-circle and, after the half-circle, either the horse returns to the wall in a half-pass position, or on a straight diagonal, or it continues straight once more down the quarter line.

This turning pattern is called the passade, which is not to be confused with the pesade, which is an air above the ground. There are several very important parts to this little exercise. First, if the rider does not teach the horse to collect the stride before beginning the passade (and later before beginning the pirouette), the horse will move into the pirouette with too large a step. When this movement is then performed off a straight centerline, for example, the first step will move way from the centerline, and the horse cannot be brought back to the centerline without a half-pass. Therefore, the horse must learn from the beginning to shorten the step before it starts the turn. This is

aided and prepared by a little shifting back of the rider's own balance. Second, the size of the turn (passade) is not so important as keeping the rhythm of the walk intact. Whether it is 6, 8, 10, 12 meters in diameter, or whatever, in the beginning, keep walking. If the rider tries to make the passade, and then the walking pirouette, too small too early, the risk is that the haunches will spin out, fish-tail, or stop, so that the rhythm is completely destroyed. Third, the pirouette must never be pulled around initially with the inside rein; nor should the rider try to finish it by pulling the horse over and around like a neck-rein with the outside rein. (Later, in Chapter 7, there will be a discussion of the canter pirouette as being one of the finest movements in dressage. This will not be the case if the early training is incorrect.) Balance is so important that just a little too much 'handbrake' will destroy it. The rider must learn to push the pirouette around with the outside leg, which is further back than the inside one. The inside leg, with the inside rein, will help keep the horse bent and flexible, but it is the rider's outside leg, with control from the outside rein, that will direct it.

At the walk, the horse must learn to accept the rider's outside leg and not just swing away from it, but step forward under its own center of gravity. The rhythm must be maintained. This does not mean going any faster,

Photo 37. If the pirouette leans much more than this, it could start to spin.

because if the horse goes too fast and leans over, the inside hind leg does not catch the weight sent over by the outside hind. The horse can then fall sideways onto its shoulders, pushing into a spin (see Photo 37) which is one of the most difficult faults to correct. If the horse learns to spin once it starts the pirouette, this spin cannot be stopped until it is finished, and even then it might be hard to stop. This spinning is contrary to the classical principles because such pirouettes are obviously out of control and out of balance. In the classical form, however (see Photo 38), the rider has such control that, at any given moment, he could ride straight out of the pirouette.

Collection in the passage will evolve almost naturally from decreasing the diameter of the circle. From the larger passage, the rider gradually decreases the size of the circle, immediately going forward, checking with the inside leg

Photo 38. Lines of reference for the classic pirouette.

Photo 39. The rider's weight has shifted over the leg that is correctly driving the pirouette (see text).

and outside rein, if the horse starts to anticipate and spin. The rider will have to be vigilant to ensure that the horse does not slow down or pivot on a leg that ceases to step actively. The hind legs should inscribe the smallest circle possible. Once again, the classical principle, which governs the training of the pirouette, pays homage to the natural gait of the horse. The pirouette should first remain true to the rhythm of the gait. In Chapter 7 we will discuss some dilemmas with this principle in relation to the canter pirouettes, and also the demands on the horse's strength.

Further to this latter point, the rider should try not to use excessive weight shifts to help the pirouette come around – which is often a substitute for not generating enough power before starting the pirouette. Suffice to say, for now, that the pirouette demands so much energy that is not a good idea for the rider to try to execute it before having learned to generate and store power in the horse.

Other than intentional, excessive weight shift, one of the most common positional mistakes is that the rider, straining to learn the pirouette, uses too much outside leg,. The leg goes into more and more contraction until the whole outside of the rider's body collapses over that hip. In consequence, the rider's weight is inadvertently shifted to the outside, setting up contradictory signals as in Photo 39.

If a hiker was carrying a tall backpack, and the pack suddenly shifted to the left, in order to stay upright the hiker would try to step under the leaning weight, and would thus step to the left. If the rider, when trying to execute a pirouette to the right, uses so much outside (left) leg that the rider tips to the left, the horse feels this and will want to rebalance its weight by stepping to the left, just like the hiker did. The left leg of the rider then works harder and harder to push the horse to the right, and the weight falls further and further to the left, thus telling the horse to step left. The inadvertent weight aids are working against the rider, negating the intended aids and confusing the horse. Since most riders, like most horses, have trouble being straight and balanced, this is a major concern.

I rarely give advice which says weight one seat bone or the other, since it usually gives riders license to tip too much, especially collapsing in one or the other hip. Weight aids are never used that way. As we discussed in Chapter 2, the rider's body is firm and lever-like, so that very slight weight shifts in a controlled one-piece body have magnified effects. In more advanced movements, such as the pirouette, subtle weight shifts and weight aids are important. Therefore, an application of the outside leg should be accompanied by the thought of the rider's own center of gravity 'leading' the horse (see Photos 40a, b). There must be no tipping over and 'breaking' at the waist, which would only weaken the rider's leverage. Instead, the back must be kept strong and the hips pushed into the turn, level and sideways, not one hip dipping down. The feeling should be like trying to push the saddle sideways, as opposed to tipping the saddle. If this was done correctly and the girth broke, the rider would be fine. If, however, the execution was incorrect and the girth broke, the rider would fall off to one side or the other.

As intimated, there is much more to be said about the pirouette in due course.

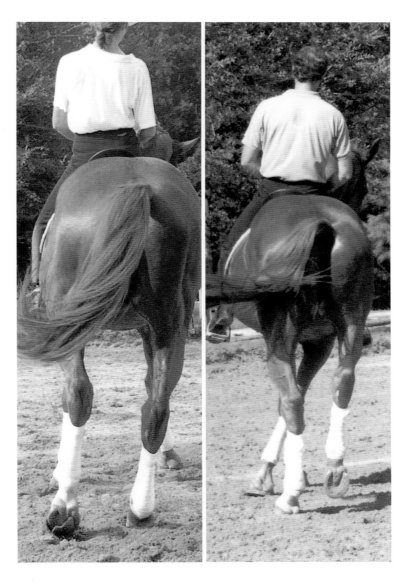

Photos 40a, b. a) Rider's weight has shifted to the outside – a common problem when using too much leg – the body contracts over that hip. b) Correct use of weight to lead the pirouette with the seat.

CHAPTER FIVE

The Campaign School – Exercises of the Trot and the Rein-back

As with the walk, the exercises of the trot also divide into the longitudinal and lateral exercises. Long and low, school trot, collected trot, medium trot, extended trot, piaffe and passage (these last two being discussed in Chapter 7) primarily define the exercises of the straight horse. They develop the horse's elastic ability to change its center of balance by changing its weight distribution from a little over the forelegs, to a more horizontal balance over all four legs, to one a little more loaded onto the hind legs. Leg-yielding, shoulder-fore, shoulder-in, travers, renvers and half-pass are the exercises of bend. These exercises promote suppleness and work toward correcting any crookedness.

Longitudinal Trotting Exercises – More Principles of Collection and Extension

At demonstrations, I often have a horse brought out and we mark the sacro-iliac joint, the hip joint, the stifle and the hock with bright discs so that people can see the bone-to-joint relationships from a distance. I lift the hind leg up and down, showing the audience the flexion and extension of the hind limb joints. Then I take the same leg and bring it forward the way a farrier would place it on his knee or on a stand in order to work on the sides of the hoof. I explain engagement. At that point, I always ask: 'If I have good flexion and extension (I am holding the leg and moving it up and down), and I have engagement (I bring it forward), do I have collection?' Some audience members jump in, but most are cautious. The answer is no, because the limb is not carrying any weight. I am holding it up with my hands. The horse has been trained to kindly lift its leg and hold it up, with a little support from the farrier, but mostly carrying weight on the other three legs. Of course this is theatrical, but it illustrates a very important principle: there can be no collection without a redistribution of weight onto the hind legs.

The practice of training the hind legs to carry weight in collection is at the heart of this classical concept. We have already discussed the mechanics of collection and extension in terms of power and the trajectory of limbs. Now we have to realize, as Steinbrecht said, that the horse's four legs do not have equal capacity to generate power, since the fore and hind limbs are not constructed the same. The horse does not move like a spider – the hind legs are the real motors. As we will see later, in looking at some faults of the piaffe and passage, if the forelegs try too hard to generate force, this can present real problems. The calm, forward stage has strengthened our young horse. Now it is time to make the horse stronger still – and more adjustable.

In Pignatelli's time (the sixteenth century), in the Duke of Newcastle's and Pluvinel's times (the seventeenth century), and then later in Guérinière's era (the eighteenth century), the whole object of dressage was to get the horse upon the haunches. To a great extent, the clear goals of jumping the horse off its hind legs (the high school airs), tested many a trainer's idea of collection. There was no question about where the balance was or, better still, where it should be. A trainer might fail, but he would know what he was trying to achieve. As time went on, the object of redistributing weight more over the hind legs remained strong. Early in the nineteenth century, Goya produced equestrian paintings similar to those of his predecessor Velazquez, who had painted the monarchs of his era beautifully in the levade. There was a long tradition of high-prestige works of art showing riders in this pose. The fine porcelain statues of the Spanish Riding School riders in perfect levades, which adorn many bookshelves around the world, are important symbols. To be seated on a horse in a good levade indicates high status. Why? Because even if one did not know how to do it – or why – everyone knew that the levade was a pinnacle achievement of collection.

High, cadenced piaffes and passages also became symbols of elegance. Being able to change the balance of the horse and redistribute weight off the forehand could save these weaker limbs in transitions, thus offering them physical relief and freedom of expression.

From time to time throughout the history of dressage, there have been assaults on this part of its practice, but no long-term results were ever achieved. One of the most intense assaults was spearheaded by the charismatic French rider, François Baucher, in the nineteenth century. Baucher's work incited a vitriolic equestrian civil war, the effects of which are still tenderly felt today, especially among French-educated riders. Baucher ignited the fire when he said: 'I proclaim it, the gathering of a horse had never been understood or defined before me for it cannot be perfectly executed without the regular application of the principles that I have developed for the first time.'[1]

This attitude was not enough for classicists to condemn him. Many great riders have inflated egos. The Duke of Newcastle was no shrinking violet! What caused the intense rebuke from riders and writers like Steinbrecht, was that Baucher was really saying that he disagreed with the previous historical concept of collection, the corner-stone of which is that the horse balances more towards the hind legs. As we have just noted the levade, which epitomized this, was held in high esteem even by those people without knowledge. The 'real rassembler', Baucher said, 'consists in collecting the forces of the horse in his centre in order to ease his extremities…The animal finds himself transformed into a kind of balance of which the rider is the centre-piece…The rider will know that his horse is completely gathered when he feels him ready as it were to rise from all four of his legs.'[2] That is what did it. Not his legacy of flexions and quotable mottoes. They were all adornments and additions to his fundamental challenge: 'The horse, when completely gathered will rise off all four of his legs' – not his hind legs!

Baucher tried to redefine collection. In his mind, everyone before him who insisted, as Newcastle had, that the whole object of the schooled horse is to get it upon its haunches, had to be wrong. Baucher said that the horse should move like a spider with equal balance in every direction. Of course, the horse is not built like a spider, and collection is not and never has been a concept of balancing a horse in the middle. Baucher suffered and his idea of dressage suffered. This was not because of equestrian politics, but because the great body of experience proved over and over that gymnasticising a horse in the classical way was healthy. To a very real degree, all the arts of collection came after the pragmatic realization of its physical value. Any riding that somehow missed that point would be an empty shell. So how does anyone miss this point!

When a horse piaffes without carrying any weight behind, with no sinking of the haunches, no rebalancing over the hind legs, this is fairly evident even to a moderately trained rider. Unfortunately, it is too late to wait until piaffe training to see that the horse and rider never understood collection. However, it is much more difficult to

[1]Baucher, François, *New Method of Horsemanship*, in Nelson, H., *François Baucher the Man and his Method* (J.A. Allen 1992).

[2]Baucher, François, *New Method of Horsemanship*, in Nelson, H., *François Baucher the Man and his Method* (J.A. Allen 1992).

really see if the young horse is collecting in the early stages of training. It is a subtle feeling. Until the rider accumulates enough experience to train horses to collect, that rider needs to work on a regular and consistent basis with someone who has done this. Occasional visual validations from horse show judges, who too often do not have practical experience of training horses, just won't work. Almost all good trainers will ride their students' horses from time to time to check on the feel and, most importantly, the progress or lack of it. When a young horse starts to try in a new movement, it may not look very impressive but the feeling can be very, very significant. The response of the rider is just as important. In training, looks do not always correspond with feel, especially in the early stages. That is how people can miss the point of collection – by trying to learn to look for it instead of developing a feel for it. Consistent, qualified help from an experienced trainer is essential.

The key to collection is that, unlike man-made vehicles, the horse has the mechanical ability to decelerate and not necessarily tip forward – see Photo 15, page 26. (In physics it is common for any decelerating horizontally shaped mass to tip forward.) By flexing the hind legs and swinging the powerful haunches down and under the center of gravity, the hind legs can be employed to do the bulk of the braking, instead of the forelegs doing this job. All the longitudinal trotting exercises hinge on this fact and are embellishments of this phenomenon. Collection develops the power and flexibility of the horse's 'motors'. Extensions are, in a sense, relief from collection but they are also proofs of collection. If a horse cannot immediately lengthen the trot, there is a good chance that the previously collected trot had no power. If nothing can be let out, nothing was being stored up. Collection and extension should be like the proverbial cannon – the same amount of gunpowder, only a different angle of the barrel.

Working Trot

The working trot is the trot of the calm, forward stage. It becomes the baseline trot, and usually in tempo it is about 160 steps (diagonal beats) per minute. From that baseline working trot, the horse can be either shortened toward the collected trots, or lengthened toward the extended trots, but always holding the same tempo. The name itself, 'working trot', derives from the requirement that the trot itself be working and also that a lot of work will be done in that gait. The working trot should be vigorously moving. The horse should be expending energy to the extent of mildly taxing the body in order to build muscle. The working trot is more or less midway in the range of trots, so its balance is more horizontal than the collected form, with weight more evenly distributed over all four legs.

In the calm, forward stage a lot of the initial working trot is ridden rising. In Chapter 2, I mentioned the importance of establishing a relationship between the rider' own center of gravity and the horse's, and this relationship with impulsion. Here, all the theory of the seat must come together with practice. The young horse has already been trained to follow the direction from the projection of the rider's center of gravity in the posting, or rising, motion – the opening of the hip angle off the solid base of the rider's legs, with the thigh turned inward, etc. This is one of the first weight aids. Already there is a marriage of the balance of horse and rider.

Now, the rider drops into the sitting trot. It is an athletic movement and the young horse may stutter in carrying the now-constant weight. The horse's back is not trained yet. If the rider 'gives up', and leans back, thereby collapsing the abdomen and gripping mostly with the lower leg, this will probably be associated with a slight pull on the reins as the rider tries to 'hold on'. What does the horse feel? There is a total abandonment of the language, which is still new between horse and rider. All of a sudden, the direction from the rider's seat is gone. The horse slows, the rider punishes it with more lower leg aids, contracts the base of the seat and leans more heavily, thereby pushing the seat directly into the young horse's back. To make matters worse, the rider pulls on the reins. All the driving into a reaching-forward bascule is arrested. The horse has no choice – either it stiffens its back in self-defense, or it drops its back in surrender. Without good position, these important first lessons of the rider's seat are a mess, and from here they just go on getting worse and worse.

What happens when the classical rider sits the first

continuous steps? First, the abdomen does not collapse and the seat bones, while now remaining on the saddle for both beats of the trot, stay pressed forward, more toward the pommel than the cantle. In this position, it is easiest for the horse to carry the rider. The engaged back of the rider directs the center of gravity to keep pushing forward and at the same time keeps the rider from leaning backwards, which would compromise the balance and disturb the horse. The thigh and knee do not move; they remain right under the rider's weight. Therefore it is no problem for the rider to cushion the young horse's back during the first full-seated steps by using a little more thigh, knee and perhaps upper calf.

This same classical connection of the thigh and knee will give the rider's seat the adhesive qualities which prevent the slapping concussion that would deaden the swinging wave in a horse's back. Riders do not lose their seats on the upstroke of the trot, even though the force beneath the rider pushes the body upward. If one were standing on the ground and an earthquake suddenly pushed the earth up, one's knees would buckle, but one would stay very close to the force beneath. Riders lose their seat when the horse reaches the high point of its stride trajectory and then falls. If the rider's legs are too loose, the rider's body continues to be propelled upward. The saddle falls, but the rider keeps going for a split second, creating a gap. The rider is now left slightly behind. The horse hits the bottom of its stride trajectory and starts back up. The rider, still falling, crashes into the upcoming horse. Their connection is broken. If the rider does not somehow get back in sync, then, like some novices, each successive collision will amplify the discord until the rider is launched out of the saddle. Good riders use the knee and thigh connection to maintain contact with the saddle so that they can add to the wave-like swing of the back and stride, and never deaden it. (I was once watching trampoline gymnasts and noticed it would often take them twenty or so bounces to get the necessary height for their aerial maneuvers. But they could stop the trampoline, even from a height of some thirty feet, in one deadening bounce. Imagine how easy it is for a rider's seat to stop the wave in a horse's back, which only rises and falls a few inches!)

Flexible hips don't just absorb the motion defensively.

They direct it and keep the horse 'in front of' the aids. Not only does this additional steadying leg support help make the seat light, it also gives the seat aids additional authority should the horse try to slow down. *Because the rider is so well balanced, there is no need to use the reins for balance. The hands, being truly independent, even allow the young horse to lean into the reins a little, thus encouraging neck extension, which will help keep the back from hollowing.* The horse is also kept straight by being channeled between the reins. This is all a function of the fact that classical lessons are complementary. The first lessons of the rising trot lead into the first lessons of the sitting trot. The horse is not confused by constant, arbitrary changes of body position by the rider.

Sometimes, in spite of the rider being in a good position, a horse will 'take its back away'. Usually, horses that do this are improperly started horses; sometimes they are lazy, with poor dispositions, and a lack of a willingness to work. If the rider has taken all steps necessary to ensure that there is nothing *seriously* wrong physically (remember, horses can be good actors!), then the rider must persist at sitting for longer periods. In these particular cases, to get up in the rising trot and 'freshen the back' is a mistake. The horse will quickly realize the difference and will convince the sympathetic rider that it is unable to cope with the additional work of the sitting trot. The rider must remind the horse that it is good for them. In re-training horses, this is one of my less favorite things to do. The rider's body will have to do all the work of absorbing the energies of the trot because the temporarily stiff back of the horse does none of the work. If the rider sticks with it and rides the horse forward, *and if the seat is not punishing*, the horse will give up its suspicion and start to relax and swing again in the back, and come up and carry the rider.

When a horse tries to keep its back stiff laterally, circling is very beneficial. The rider can't go very far in the working trot before realizing that the horse is stiffer on one side than the other. When horse and rider are going down the long wall, or are otherwise on a straight line, and the horse (in this case, being stiff on the left) leans into the rider's left leg and rein, the rider must not overuse the half-halt or checks on the stiff rein. It is too easy to make the horse even more crooked because the neck will give in before the body does, and the body is the real source of the problem. Instead, the rider should try to keep the reins steady, but use a circle to the left. Remember the rowboat? To turn to the left, the right oar needs more energy. Whenever one rein is too heavy it is almost certain that the other is too light. The horse is not reaching into the bit on the right side, but is staying contracted on that side – commonly called the hollow side. The rider must make the right hind leg drive the circle and stretch the right side out. Of course, the rider's inside leg must encourage a softening in the ribcage. Remember, though, that a rider who overbends to the left in an attempt to remedy the stiff side will end up with two short sides (see Photos 10 and 11, pages 21 and 22).

At this stage in training, we are just about to begin collection, but we are not mastering it yet. So, to get the hollow or short side to stretch out, the rider should keep using circles strategically when the horse leans at its worst, and will thereby thwart the horse in its attempts to be crooked. Then, as the horse strengthens with exercise, it will also grow straighter instead of the other way around.

Collected Trot

The collected trot is developed from the working trot and becomes a trot in the same tempo. However, the collected trot covers less ground because the body travels in a shorter and higher trajectory. There is more flexion in the limbs of the collected trot than in the working trot – but then again, there is more flexion in the medium or extended trot than in the working trot. What is really different is that, in the collected trot, the rider restrains the forward urge by keeping the horse's feet more consistently under its mass. The result is that, when there is a complementary extension of the limbs, the force is more vertical. The flexing and extending rhythm of legs is not interrupted; it is adjusted. The rider is almost balancing the horse's body back so that the horse's legs can push the body up. Since the hind legs do the lion's share of the pushing, by definition, more weight will be placed on them. Of course, this is not accomplished by holding the horse back with excessive rein aids. I have already discussed the physics of the rein aids. If a rider pulls on the reins, the braking action will tip the mass forward just

as your automobile tips forward when you apply the brakes.

The Value and Execution of Full Transitions, Square Halts, and Half-halts

Full Transitions

As I have said, a working trot is one that is balanced fairly equally over all four legs. If the rider can stop this trot without allowing the horse to lean to the front or brace its forelimbs and thus brake the impulsion, there will automatically be moments of collection before the full arrest of the forward motion (momentum). The Duke of Newcastle said this hundreds of years ago: 'The best exercise I know to put the horse upon the haunches is to trot and stop, trot and stop'. However, the secret is all in *how* you stop.

If a rider undertakes a course of transitions for training purposes and, at each halt, uses the reins to stop, exactly the opposite result to Newcastle's advice will be achieved. The horse will be trained to stop perfectly, even very quickly – on the forehand. The result may be obedience, but there will be no collection. However, if the rider stops the horse by firming the body, closing the thigh and locking the hips from further motion, then when the horse tries to lean, it will be solidly blocked. At this point, early in training, there may be weight in the reins – in fact, there will almost certainly be weight in the reins. However, the rider does not pull back, but simply does not allow the horse any pulling forward either. It is all very ethical. This is very important. When the horse cannot lean and the rider's position is quiet but engaged (legs firm, heels down), to prevent the horse's haunches from escaping to one side or the other, the horse will have to use its hind legs to decelerate. If it does, the rider is on the way towards collection. Repetition will train the form and build the strength, so that the horse will learn to tip to the rear. In learning collection, both horse and rider must learn that *neither* is allowed to pull on the reins.

Square Halts

When a rider rides into a halt transition with good power, and the balance is focused more toward the haunches, the halt will naturally tend to be square. This is because the horse stops itself with good use of the hind legs and settles down onto the forelegs. It finally balances over all four legs, which seek the four corners of the earth, as it were, to stop and hold the power coming down. If the horse stops lazily, that is, the feet are all spread out, the rider must not look down to correct the feet after these initial transitions. This would teach the horse that it is all right to stop anyway it wishes, because it will be allowed to correct and square up the legs afterwards. Rather than trying to correct the foot placement, the rider should trot off again, crisply. Any lagging leg will have to get in position quickly to drive. If this is repeated over and over, the halt is not taken by the horse to be a rest period, but it is almost on alert to stop to listen. The horse will then start getting in the habit of preparing itself for the upward transition by not letting the downward transition 'fall apart'. Without even looking at the feet, the rider must be able to feel engagement, and must keep up the energy. Then, the halts will usually square up all by themselves.

However, if after a while the horse still habitually seems to rest one leg in the halt, the rider may have to correct this leg. In this case, it is preferable to halt near a mirror, so that the rider can check the horse's legs without leaning over in the saddle and looking down, which will unbalance the horse. Furthermore, since tapping with a whip or spur to square the horse almost always follows this leaning-look, the horse becomes suspicious, by association, about shifting weight in the saddle. The horse may begin to get fidgety. So now there are two problems: one, the halt is not square, and two it is not immobile.

If the rider simply glances in the mirror to assess the legs, position and weight will be unaffected. If the left hind is out of position, the rider may attempt the correction by a tap with the whip or a bump with the leg on the left side, the theory being to remind the horse to put weight on that foot and bring it under the body. The problem here is that whip or leg aids on one side mean engage that leg – move it up and under. If the horse stops with its left hind leg lagging way out behind, it makes

sense to tap that leg and bring it up. However, if, for example, the leg is under but resting and the rider taps it with the whip, the horse will only lighten it more in attempting to answer the rider's aid by stepping up. If resting one leg in this way becomes habitual, it makes more sense for the rider to use the opposite leg – the rider signals the right leg to move, even if it is square. As soon as it prepares to engage, it takes the weight off itself and transfers it over to the left. The horse must then stand up square on the left or, theoretically, it would fall down. Any groom who has ever tried to put a bandage on a horse that cocks a hind leg knows this method well – tap the other hind foot and the one the groom wants to wrap will stand straight. If the rider keeps attacking the empty, unloaded leg, this will only make that leg more and more unstable.

Even in the halt, the rider must always think of follow-through. In tennis or golf, for example, the player does not meet the ball and stop; the follow-through is an integral part of the action. It is the same in riding. The halt has to be considered a space in the ride, just like a pause in music, where the silence retains an electricity. The power is held in suspension – in control. For this very reason, excessively long halts should be avoided, as they tend to let the young horse's mind wander. Instead of building concentration and attention to the rider, a 'what's coming next?' attitude, the horse can be trained to become bored and wander mentally. However, all of riding is balance in various forms, so it should also be evident that a rider who goes overboard and does too many brief halts can make the horse nervous and unsure. Like a good sheep dog, an intelligent horse learns to think for itself and to anticipate. Yet it never forgets that it is part of a team, and this functions best if the horse and the rider work together.

The Half-halt

When the horse can execute full transitions between gaits, the rider will need to establish a technique for rebalancing within a gait (because otherwise it would be necessary to keeping stopping in order to re-establish balance). This technique is the half-halt and, in a very real sense, it is simply half way to the full halt. In riding literature, this term can often be very confusing. There are endless different descriptions of rein aids (light, heavy, outside, inside, both) and driving aids (seat, back, seat without back, legs with seat, legs without seat, etc.). The reality is not that these descriptions are wrong, but that they can have such great variation because each application is dependent on the horse, and how much it takes to get the horse back into balance. Thus the real definition of each half-halt is peculiar to its use.

Essentially, the half-halt is a technique designed to change a horse's balance – always toward the hind legs. The half-halt, or multiple half-halts, can be used in the middle of the trot phase to rebalance the young horse if it starts to tip further and further onto the forehand. The half-halt can also be used if the horse is currently in good balance, but a movement that needs more collection is coming up, and the rider needs to balance the horse even further back. Since balance itself is so dynamic from horse to horse – and even from day to day on the same horse – adjusting it will be even more variable and dynamic. In one instance, it can be a light check on one rein if the horse leans slightly toward one shoulder. In another case, it could be both reins and a solid, engaging back and even the use of pressured legs to set up a canter pirouette off a straight line, for example when a horse is going too much forward. If the horse is crooked, or bent, the half-halt can be purposefully unequal in one rein or the other, on one side of the body or the other. It is essentially a levering technique, so the reins are always used in conjunction with the back and seat, and sometimes also the legs, when riding. (The half-halt can also be used in in-hand work.)

In a full halt, the rider's hips stop, signaling the horse's hips to stop. In a half-halt, there is only a momentary arrest. Half-halts are normally used in repetition, and must be short in duration. If the rein aids are held on too long, instead of insisting on self-carriage, the reins become the support of an invisible cane. The best half-halts work like descente de main – a momentary arrest, as the hind legs come under more. The rider remains in good position and releases the reins to see whether the horse is carrying itself any better. If it is, the rider tries to leave the reins as light as possible until the balance falters, and then comes another half-halt and another release. (If the half-halt lasts too long, it will actually have the opposite effect.) The best riders use more and smaller half-halts to keep track of

the balance, rather than one or two big, wrenching ones. It becomes a conversation of feelings, not unlike a high-wire walker with a balance pole. As with the circus artist, the rider constantly makes minor adjustments for the smoothest progress.

The School Trot

The school trot is even shorter and more collected than the collected trot. The hind legs carry even more weight. It is often used as a preparation for the ultimate collection of the piaffe. Trainers who think of it as obsolete will often unknowingly use it in the exercise of collected trot to almost trot-on-the-spot and back out into collected trot. This evolving process of continuous collection of the trot will culminate in the piaffe and passage, which will be covered in depth in Chapter 7.

Medium Trot

On the other side of the working trot from the collected form are the medium and extended trots. One of the first things that comes into play in the development of the longer trots is speed. If the trots are all to remain at the same tempo regardless of whether the horse lengthens or shortens, then it must be understood that speed will be a by-product of lengthening. If the horse takes twenty collected strides and twenty extended strides at the same tempo, it will cover much more ground in the twenty extended strides than in the twenty collected strides, in the same amount of time. Covering more ground in the same time means it is moving faster. Thus, when introducing the medium trot, the rider must know that it isn't the raw speed of travel that is to be kept the same as the working gait; it is the tempo. In other words, the rider cannot, and should not, stop the horse from speeding up when it lengthens, but the rider must watch that the tempo does not increase. Depending on the degrees of cadence, swing and balance that the horse has in its natural stride pattern, it can be easy or difficult to introduce the lengthened trots.

To begin with, a rider who has natural gifts, or has

practiced well, can remain sitting in the trot, which should afford the best control. However, if the horse is naturally a little short-striding or tight in the back, it is probably better to use the rising trot, so the horse will have no excuse not to free up the back a little for the longer reach.

Some years ago, I remember seeing articles in good equestrian magazines about the difference between 'leg movers and back movers'. This can be a good way to think about the training of extensions. Back movers are elastic in the back when power is added to increase the limb and gait suspension. They are more like our human high jumpers, bounding to gain loft, maximizing the vertical force, rebounding off their seemingly rubbery bodies and legs. Horses with longer backs tend to be more elastic than short-backed horses, but this is not always so. If the back gets too long, it gets weak and even if such horses seem to lengthen well, they cannot collect. Horses built like this are often impressive at the lower levels for their beautiful, long movement, but seem to disappear in the medium levels. Leg movers seem to have adequate reach in the shoulder, but they move closer to the ground than back movers. While they can show good reach, the back seems stiff. The limbs move like the legs of tin soldiers.

My experience is that the actual length of the horse's back is not the key as to whether it will be a leg mover or a back mover. It is simply that, if the back is too tight, the horse will naturally be too stiff to be a back mover. For horses of this sort, it can help to introduce lengthening in the rising trot. Also, it can be helpful for the rider to introduce some of the longer steps on a very large circle. Here, the horse will have to stretch the back a little to accommodate the requirements of the curve, and this 'letting go' will help show the horse how to keep freer in the back while adding power. These horses want to be like the human sprinters – as soon as one leg finishes driving, the other one is engaged. It is as though they feel the rider's leg and seat and immediately assume that more speed is required of them.

The following technique is one that can be easily misunderstood, yet it is the secret to turning ordinary movers into good movers. It is one of the best ways to free up the horse and get more energy into the stride, but it is not the easiest way. The rider should stay in the sitting trot

and reduce the tempo. When it can be kept regular (and this, oddly enough, may mean using a lot of interrupting transitions to teach the horse to wait in tempo), the rider will then try to amplify the stride and increase the cadence. This does not mean faster, nor does it mean using a lot more leg aids. It is done by using the back, seat and weight. The feeling is a little like bouncing carefully on a trampoline with a small, very subtle jump. The rider's body must be firm to drive the energy wave, but flexible enough not to shock it. As the horse's mass falls in the downstroke of the stride, the rider pushes it down by deliberately letting the hips and seat push down. Of course, the horse is moving forward so the wave will be moving forward also, as well as up and down. Then, on the recoil, the rider's thighs adhere to the saddle and the rider tries to lift the upstroke just a little higher and forward. The seat bones stay in contact with the saddle, and thus in contact with the back. The rider must have a good seat, because any punishing concussion will stiffen the wave immediately, just as if someone steps onto a trampoline while someone else is jumping, and the bounce is deadened. If, with a firm abdomen, the rider repeats this action of exaggerating the rising and falling, the rider's body will gain more vertical force because it is not absorbing energy by crumpling. The rider will feel the horse free up. It is as if the rider's weight is being used to massage the stiff horse. There will be a harmonic amplification in the undulation of the stride – the 'wave' will grow. Once the rider can amplify the cadence until it has more suspension, the tempo can be taken back closer to normal, power being added with the leg aids.

This amplification of stride is only possible if the rider has a strong, flexible and balanced seat. If the rider is chair-seated, or the attempts to 'bounce the stride' are too crude, then instead of getting the legs to flex and extend more, the back will simply sink and hollow. Although the rider will feel an increased undulation, it will have no effect on the horse's legs. If the legs don't flex more on the downstroke, it will be impossible to get more force from the extension on the upstroke. Needless to say, if any of the muscles tense in this technique, it won't work.

The lengthened trots are best introduced along the wall. The clean line of direction will help to keep the horse straight when lengthening. If the horse holds too much residual crookedness and the stride lengthens it will become uneven and, if more power is added or the shape is lengthened further, the horse will naturally break into canter. A second, associated, problem is that if the horse is not straight and the rider lengthens the stride across the diagonal, the crooked horse will drift in the free space. Then, when the rider tries to push the drifting horse back on line, the rider's strong leg aid again gets perceived as a canter aid, and the horse breaks gait or loses power because he is fighting the correction from the leg. This actually ends in a shortening, or quickening, of the stride. Both problems are corrected by the rider making sure that the horse is very even and straight before opening up the frame.

In most cases, rapidity of steps signifies tightness, tension and speed. However, with some 'bad' movers, sometimes the only way to open up the stride is for the rider to teach them to stretch their stride by picking up the tempo. This teaches the horse that it must drastically increase the effort of the trot. Once the horse has begun really trying, the stride will lengthen. After a while, the horse will begin to understand that it has this new kind of gait which, albeit too fast, has more length. At this point, the rider begins gradually to slow the tempo back down, but retains the length. Eventually, the horse will stay more lengthened when the tempo is slowed to a more normal rate. The obvious risk here is that the rider will make the horse tense or nervous if this strategy is kept up too long. There have to be constant checks, assessments and breaks. This way, when the trot is returned to the normal tempo, the horse is settled. I am reminded here of the words of Nuno Oliveira: 'A lot of riders know inside rein, outside rein, but few know how to work the horse the degrees between nerves and relaxation.' One has to be a good rider to learn this.

The medium trot is really self-explanatory insofar as it lies between the shorter collected trot and working trot, and the extended trot, which is longest of all. A good medium trot will show that the rider has control of the lengthening process. It is also useful for practicing the accordion-like back exercises. If the extended trot were used to lengthen the stride in everyday practice, the extreme effort would be too demanding for more continuous training repetitions.

Extended Trot

The extended trot is the ultimate length of trot available to a given horse. Obviously, different horses will have different sizes of extended trot. The extended trot should show nearly equal activity of the hind and forelegs. The cannon bones should be approximately parallel when in full extension (see Photo 41). If the fore cannon is angled at 45 degrees to the ground, the opposite hind cannon should show a similar angle. Extended trots that show dramatic reach with the foreleg, but an unmatched hind leg with half the reach, have to be considered faulty. Too much disparity will demand that the horse hollow its back as in the Spanish walk, which is not the aim of the powerful, gymnastic, extended trot. When executed correctly, the extended trot shows the maximum of swing, elasticity and strength (see Photos 42, 43 and 44). It should never appear restrained, tight or false in any way. When it is coupled with smooth, collecting transitions, it can be a proof of mastering the forces of impulsion. Furthermore, when this is done with light reins, it approaches art.

Photo 41. Excelso in extended trot. It is an old rule of thumb that, in extension, the fore and hind cannon bones should be approximately parallel.

Photos 42 and 43. A phase of extended trot that is not often depicted. Whether the horse is a Baroque type or a modern type, the requirements are the same. Both horses are about to unleash the power of a coiled hind limb that will propel them into the air (see Figure 20 page 83). Immediately after this phase comes the extension of the hind limb (see photo 44). Where it is correct – elastically moving – even a trot this powerful is comfortable as well as exciting.

Photo 44. St. Graal – extended trot.

With the invention of faster and better cameras, closer and closer examination of the gaits of horses is possible. It was not so long ago historically that Muybridge made his revolutionary photographs, which proved unequivocally to some skeptical people that the horse has moments of suspension, when all four feet are off the ground. At present, riders are up in arms about analysis that shows impure diagonal rhythms at the extension, such as the hind leg breaking off the ground before its diagonal partner.

Some years ago, I hosted a lecture by Dr. Doug Leach, who was a noted researcher in equine locomotion. (For more information on this, please refer to the chapter A Fog of Walks, in *Exploring Dressage Technique*.)[3] Dr. Leach spoke about rotary gallops, transverse gallops, cross-cantering, right leads, left leads, and at one point in the lecture he went on to say 'Surprise, surprise – gaits do not exist!' He

[3]Belasik,P., 'A fog of walks' in *Exploring Dressage Technique* (J.A. Allen 1994).

explained that, if one were to analyze carefully the locomotion of horses, one would determine that there are continuums of changes in the patterns of limb movement. One researcher (Hildebrand) in California, after defining over 400 strides, concluded that there is no such thing as 'stride'. Anyone who has watched foals has seen gaits that are not recognizable. As Dr. Leach said, 'We, in our simplified way, categorize and selectively train for gaits'. To me, this science will never be at odds with the art form of dressage riding. It will be helpful. If force plate analyses show that horses assumed to be collecting are not really shifting weight at all, this will help us to understand why, and it will have a positive affect on our judgment and also, therefore, on our training. Since the classical consensus is so simple and natural, analytical scrutiny can only help to describe it, not disprove it.

Part of the naturalness of classical riding is that it is an art, purposefully limited by the natural bodies and minds of both the horse and rider. The use of performance-enhancing chemicals is intentionally limited. There are also restrictions on the use of equipment. Computers will not be put into bits, and electronic devices will not be installed in saddles – not because it can't be done, but because we will not let it. The dressage rider and trainer must insist that their work takes place in real time, real space, and not in cyber time or cyberspace. We revel in the antiquity. There is a beautiful redundancy built into it – each generation studies the same thing. Like a father teaching his child fly-fishing, it is about the whole process, the life of the process, not the end result.

Lateral Trotting Exercises

Very often in training one finds that, when different kinds of exercises are juxtaposed, they can have a greater value than if they are always carried out separately. This is why the classical longitudinal and lateral exercises are almost always woven together in dressage practice. As we have seen, the longitudinal exercises develop connection. They unite the horse into 'one piece', and enhance its ability to shift its center of balance from front to back. The lateral exercises keep the horse's body flexible. These exercises of

bend can also remedy the natural one-sidedness that is inherent in almost all horses.

How do they do that? If a boat had two motors on the stern and both motors were equal in power, the boat would for the most part travel straight. Likewise, if the horse propels itself equally off each hind leg, it will travel in a straight line. In order for the horse to move off that straight line one leg will have to exert more force than the other, so that the horse's mass will be lifted and either projected sideways, obliquely forward or on a bias over the less loaded leg. This is the secret of the gymnastic value of the lateral exercises. These exercises are mostly designed to make one particular leg work harder than the others. Therefore, if the horse is lazy in one leg (or blocking that leg with stiffness in the torso), all the rider has to do is to match the exercise to the leg that needs to be strengthened, or to the side that needs to be contracted or stretched.

There is a simple rule of thumb to determine which leg is using more force or working harder. Whichever hind leg is crossing over in front of the other will be the limb that is doing more work and carrying a greater load (see Photos 45a, b). To use the analogy of the boat with two motors again, one leg will be directing the line of travel. That one leg, as the stronger motor, will be using more power and propelling the horse's mass off a straight line. If both hind legs were to propel the horse equally, it would go straight. But, of course, the horse also has two forelegs which can also generate power. Usually, both sets of legs are synchronized, with the stronger hind legs dominating the direction of travel. However, if the forelegs are too far out of line, they can, by themselves, disturb the straightness. Here is an example to illustrate this point. A rider is leading his horse down a straight track, walking very close to it at its left shoulder. Both of the horse's hind legs are engaged equally, and the forelegs travel straight. The energy seems to push the forehand straight in front of the hind legs. The rider is carrying the reins lightly, but there is hardly any need to hold them, as the horse walks resolutely forward. Then a biting fly lands on the horse's right side near the saddle. The horse swings its head and neck around to the right and, as it does so, its left shoulder slams into the rider, pushing him aside, and the horse almost steps on him as its own left forefoot is forced over.

Photos 45a, b. a) In this half-pass the right hind crosses over – it is the load-carrying leg.

b) Here, the right hind is driving the half-pass to the left – the right hind crosses over then it drives.

Thus we see that, if the neck bends excessively, or the shoulders and a foreleg move sideways, then straightness is affected even if the hind legs are perfectly matched and stay straight. This is why, in all the lateral exercises, we seek a uniform curve in the horse from tail to head. Too much bending of the neck in one direction can force the shoulders off in the opposite direction (see Chapter 3, Figures 15 and 16). If the rider keeps pushing a horse in this pose from behind when the shoulders are misaligned, the shoulders are driven over even more, sliding sideways, in the same way as an ice hockey player might check an opponent by driving his left shoulder into the opponent, with force from his right leg and planted skate. The result is that the energy shoots out to the side.

It is a law of classical equitation that forward movement takes precedence over sideways movement. When the horse slides sideways through a bulging shoulder, the rider cannot control the amount of bend and therefore the direction of the exercise. The horse becomes disconnected near the withers; its body is in a false position. Eventually, the muscles pay the price. This is one of the primary reasons why bending the neck of the horse is more than just a bad habit. It is a serious fault. The rider teaches the horse to disconnect the neck. When this is done, the rider cannot be disappointed or surprised by the loss of control, or the realization that the horse is not 'through', or begins to travel unevenly. Catching the errant shoulder with the outside rein might be a temporary correction, but it is not a solution. The horse has to be made to reach honestly, thus connecting the neck and the back, rather than bouncing the head and neck alternately between the inside and outside reins like a ping-pong match.

Leg-yielding

Leg-yielding is the most elementary lateral exercise. It is totally self-explanatory, since it asks the horse to yield sideways away from the unilateral pressure of one of the rider's legs. In this exercise the horse will show an approximately equal crossing over of both the fore and hind legs. The horse is bent a little around the rider's leg that pushes the horse sideways (see Photo 24, page 58).

There is a basic biomechanical law that states that, the more the legs scissor or criss-cross, the less they can drive the horse forward. Lateral movement has an inverse relationship to forward impulsion. The more you go sideways, the less you can go forward. This, of course, highlights the main use of leg-yielding, which is to *increase flexibility*, not build strength. When leg-yielding is used judiciously (that is, without radical sideways movement, without powerful attempts at impulsion, and without exotic patterns of bend and counter-bend), it can be a very important part of the stretching, warming-up exercise.

Leg-yielding was not universally praised or received as an exercise when it was first introduced. Seunig's masterpiece, *Horsemanship*, written in the first half of the least century, calls it a 'completely unnecessary lesson'.[4] Along with many other middle European trainers of this time, he cites and probably exaggerates its disadvantages. However, as the century progressed, leg-yielding became more universally accepted. The general consensus today is that leg-yielding is not a panacea. It should be used without too much bend, and can be useful as an elementary lateral exercise (see Photos 46–48).

[4]Seunig, W., *Horsemanship* (Doubleday 1956).

Photo 46. Leg-yielding along the wall; the spine is relatively straight. This is often used as a precursor to teaching shoulder-fore and shoulder-in.

Photo 47. Three-track shoulder-in. You can see how the bend and collection of shoulder-in are developed from the straight leg-yield.

Photo 48. Four-track shoulder-in. More displacement of the shoulders does not guarantee more collection or more bend.

Shoulder-in and Shoulder-fore

The shoulder-in and the shallower shoulder-fore are pre-eminent lateral exercises. Their invention is credited to Guérinière, although it is clear, as acknowledged by Guérinière, that the English horseman, William Cavendish, Duke of Newcastle, had laid down much of the groundwork. In *A General System of Horsemanship*, Newcastle had written:

You must walk the horse in his own length drawing the inward rein, and helping with the inward leg which always works both the shoulders. [It seems clear that Newcastle purposefully pushed the croup out to isolate the shoulders.] For the croup is put out and the shoulders nearest to the centre, and the part nearest thereto will always be more restrained, laboured and confined than that which is farther off...Thus you see he keeps his shoulders within his hind legs which prevents him from being entire (that is refuse to turn) [stiff] and renders his shoulders supple and pliant.

I think Newcastle knew exactly what he was doing. He seemed to focus on the shoulders in order to free and control them. Guérinière's genius was to realize that, so long as the balance and focus were on the shoulders, that emphasis was its own worst enemy. He knew that the circling was a problem, so he took the inside bend along the wall: 'The circle is not the best means of suppling the shoulders since a thing constrained and under its own weight cannot be light.'[5]

When Guérinière took the movement along the wall he also changed the focus to the hind legs – particularly the inside hind, which had to step under the horse's center of gravity:

Each step taken in this posture carries the inside hind leg forwards under the belly and brings it over the outside hind leg, which it can only do by lowering the haunch; it is thus always on one haunch in one direction, and on the other haunch in the other direction, and learns in consequence to bend its hocks under itself, this is what is called being on the haunches.[6]

Once the weight came off the shoulders and was transferred to the engaged, collected hind legs, (see Photo 49),

[5]De la Guérinière, F.R., *School of Horsemanship* (J.A. Allen 1994).
[6]*Ibid.*

Photo 49. Once the weight came off the shoulders and was transferred to the engaged, collected hind legs, the shoulders became freer than Newcastle could ever have dreamed of.

the shoulders became freer than Newcastle could ever have dreamed of. But there is a caution here. The rider has to be careful not to let the horse drop its inside hip excessively. If it does, it can be avoiding flexing its hock. Imagine the way a person with a cast on their knee would swing their whole leg from the hip. The danger would be that the horse's stiff inside leg would pass by the belly and the center of gravity, and the hock would not flex. The whole exercise would lose gymnastic value. Guérinière is clear that the inside hind must go under the belly, and that the hocks must flex. This seemingly small distinction points to the way the modern shoulder-in on three tracks has evolved slightly from the four-track shoulder-in of the eighteenth century, which will be discussed further on.

In the shoulder-in, the rider's inside leg encourages the horse sideways but also forward, with its head looking away from the line of travel. The rider's inside rein can help signal and create the inside bend: 'Its head and shoulders must be turned somewhat towards the centre of the manège, as if it were desired to turn in this direction, and when it is in this oblique, curved position, it must be made to move along the wall, aided by the inside rein and leg' (Guérinière). Ideally, however, the inside rein becomes softer because of the bend in the area of the ribs created by the rider's increased inside leg aids. Since this curve to the inside shortens the inside profile of the horse, the formerly equal length of rein is now affected. The inside rein softens (slackens) as the horse bends toward it. By the same token, it is not necessary to tighten the outside rein. It will tighten by itself as the horse stretches the outside, forming a longer curve. All the rider needs to do is hold steady with the outside rein at its existing length if the horse tries to bend too much to the inside.

Riders who try to create displacement of the shoulders by using the outside rein defeat the gymnastic benefits of the shoulder-in. Not only do they remove the bend, they also kill impulsion with 'handbrakes' and put the horse on the forehand, where Newcastle had him. When the movement is created with more inside leg and less outside rein, the horse learns engagement and goes 'uphill'. In the case of the shoulder-in, the engagement and collection are unilateral – that is, the loading is asymmetrical on one hind leg, namely the inside. Herein lies its further genius as an antidote and cure for the natural asymmetry of all horses.

Unlike the sideways traverse of leg-yielding, the shoulder-in must be ridden forward with inside bend whether it is ridden on a straight line or a curved line such as a circle. It could be described as moving on a bias. For a long time, there have been arguments as to whether the shoulder-in is a three-track or a four-track movement. It seems quite clear that Guérinière intended it to be on four tracks. This is the way it is still practiced at many classical schools around the world. If one stands behind the horse in a four-track shoulder-in, all four feet and legs will be visible (as in Photo 50); whereas, if the horse were traveling straight, one would see only the two hind legs, which would block the view of the forelegs. (The straight horse would leave two lines of tracks on the ground. Even today, some people still refer to all lateral work as 'two-track' work, as opposed to straight work being on 'one' track. This description cannot take into account differences of three or four tracks, and it is

Photo 50. Shoulder-in on four tracks.

so confusing that I will not address it anymore.) Now, it is possible to leg-yield along a wall (as in Photo 46, page 103), and when one watched from behind or in front of the horse, one would also see four tracks. The difference is that in the shoulder-in there will be lateral bend throughout the horse's body whereas, in leg-yielding, the horse will be relatively straight. This bend changes the exercise from one of improving flexibility to collection.

Today, the two distinct executions of shoulder-in, three-track and four-track, still remain in use. If the horse's hips remain parallel to the wall, as in normal trotting, and the shoulders come in to leave three lines of tracks (the outside foreleg on the same track the inside hind – see Photo 51), this shoulder-in can actually be more demanding than a four-track shoulder-in, which has the shoulders even further to the inside. Although the displacement of the shoulders is less in the three-track version, there can be more torque in the body because the haunches, or hips, are kept parallel to the wall (Photo 52). The barrier of the

wall and/or the rider's outside leg, positioned slightly back, prevent any escaping of the haunches. Furthermore, when the haunches are kept straight, the movement cannot turn into a leg-yield with the inside hind leg crossing under and past the horse's center of gravity, with the hip dropping down. Instead, the inside hind leg has to step right under the barrel of the horse, which has been carefully placed by the rider directly in its way. It cannot possibly escape carrying the load unless the horse completely stops going forward. The four-track shoulder-in allows the hips to be bent a little, slanted at a slight angle from the wall. Therefore, even though the shoulders can be further in, there can actually be less bend in the body in this form of shoulder-in. One benefit from this shoulder-in is that, by

Photos 51 and 52. Front and rear view of shoulder-in on three tracks. If the horse's hips are kept parallel to the wall this form of the movement can be more demanding than shoulder-in on four tracks, because it produces more torque in the body.

allowing a little latitude in the angle of the hips, there is a nice safety valve giving protection from too much torque if the impulsion gets too strong.

Although more has probably been written about the shoulder-in than any other lateral exercise, there is no definitive formula for its execution. A shoulder-fore, which just moves the shoulders slightly away straightness, and gradually proceeds to more bend, usually introduces this exercise. The shoulder-in does, however, have one definite requirement. Whichever form of the movement you choose to ride, the shoulder-in must be uniform and symmetrical in both directions. Remember that symmetry

in form does not necessarily mean symmetry of effort. One direction will almost always be more difficult than the other. The object is, through practice, to close this disparity, which will be proof that the horse is becoming more evenly balanced, supple and strong.

Travers and Renvers

The travers and renvers are really identical twin exercises. They are virtually the same yet, like twins, they are a little different (see Photos 53 and 54). Their differences lie in

Photo 53. Travers.

Photo 54. Renvers.

execution and, in particular, their relationship to a reference wall or straight line.

In travers, or haunches in, on the right rein, the rider's inside leg (right) remains near the girth, or under the rider's hip, to keep the horse curved around that leg. At the same time, the rider's outside leg (in this case, the left) slips back a little and displaces the hindquarters toward the center of the arena. The horse continues to look straight down the wall and doesn't flex its head inside. The curve starts from the poll and continues evenly to the tail. As in all such cases, the inside rein should become softer by virtue of the horse's lateral shortening on the inside of the curve, while the contact in the outside rein will increase as the horse stretches the outside lateral. The horse's outside (left) hind leg will step across and in front of the right hind leg. This leg drives the horse forward by stepping up and under the belly toward the center of gravity, where it will lift and propel the horse's mass on a bias left to right.

In the renvers (Photo 54), when traveling to the right (clockwise), the horse's shoulders will be displaced to the right to allow room for the hindquarters to curve toward the wall of the arena. The bend will be around the rider's left leg, with the rider's right leg slightly further back than the left and pushing the hindquarters to the left and forward.

The renvers and travers are the first lateral exercises in which the horse is looking in the direction of travel. Since most horses seem to love to be crooked, teaching the travers is usually not too difficult if the rider does not ask for too much displacement at first. The leg aids should be more pulsing than continuous. Strong, continuous pushing will often make sensitive horses suspicious and cause them to tighten in the barrel. The travers is also the easier movement because the rider retains the same bend as in the previous corner. The rider proceeds through the corner on the right rein. The horse is bent to the right. As the horse finishes the corner, the rider exaggerates the outside leg and bend, and the horse is in travers. In renvers, however, the bend must change. The horse travels through the corner on the right rein with right bend. As it finishes the corner the rider continues with the bend as if to ride a circle or shoulder-in. The shoulders must come off the track to give the horse room to bend left. Then, quickly but

smoothly, the rider changes bend from right to left. The horse's spine feels as if it makes a slalom turn from head to tail, rather than just snapping from one bend to the other.

The renvers can be difficult at first when trying to move the shoulders off the wall and change bend. The track often has a strong, seemingly magnetic, pull. Furthermore, the reference line of the long, perfectly straight wall looming in front of both horse and rider will make the horse that is learning the exercise seem all the more wobbly. Persistence will pay off. If the horse seems trapped by the imposing wall, the rider should make the first attempts away from the wall, even toward the quarter line. It will be easier to move the horse over in the free space. Once the horse becomes familiar with the aids, the movement can be perfected along the wall.

There is no better preparation for the half-pass than travers and renvers, and there are no better exercises for correcting faults in the half-pass. In regard to this, some trainers have said that the half-pass is nothing more than a renvers or travers on a diagonal. This points to a misunderstanding of the lateral exercises. The travers and renvers have a specific relationship to a line or a wall. That is, the shoulders are parallel to that line or wall. It does not matter in which direction that line travels – diagonal (across the arena), or along a wall – it is still a straight line and the shoulders stay parallel to it. Obviously, in travers and renvers the forefeet will never criss-cross or scissor as they will in half-pass, so the latter is a very different exercise.

There is another matter to consider when teaching these bending exercises. Riders should be careful not to use the whip too much to displace the quarters. The object of these exercises is to train the horse to move from the leg. The proper use of the whip is more for discipline if the horse ignores the rider's leg. It should not become a magic wand that actually initiates and guides lateral movement, or the horse will never learn the lessons of the leg.

Half-pass and Counter-change of Hand

The half-pass is one of the most beautiful movements in riding. The horse moves obliquely forward. Later, in the counter-changes of hand, the horse will couple traverses to the right and left, back and forth in a dance that will betray any one-sided crookedness and glorify correct training. What makes the half-pass unique is the way it travels in two dimensions — forward and sideways at the same time. All the other lateral exercises are ridden on what I have called a bias. By this I mean that, once the movement is set up, it travels in one direction; one part of the horse, whether haunches or shoulders, stays parallel to this one straight line. In a sense, even if these movements are executed on a circle, they stay true to one line. However, the half-pass follows two lines, one forward and

Photos 55 and 56. In half-pass, the forelegs cross and the hind legs cross.

one sideways, at the same time (Photos 55 and 56). Both forehand and hindquarters follows this sliding-forward line, thus making both the fore and hind legs criss-cross.

In a half-pass to the left, the horse is bent to the left. The outside hind (right) will cross over in front of the inside hind (left) and propel the horse from right to left (Photos 57 and 58). The forelegs will follow a similar pattern, crossing in harmonious symmetry with the hind (Photo 59). If they don't, the traverse will not be steady: the shoulders might be left behind, they might speed up, and haunches might swing out ahead, or lag behind. Therefore, both ends of the horse must move sideways together and stay in the same relationship until that half-pass is completed (see Photo 60).

Photos 57 and 58. Mime, half-pass left, showing crossing of the hind legs.

Even though the half-pass has two requirements of direction, one forward and one sideways, they are not of equal importance. In all classical theory, forward riding takes precedence over going sideways. The full sideways traverses that can still be seen in the bullrings of Spain and Portugal have almost disappeared from modern training. The reason for this is the same reason why leg-yielding has never had a universal acceptance. Sideways movement has an inverse relationship to impulsion and forwardness. The more the horse travels sideways, the less it can move forward. This is not just for the obvious reason that they are contradictory directions. More importantly, it has to do with the mechanics of the hind legs, which are built to propel with much greater facility (and are thus stronger-acting) on a longitudinal as opposed to lateral range of motion. After a certain angle and size in the sideways steps, the driving hind leg will go past the center of gravity and the sharp angle will force the leg out of its carrying ability and demand that the forelegs push. In this

Photo 59. St. Graal in half-pass; legs crossing in perfect symmetry.

Photo 60. Here is a half-pass with much scope. Trainers must be careful to evaluate half-passes both from in front and behind. This half-pass is correct but, from this angle, it looks as if the haunches are leading. A salutary illustration that you cannot teach riding from a chair at the side of the arena.

pose, it will be impossible to collect the horse, which is the only thing that will give it true freedom and lightness of the forehand. Thus we return to Newcastle and Guérinière. Newcastle in trying to free the horse up with severe traverses, which only put the horse further on the shoulders. Guérinière, in developing collection, obtained the most lightness from it. Today, the requirement that the shoulders lead in the half-pass is homage to this principle. The hind legs must push the shoulders cleanly and never

fish-tail like an overpowered car on a slick road. Riders who try to show off great lateral sweeps usually show only that they don't understand the principles of impulsion or collection.

Probably the easiest way to introduce the half-pass is to

turn down the centerline, for example, to the left. While the horse is established in a left bend, the outside leg (right) begins to push the bend over to the left wall. The rider keeps hold with the inside rein and leg to maintain the bend. The rider must try not to push the movement over with the outside rein, but neither must the shoulders be allowed to escape. The steps must be gradual and at a shallow angle. If the horse understands the shoulder-in, travers and renvers, it should understand quite easily what is being asked.

As soon as the horse understands the exercise, it must be trained from the wall. Whereas the mysterious magnetic attraction of the wall helped pull the young horse over in its first half-passes, now the rider must train the horse to overcome its grip. One of the most traditional exercises is to come through the corner and establish a shoulder-fore or shoulder-in. Once the bend is set and the shoulders are leading the rider changes driving legs and the outside leg pushes the horse sideways. Horses that are not set in their various bends (that is, holding the bend of each particular lateral exercise by good impulsion), will not be able to change without collapsing somewhere in the body. The neck or back or shoulder will bulge. The advantage of starting from the shoulder-fore or shoulder-in is that, if the horse anticipates, the rider can wait and time the half-pass departure for whenever the horse's attention is re-established. The other obvious advantage is that the shoulders are in the proper position (leading) for a classical half-pass. The disadvantage is that the rider and horse must both change driving legs, from the inside leg which moves the shoulder-in, to the outside leg which must move the half-pass. Starting from the travers would retain the same driving leg, but it would break the most important rule of never letting the haunches lead. Thus, the shoulder-in preparation is advantageous on balance.

In the counter-change of hand we switch from half-pass in one direction to the other. It doesn't matter how many are done in a row: they would simply be multiple counter-changes of hand. The counter-change of hand presents an interesting theoretical question, which translates into a moderately difficult technical problem of execution. If, in the half-pass, the horse is supposed to lead with the shoulders and have the haunches slightly following, how will the rider and horse change direction and honor this

requirement? There must be a moment of straightness before the change into the other direction. If the rider were in a half-pass to the right with the haunches following and suddenly switched direction, the haunches would now be leading to the left. There has to be a buffer for straightening.

The easiest way to practice this is to half-pass toward the wall from the centerline. As the horse approaches the wall, the rider brings the haunches over a little more with the outside leg, so that the haunches and shoulders touch the track at the same time. The rider should hold that new position for a moment and then straighten the horse. (If one were just to ride to the wall and let the wall stop the shoulders and then keep riding until the haunches touched the wall, concise changes in the free space of the arena will never be possible. It is best to learn early on how to 'taper off' the half-pass.) Then, when the half-pass is taken out into the middle of the arena, the rider imagines a wall or straight line as the target and straightens the horse along that line. In the beginning, it is very important to ride straight for a while before initiating the second half-pass. Horses learn to anticipate the movement, and take over. If this happens, both control and correct execution will be lost in the multiple changes. If the rider always pays more attention to the straightness in between half-passes than to the half-pass itself, this understanding of the classical principles will bear fruit later.

Much attention must be paid to symmetry in the counter-changes. Almost all horses will have a freer half-pass in one direction than the other. If the rider isn't careful, the freer half-pass will go over further than the stiffer one. If, for example, the half-passes are made to the left and right of the centerline, the rider will then be unable to make it back to the symmetrical halfway point. Until the horse's training reaches such a point where the half-passes are symmetrical, it is better for the rider to think of overall distance rather than number of strides. Practice coming 5 meters off the wall and returning in the same distance. A typical exercise might be to come through the corner on the long side and begin a shoulder-in then, when in control, half-pass to the quarter line (or even less far than this). Straighten up then, when in control again, initiate a slight shoulder-fore and then return to the wall in half-pass. Never rush the straight section in the middle. The control that is instilled now will pay off tremendously later on. As training progresses, the straight buffer will become smaller and shorter, and the half-passes will cover more ground, but all must be achieved in a natural progression.

Rider Problems in Lateral Work

The practice of lateral work challenges the rider's position, particularly if the horse is resistant or difficult. The reason why lateral work is good for the horse, in respect of correcting its asymmetry, is the same reason why it is difficult for the rider. In general, whichever leg of the horse drives the particular lateral exercise will be controlled by the rider's leg and weight aids. When Newcastle spoke about the position of the rider's lower leg, he said: 'The rider should keep his hams [calves] stiff having his legs neither too near, nor too distant from the horse, that is to say they should not touch the horse's sides, because of the aids which shall afterwards be explained'.[7] Here, he was talking about the requirements of lateral work. If the rider's calves are planted on the horse, there will be no dexterity or feeling in the lower legs. The classical 'draped leg' is one that hangs from the seat and thigh, always alert as an aid, but it has no major function for balance. If the rider is gripping with the calf, light and expressive lateral work will be impossible.

In really good riders, the lower legs seem to have the dexterity of the hands and, when this is coupled with the weight aids, their relationship in the lower body is similar to the relationship of the hands and the weight aids in the upper body. Take the left half-pass, for example. The rider has the horse bent around the left leg, and the right leg is slightly back and pushes the horse to the left. When traveling straight, the weight of the rider is perfectly balanced. In the half-pass, the rider leads with the hips and center of gravity in the desired direction of travel, in this case, to the left. Suppose the horse resists the aids of the right leg, and the rider uses more strength. The increased contraction of the right leg travels up the rider's whole

right side. Finally, the rider begins to collapse or fold over the right hip. The weight aids shift to the wrong side. Now, a destructive war takes place between the rider's aids. The more unilateral leg strength is used, the more the balance of the rider is disturbed. The aids negate each in a furious burning-up of energy. The horse is confused because the leg says go, but the seat says stay.

In contrast, good riders have good seats and very good balance, with light leg aids. Most of the time the horse will respond to their shifts of balance alone. When the leg aids are used, they are light, but fast. If the horse doesn't respond to the leg aids, such riders might follow up quickly with the spurs or whip. They don't increase the pressure of the leg aids with each subsequent repetition. In some cases, they probably lessen it. (I remember in grammar school I had one teacher who would progressively lower her voice as the class became too loud. On straining to hear her, the level of our own voices went down.) The rider always has to be careful not to sacrifice position to get a movement. This trade-off never works, and it begins to poison the dialogue between rider and horse, which can lead to serious breakdown in the more subtle communications that are soon to follow.

A second general area of trouble for the rider in the lateral work lies in the hands. I have described previously how, when an otherwise straight-traveling horse swings its head and neck to the right to bite at a fly, the shoulders will bulge and be displaced to the left. The horse's head can account for five percent of the horse's weight. When it swings sideways it has significant wave-like effects through the body. This is one of the reasons why so much classical instruction requires steady hands. The thinking is to establish a solid connection through the back and neck to the bit and never to bend the neck back and forth.

If the rider uses too much inside rein in the lateral exercises, this can overbend the neck, disconnect it from the back and hindquarters, and force the shoulders out (as in the biting fly). This mistake is almost always followed by a correction from the outside rein. Too much outside rein in the lateral exercises is even worse. The first thing it does is eliminate the curve or bend, which is a primary objective of lateral work. If the rein effect doesn't go through the body, then it can warp the neck into an 'S'

[7]Newcastle, William Cavendish, Duke of, *A General System of Horsemanship* (Winchester Press 1970).

curve, thereby shortening the overall length of the neck and stiffening the horse's back.

Bending in the lateral work must uphold the fundamental principles of all bends. The rider must get used to moving the horse's ribcage or torso, and it is upon this area that feeling and thinking must be concentrated. When one pushes or weights with one leg, one wants to feel the energy move into one's other leg through the horse's torso. The rider should feel this effect in the seat. The rider also has to think of a concept of uniform extension or bend in the horse's spine, even though the spine is not uniform. It is rather like a fishing rod – it is potentially very flexible at the tip (neck), but gets stiffer further back towards the hips. For riding, in the early stages, the front end is too flexible. It is the site of many evasions. To compound this, the torso can be too stiff, bolstering up natural crookedness and contributing to asymmetries. Therefore the rider is always trying to firm up the flexible end and increase flexibility in the stiff end, thereby making the horse more uniform in its bending.

Riders who are always developing or correcting bend with the reins are missing the point. It is one thing to guide back an errant shoulder with a rein aid, but it is quite another to be guiding all movements with the reins. As the great Richard Wätjen said, 'The rider should not try to support the movement by the aid of the rein; this never leads to true success. Leg and back aids must always be predominant. The horse must learn to move in self-carriage and must only be guided and not pulled by the rider.'[8]

Rein-back

I have included the rein-back in this chapter primarily because, like the trot, the movement of the legs occurs in diagonal pairings. The rein-back can be a clear proof of the horse's 'throughness' and acceptance of contact. Correctly executed, the rein-back takes place as follows. The horse acknowledges the driving aids of the rider and its legs step upward to develop motion. However, because the horse respects the rider's passive hand, it won't go

8Wätjen, R., *Dressage Riding* (J.A. Allen 1958).

through this barrier, but instead softly steps back and away. The rider follows the horse's backward movement with the passive hand, not pulling it back, but acting as if the 'wall' in front of the horse were retracting, until the rider wants the horse to stop. The rider then relaxes the hand and 'opens the front door'. If the rider tries to pull the whole, stiff horse backwards, there is no yielding in the neck and back. The resistant horse drags its forefeet through the sand. Even worse, the hollow horse feels the pressure on the bit and back, and panics because its hollow back has locked its stifles and hips, which cannot flex.

To me, the key to training a confident and reliable rein-back is patience in the first few attempts. It is very important to establish a good square halt, with the hind legs engaged and the horse's back up and round. The feeling should be as if one were going to turn into a walk pirouette. The horse is thinking 'collect', then the rider stops. At first, instead of trying to get three or four steps, the rider should just try to get the horse to lean backwards. That is, to accept the 'barrier' of the reins. Then, when the rider's back and legs engage, and the horse's leg is about to rise from the ground, there is no room to go forward. Thus, the horse should obey the commands of the rider's seat and leg to move, but now the hand sends a contradictory message by giving the horse nowhere to go. As illogical as it probably seems to the horse, by this time it trusts its rider and it will try. The only open door is behind the horse, so it moves toward it to see if it opens.

To me, this is a big leap of trust from the horse. It is much more important than big steps. From that single, small, step backwards, through repetition, the horse will learn to take any number of backward steps and then walk forward when the rein changes to open the front door again. The horse should never be afraid of stepping backwards. It should step up with free legs in an easy, confident rhythm, not rush or dive down in its head and neck.

When the rein-back is coupled with a forward walk, a transition, or even twice backward and forward for a predetermined number of steps, the horse and rider should show such control that the step does not square up at the end of the rein-back. When correctly executed, the horse will stop the stride with the natural straddle that occurs when the legs are moving as diagonal pairs. The horse will then move forward smoothly (usually to the walk), and back again if necessary.

In this relatively simple list of exercises, there is an infinite number of combinations and applications that can expose a problem in riding and then show the way to correction. It is when they are not thoroughly understood in the classical sense that they are stylistically altered and then imitated. That is always when there is the most potential for harm to the classical system, and ultimately to the horse. Charismatic personalities may champion their own biases rather than the classical way. People follow this and, depending on the power of the trend, there is the possibility of much destructive practice.

Long ago, Guérinière warned his contemporaries about the danger of imitation without true understanding. However, at no time in history has unknowledgeable imitation been more of a danger than now, at the beginning of this twenty-first century. The world is completely connected. Information passes instantly. For instance videos and other technology make trainers and riders around the world accessible to each other. Trends get started and these can be manipulated and marketed so that, within months, there is global participation. In the past it would have been too difficult to get such a unified message or to reach such a large audience. The isolated pockets of classical horseman ensured legitimate variety as well as scrutiny. They edited trends. In this new century, true horsemen and horsewomen will have to find a way to stay alive and independent of the grand multinational promotions, where the message is always quick and easy, aimed at the ego and entertainment of the human individual, not the heart and soul of the horse. In this time of ultra-communication, when we constantly celebrate connections, we need to celebrate humanity's connections with Nature and not humans' connections with themselves.

CHAPTER SIX
Exercises of the Canter – the Modern Masterpiece

If, in terms of the horse's gaits, there is one area of expertise where the modern horseman could feel confident in comparison with the old masters, it is in the canter. In the last hundred years or so, the work in the canter, more than any other gait, has shown the most notable changes. Oddly enough, the classical dressage schools cannot really take the credit for initiating the advances in the canter, even though they have perfected them. The understanding and development of the new exercises for the canter came from three main areas in the late nineteenth and early twentieth centuries – jumping, racing and the circus (not necessarily in that order of precedence).

After the dissolution of the French monarchy and the school of Versailles, equestrian field sports became increasingly popular. Hunting, and with it jumping and racing, began an ascendancy that continued into the twentieth century.

In the early years of that century, it was Federico Caprilli's revolutionary jumping style that changed the face of riding. His work was often a direct reproof aimed at high school dressage. A very strong case can be made that it was because of Caprilli's new ideas about balance, and freedom for the horse's neck, that dressage changed. Unlike the practice of the previous centuries, the modern notion of dressage could not conceivably involve only collection. Today, the horse must be able to collect and extend with equal facility, to the point where, under the most knowledgeable eyes, the transitions within the gait are a more important test of training than the gait itself. Furthermore, almost all of Caprilli's ideas were developed in the canter, the gait most widely used for the popular outdoor sports, in which changes of direction obviously occurred. It is a certainty that flying changes were deliberately practiced then.

In racing, the whole raison d'être was the development and comparison of the horse's ability to gallop, the four-beat gallop being, as it were, a child of the three-beat canter. Early technical innovations, such photographs and film, clarified the biomechanics of these gaits. Then, in an ongoing process, technological and genetic advances, which fueled the incredible and seemingly unlimited racing industry, spilled over into other equestrian sports. As multidisciplinary sports grew in popularity breeders produced horses with better and better canters,

Finally, in the continuous pushing of novelty to the limits, circus riders like François Baucher and James Fillis tried to do everything to the canter. Much of this work, such as canter on three legs, canter backwards, etc., was held in disdain by dressage purists, because it seemed too far removed from what came naturally to the horse. However, it was very difficult to continue to argue that multiple flying changes were also unnatural. Flying changes were and are exhibited by free horses all the time, even in multiples. Yet, even as late as the middle of the twentieth century, some authorities argued that the flying change on every stride was not classical. Whatever the resistance, by the end of the century, the acceptance of one-time changes as a legitimate classical movement was virtually universal.

The canter is the only dressage gait which has a distinct left or right leading side. If the horse is cantering to the left and is on the left lead, the sequence of footfalls would be right hind, left hind and right fore at the same time, and finally the left fore (see Photos 25–28, page 59). If the horse is cantering to the right and is on the right lead, the sequence would be left hind, right hind and left fore and finally the right fore. At the end of each of these sequences is a moment of suspension, and then the cycle repeats itself. The horse has the ability, however, to change this cycle in mid-air. Galloping racehorses can make a similar change, for which fatigue will often be the reason. In racing, the flying change occurs in the forelegs first, and then in the hind. In dressage, any change must be deliberate and must occur first in the hind legs and follow to the front as a constant homage to the rear end being the power source. Because the flying change has to be so controlled, it is not taught to the horse or practiced until both leads of the canter and counter-canter are secure, and the horse is capable of carrying the balance a little more toward the rear.

By its nature, the canter has a slight twisting feeling, which is caused by the sequence of footfall. Since, when the horse is in the moment of suspension, both hind legs are moving up under the belly, it also has a distinctive rocking action. Because of this rocking action, the canter is easier to sit than the trot. Since it has a climbing feeling in front when the horse's hind end is curling under, it is a gait in which inexperienced riders can get their first feelings of collection or at least engagement.

Confirming the Rider's Seat

Once the working canter is established to the point where the horse will not speed up or slow down, nor change leads without the rider's signals, then collecting and extending the stride from the baseline canter can

begin. One of the most important features that determines whether a horse is ready for more advanced canter work, is also applicable to the rider. That is, there must be the capability for the canter to be maintained by the rider's seat. The horse must be following the rider's hips and seat for direction and tempo, and not the other way round. Over a long period, and especially after correcting so many riders with faulty seats at the canter, I have noticed what seems to be a typical phenomenon here. The rider gets the horse to canter, the canter becomes increasingly disunited, the rider's seat starts slapping the saddle, there is a gap in the timing and with each stride, this seems to magnify. Left to their own devices, such riders will usually fall backward to find the back of the horse. In order to alleviate the concussion, the rider lets go in the abdominals and, if that is not bad enough, even lets go in the neck, so that the head begins to bob. Usually, such riders kick or grip with the calf in order to generate some speed.

Once a rider learns to do this, it is amazing to me how deeply it gets imbedded as an unconscious action. Every time there is trouble, the rider's position will soften to this defensive collapse. Anatomically, this reflex position is very destructive to learning more advanced dressage movements because it actually stiffens the rider in the hips and freezes the center of gravity and the balancing mechanisms. This makes the rider's position 'dead' and lacking in agility. Instead of learning to make the back and abdominal muscles stronger and use the hips to adjust balance, the rider lets go with these muscles and resorts to the gripping calf. This simple fault in the fundamentals can control riding style for the rider's entire life! Some go on as professionals and inculcate these faults in the next generation of riders. These riders often sit just slightly behind the motion, ramrod straight in the upper body, almost as a disguise to hide the faulty seat. Their legs are just slightly too far out in front and thus unable to really take any weight off their punishing seat. Depending on the Spartan qualities of the individual, such riders will often endure a painful backache as their stoicism conceals their mistakes.

However, the horse always reveals the seat. In such cases smooth collection is impossible, because the horse's back is also in a defensive mode. The hind legs cannot make the necessary adjustment (get under quickly when called for), because the rider's weight is holding the back down which, in turn, is keeping the lumbo-sacral joint from flexing. The back has no mobility and the croup just can't tuck under. And on it goes, hips freezing hips.

The enigma for many riders is to realize that flexible, educated hips are a result of very controlled abdominal and back muscles. If a good rider is not wearing a coat, but happens to be wearing a belt with a buckle, the observer will see how still and purposeful that rider is upon a particular horse. The belt buckle is not dancing all around, flying in and out. It is as if the back and thigh move the hips, and the hips move the saddle, and the horse follows the saddle.

The classic position requires good balance. The rider's buttocks stay soft. The rider is supported on bones, not on flesh. The thighs are strong and flexible. The legs are well positioned under the rider's center of gravity. The abdominals and back allow no collapse. If the tempo of the canter begins to slow down, the rider pushes it back up with the seat. If an instructor is really vigilant, and does not allow pupils to collapse when they start losing the tempo, the rider will have to speed up the action of the hips to get back into synchronicity with the stride, then continue to control the tempo with the hips. The leg is more of an auxiliary aid. If the instructor does not give up in these endeavors, but keeps the pupil straight – even at the risk of being initially stiff – and only allows the rider to maintain position by moving the hips to keep the canter going, the instructor will be giving the rider one of the greatest gifts in riding. So much of what happens in the canter is a result of athletic, but often very subtle and accurate, positioning of the seat and hips, or one individual hip and then the other. The rider does not have to *drive* every stride but must *ride* every stride. The seat becomes the conductor, always controlling the overall tempo while allowing the other parts of the body to 'go solo'. That is what I mean by not advancing to collection or extension until the rider can control the rhythm of the gait with the seat. The only way to control the rhythm with the seat rather than the calves is to master position. This does not mean sitting like a statue, but it does mean using the rules of position to develop feel in the seat and, in particular, the hips.

The Collected Canter

To collect the canter, the rider almost simultaneously begins to push the gait a little while closing the fingers and making the hand more passive. This dams up the power so that the trajectory of the stride begins to climb, covering less ground forward but becoming higher in its steps. As have already made clear, this is not accomplished by increasing the leg aids but, if the rider pushes with the seat, when, and how much?

In the trot, which is more horizontal and more staccato in its rhythm than the canter, the driving seat might seem, paradoxically, a more steady or continuous means of pushing the horse, when needed, in these steady packets of energy. The canter, however, is different. There is really only one part of the stride during which the rider can push effectively. The rider *could* push constantly but, in order get more engagement, the push needs to come when the forehand (ideally, the one leading leg) is on the ground. This is the moment in the stride when the hind legs are up off the ground and the horse's hips are going to swing under. If, at this point, the rider initiates more drive with the seat, the horse's hind legs will be pulled along by the seat. Thus the hind legs will come a little further under than they would without any encouragement. This further underside engagement of the horse is only possible if the topside (top line) stretches while the abdominals contract. If the rider were to drop down on the back of the horse at this moment and grind into the back muscles to try to drive the hind legs under, it would have exactly the opposite effect. Upsetting the stretch of the top line would directly affect the underside engagement. This is another example of how the principles of muscle movement – namely alternating contractions which feel like contraction and sympathetic extension – determine much of the training, whether laterally (one side to the other), or longitudinally (the top to the bottom).

What makes dressage so amazing to me is, like ballet, the level of sophistication that is layered on these natural biomechanical phenomena. There is even more to this, and I have personally experienced these sophisticated principles work just as magically in reverse. Handicapped riders, ill-conformed horses, diseased and injured bodies, realize amazing recuperative powers from dressage.

Sophisticated movement gets sophisticated results for everyone.

To return to the mechanics of collecting the canter, the classical rider with a light seat but strong and flexible back pushes forward as the horse begins to rise in front of him. This forward push draws the rear end further under the belly. The rider's seat, crowding the pommel, does nothing to impede the horse's back muscles from stretching to allow the underside reach. Let me be quite clear on this. It does not mean that the rider stands up off the horse's back entirely like a jockey. This might get the rider maximum engagement, but in dressage, immediacy of response is necessary to extend then collect, collect then extend, etc. The seat must always be there, because it is the center of balance. That contact with the horse becomes a kind of gyroscopic command center.

As always during training, the legs reinforce the instructions of the seat. They do not do all the work themselves. They remind the horse to follow the rider's seat. This is a very crucial moment in the canter stride, which will become quite apparent in the flying changes.

In the collected canter, the rider encourages more engagement of the hind legs with seat, back and legs and simultaneously restrains or contains this power with the reins – but must be very careful not to let the horse 'lie' in the reins. This will defeat collection and tip the horse onto the forehand. The mass of the horse is held, in a sense, over the hind legs so that the horse is taking a shorter stride, learning to carry the weight longer, flexing the hocks, stifles and hips more. If the rider pays a lot of attention to maintaining the same tempo, then the horse won't 'cheat' thereby making the stride shorter by just slowing down. Instead, it will make the stride shorter by collecting it, and the stride will keep its jump.

As in so many lessons of dressage, the sensations of collection might not be crystal clear at first, but they will become more discernible with experience. Even in the early stages, the less experienced rider will not be lost if the basic principles are adhered to. In this case, tempo is crucial. Even if you can't exactly feel it, count it out. If the rider maintains the same tempo and shortens the stride, the horse and rider *will* be collecting. With practice, the definition will increase. Just as muscle definition increases with practice, so will the definition of movement.

The School Canter and the Terre-à-terre

The school canter is a very collected canter. The term is not used very much nowadays although, whether riders want to admit it or not, the exercise remains very much alive today. One sees it most often when riders are strengthening their collected canters by making transitions from a collected canter to 'one on the spot', and back out. Although the canter is not literally placed on the spot, the rider tries to collect it to the size of the pirouette canter while remaining straight. Like the canter in the pirouette, the school canter is often four beats. Among the older masters, there was a very clear distinction between forms of four-beat canter: a canter that breaks down to four beats because of lack of power and impulsion, or a canter that lazily spreads out its load over the four legs like spokes of a slow wheel, or a canter where the diagonal pairing dissociates because the hindquarters have taken on a levade-like load.

The terre-à-terre is a very collected canter that rocks back and forth from hind legs almost as a pair to the forelegs almost as a pair. The terre-à-terre is still used, with the piaffe, as a collecting preparation for the airs above the ground in French schools. Its role in this context will be discussed in Chapter 8.

The Medium and Extended Canter

The medium and extended canters are both extensions of the canter stride itself. The extended form is the maximum, and the medium is a steady, long stride between the working canter and the extended canter. The canter must obey the same laws of physical motion as all the gaits. As the horse lengthens the stride, it must keep the same tempo. Even when it does, the horse will pick up speed. Unlike racing, speed is not the object of dressage exercises. It is, however, an irrefutable reality. Dressage trainers must learn to take speed into account. For instance, extensions without speed are false.

When a horse is frightened, it will run away from danger. The more frightening the object or situation, the faster it will try to run. Therefore, eliciting speed can induce excitement. This can happen in the extended canter, and the horse has to be trained to handle the excitement of this gait. If tension or fear were to become associated with lengthening the canter, collecting it subtly would be impossible.

The extended canter is the largest, longest and consequently the fastest form of canter in dressage. When it is coupled with a transition back to a collected canter, it becomes a very important test of physical and mental agility. The horse must have the physical strength to arrest its considerable mass from its most powerful inertia and smoothly slow it down without changing the tempo of the strides. It must also have the emotional stability to remain obedient to the rider when it is asked to fly powerfully forward for a predetermined distance, and then gather.

The most common fault in the extended canter is that the rider does not lengthen the stride in an 'uphill direction' (see Photos 61–64) – keeping contact with the reins and guiding the neck up and out so that, as the power increases, the forehand feels as if it climbs. This is possible because lengthening in dressage does not last for too many strides; the acceleration can keep the 'bow of the boat' up if too much weight is not placed there. However, if, in going for maximum reach in the lengthening, the rider drops the reins, allowing the horse's head and neck to drop down, the balance will fall on the forehand as in the galloping racehorse.

The second common area of trouble is in collecting the extended canter when it is done abruptly, or if the horse is not well trained. In such cases, the horse will feel the added work of collecting and deceleration, and change leads to relieve the workload on one hind leg, thus defeating the gymnastic demands of the exercise. The best practice is to gradually develop more strength by working on the transition to and from collection in the medium canter, where it is less taxing and the rider can perfect the fundamentals of the exercise.

As some of the exercises become more and more physically and mentally demanding, the rider has to be careful. Most horses, after some initial reluctance, will try to do

Photo 61. In right lead, the left hind strikes the ground as the first beat of the canter.

Photo 62. Second beat: the diagonal pair.

Photo 63. Third beat: the single leading foreleg.

Photo 64. The suspension phase of canter is often a magical moment of stillness in the midst of an outpouring of great energy.

the new exercises. However, the rider has to be sure that the horse is strong enough to do what is required, and must then be careful not to fatigue the horse. If the horse is too weak, or too tired, it will be unable to perform the exercise correctly, for instance, with deep-set haunches. Consequently, the horse may be more or less obliged to 'cheat' in the exercise. I think this is one of the most common sources of faulty movements later on. The fault germinates from an evasion. The rider assumes it is disobedience and tries harder. The horse gets more frustrated and, even if the existing evasion does not get magnified, new ones creep in. Good riders do everything they can to get a new exercise started correctly, maybe accepting fewer steps in it, or making the patterns more generous. Getting a fundamental correct does not mean it has to be completely polished. The rider has to know the most important objectives of each exercise and work in that direction, without becoming obsessed with small details that are not that important in the big picture.

Counter-canter

As we have seen, most horses are not straight in the dressage sense, which means that the sides of the horse will not be symmetrical. In one direction the horse will be softer and will have a tendency to bend easily, or even too much. In the other direction the horse's body will feel stiff. Over the years, there have been many opinions as to which side is the problem side. It seems fair to say that, today, we appreciate the interconnected nature of the horse's body and understand that most problems are dual. If a horse is too stiff to the left, it is usually too soft to the right, and vice versa. In the basic canter, one of the most difficult tasks is to make the asymmetrical horse straight: very often the horse will canter fairly straight on its stiff side, but carry its haunches crooked to the inside on its softer side.

The importance of correcting this fault is recognized by all factions of riding, and the attempts to correct it run the whole gamut of methods. However, one of the oldest methods, which originates from riding in a school or a building with walls, is the counter-canter. When the old masters encountered a horse that carried its haunches to the inside, away from the wall and towards the middle of the arena, they simply reversed the direction of travel and rode the problem canter in the other direction. Now the wall trapped the escaping haunches. As the rider practiced this exercise with the horse's body molded by the wall, the crooked true canter was made straight by riding it in a counter-direction, hence the name counter-canter.

As soon as one knows why the counter-canter was invented it will be evident how to ride it. If there were no wall for guidance, the rider would use legs and seat to take out the excessive bend. In more recent times, however, we often see the counter-canter ridden with too much bend. Always, the cause of this is a trainer with insufficient knowledge of theory. Even a perfunctory review of equestrian literature will reveal what we have already explained: that the counter-canter was devised as a straightening exercise. When it is ridden with too much bend, this defeats the purpose of the exercise.

The counter-canter can eventually be performed on straight lines and circles, but it is easiest to start the exercise on the shallowest of serpentines. For example, in left canter the rider passes through the corner onto the long wall and gradually curves off the track until the horse is a meter or two out from the wall. Then the rider curves the horse back to the wall, holding the left canter. If the horse does not break gait or change leads, it has taken its first steps in counter-canter. The bend of the serpentine can be gradually increased until it can be ridden out to the centerline and back. This process can be continued until the horse can do a three-loop serpentine with the first loop in true canter, the second in counter-canter, the third in true canter.

Some horses will find the figure of eight easier if, in the beginning, it is deliberately ridden a little lopsided. That is, the circle in true canter is ridden a little smaller to leave more room for the circle in counter-canter. If a shorter diagonal is ridden, the rider can leave almost half of the arena for a large, generous counter-canter half-circle. At first the rider should stay off the track to allow some cushion if the horse tightens up and needs a little more room. Later, the pattern will become more precise

At first, in the counter-canter, the rider might have to allow the inexperienced horse some additional length in the frame to keep it on the counter-lead. After a while,

however, the counter-canter should be virtually identical to the true canter in size and tempo.

Lateral Work at the Canter

Shoulder-in

Essentially, all the lateral exercises of the trot (see Chapter 5) can be repeated in the canter. The shoulder-in at the canter has the same gymnasticising benefits as the shoulder-in at the trot – and more. If there is a gait that is the running gait, it is the canter or gallop. Very often, when training the horse for more engagement and collection at the canter, the horse will misunderstand the increased driving aids and simply run faster. The shoulder-in at the canter is a wonderful remedy for this. The natural collection that the shoulder-in demands teaches the horse to differentiate between the rider's leg aids; to understand that leg aids do not always or only mean 'forward'. In short, because the canter is the gait in which the horse is most prone to running off, the shoulder-in becomes a useful tool to prevent this without resorting to grabbing the reins.

The shoulder-in is also a very useful exercise for lightening horses that want to pull into the reins, which is almost always an attempt to relieve the increasing weight-carrying demands on the hind legs. Again, the redistribution of weight off the forehand lightens the entire front of the horse.   Finally, as an exercise, the shoulder-in has the usual benefits of addressing one-sided crookedness – often so prevalent in canter – by gymnasticising the horse's body with a bending regime.

Travers and Renvers; Riding along the Wall

As has been previously discussed, travers and renvers are twin exercises They are identical except in their relationship or reference to the wall. This relationship to the wall is, of course, crucial. In the simplest analysis, the travers, in which the horse travels with a bend in the direction of movement, will ask for the horse's haunches to be off the wall, whereas the renvers will place the haunches on the wall. (For exact mechanics and descriptions of these movements, see Chapter 5.) Whenever the horse is moving in open space, the haunches become more difficult to control because the door becomes open for their escape – which is a function of any horse's natural crookedness. Now, certainly, there will be a time in the horse's training when it will need to be tested in the open without the support of the wall, but, as has been stated before, this is unwise in the early stages for a very simple reason. If the wall is unavailable for guiding or controlling the hindquarters (in this example), then the job must be taken over by the rider's legs. This will compel the rider to use too many leg aids, with the young horse bouncing around between the rider's legs. Using the wall allows the rider to use fewer and lighter leg aids until the horse's body is educated to the form of the exercise, at which point moving the exercise to a different location is easy. A case can be made that modern riders, who have been influenced by the move towards outdoor riding and away from school riding as a whole, do not make as good use of the walls – and thus use more and heavier aids – than the school riders of the past, who almost always rode inside small buildings. To become obsessive about riding and training young horses and riders away from walls seems obstinate. If one thinks of the wall as the beautifully straight line that it is, one can use it to train precision and healthy uniformity into the lateral exercises.

The renvers has many gymnastic applications by itself, but it can be also be used constructively in combination with other exercises. Examples include: with passade, to prepare for and correct flaws in half-passes; with small circles, on three or four tracks, as preparation for pirouettes; with shoulder-in for increasing suppleness and obedience; with counter-canter for obedience if a horse gets too exuberant about flying changes, etc. It really has unlimited applications – so long as the rider/trainer keeps in mind a fundamental principle of designing good jumping courses. That is, there is a fine line between a challenging gymnastic combination and a destructive trap. However, there are so many tested classical combinations of exercises that it seems almost inconceivable that anyone should need to invent new ones.

Obviously, because of the 'sided' nature of the canter,

certain combinations of lateral exercises, which are useful and attainable in trot, are impossible in canter. For example, in the trot, a shoulder-in left can be changed at the wall to renvers. This is an excellent exercise because it changes bend while leaving the left hind as the driving leg. Horses do not get tangled up switching their hind legs. In the canter, however, this exercise is impossible. It is always up to the rider to understand the objectives of each exercise, and to use different combinations to enhance the training of different horses. This is part of the art of riding. The work is not only good physiotherapy, but it also becomes the basis for good choreography.

Half-pass

There are two paragraphs concerning lateral work in the *FEI Rules for Dressage Events* that are so succinct and so important that I would like to quote them verbatim:

Article 412, Paragraph 2:
As all bending or flexion at the poll and neck has repercussions on the whole spine, the bend or flexion must never be exaggerated so that it impairs the balance and fluency of the movement concerned; this applies especially to the half pass, where the bend should be less evident that in the shoulder-in, travers and renvers.

Article 412, Paragraph 3:
At the lateral movements the pace should remain free and regular, maintained by a constant impulsion, yet it must be supple, cadenced and balanced. The impulsion is often lost because of the rider's preoccupation mainly with bending the horse and pushing him sideways.

One would think that, since these rules are so clear and since they concur with the classicists' ideas, there could be no misunderstanding in any camp of dressage. Yet, today, half-passes can be either a pinnacle of achievement or they can be grotesque parodies, with horses stumbling sideways, paralytically tangled up by riders. Why is this? In the first place, it is a proof of Guérinière's cry:

Practice without true principles is nothing other than routine, the fruit of which is a strained and unsure execution, a false diamond which dazzles semi-connoisseurs often more impressed by the accomplishments of the horse than by the merit of the horseman. From this comes the reason for the small number of well-trained horses, and the paucity of ability one sees at present in the majority of those who call themselves horsemen.... The dearth of principles renders pupils unable to distinguish shortcomings from perfection. They have no other recourse but imitation, and unfortunately it is easier by far to fall into bad practices than it is the acquire good ones. [1]

So long as international trainers declare such movements as the half-pass to be nothing more than a travers or renvers on a diagonal, then the misunderstanding of the 'principles' will continue to be fostered. In a sense, this is easier to correct than the second reason.

One sees so much variation in what are essentially clear movements like the half-pass. Because performers try to distance themselves from the pack, they often try to embellish or exaggerate certain movements, which first leads to distortion, and then may ultimately destroy the purpose of the exercise. The ego has to be held in check. The mindset should be closer to that of the carousels and quadrilles – groups of horses and riders so well trained in the classic exercises that they are almost indistinguishable; a *corps de ballet*. There should not be a grouping of riders in some sort of race, each trying to outdo the one before. Imagine the childishness of such a sight at the ballet!

As in all lateral work, the rider must constantly keep in mind the inverse relationship between cross-over and impulsion. It is the duty of classical practice to *understand* each exercise and not just imitate. The rider has to be careful not to put too much bend in the horse or allow the haunches to get ahead and lead the movement, for all the same reasons that we discussed in the trot.

Counter-changes of Hand and Zigzags

In order to change from the right half-pass to the left half-pass or vice versa, while remaining at the canter, the horse will have to perform a flying change of lead, which will be discussed next. Although there were many lateral exercises practiced in earlier times, there is, to my knowledge, no mention of flying changes until well into the nineteenth century. Certainly, multiple flying changes are not

mentioned before this time. It seems that the introduction of deliberate, multiple, repeated changes as an exercise began in that era, and credit for one-time changes (a flying change every stride), is usually given to the French circus rider, François Baucher.

When flying changes were coupled with the old lateral passes, this marriage produced a rather new exercise. This shows that dressage has evolved, and will probably continue to evolve. How it will change should be interesting, but it may not be with new movements. Although people have 'invented' many novel ways of going, no new movements or exercises have been added in almost one hundred and fifty years. It seems that the work of more recent riders has been to polish the now complete collection of exercises. However, this collection honestly had to be considered incomplete before the addition of the canter flying changes. Classical dressage has always had a goal of perfecting what comes naturally to the horse, and certainly flying changes occur in the natural, free-moving horse. Yet they were not seen in school riding. (It is my own feeling that there is now no necessity for anything new to be added, but the airs above the ground need to be revitalized. They are so rare at the present that the average dressage rider has no idea of their importance as complete proofs of the mastery of balance.)

The requirements of the counter-change at the canter are basically the same as the trot. In the counter-change of hand, the horse must neutralize the bend of one half-pass before it begins the next in the opposite direction. If this is not accomplished, the haunches, which are and should be trailing the shoulders in the first half-pass, will be ahead and leading when the direction is changed. Hence, the moment of straightness that should occur in the counter-change of hand at the trot. However, this becomes somewhat more difficult at the canter because, at that moment, the horse must execute a flying change of lead. In training, it is so important to be straight that as many straight strides as are necessary should be used to achieve this before the next half-pass is begun.

When several counter-changes of hand are executed in succession, the exercise is commonly called the zigzags. In higher level riding, these successive counter-changes are required to contain a precise number of strides in each direction. When this movement is performed to the right

[1] De la Guérinière, F.R., *School of Horsemanship* (J.A. Allen 1994).

and left of an imaginary line, any asymmetry in the training will be exposed. If, for example, the horse's right half-pass is freer than the left, then it may travel further during the same number of strides. If the half-passes are performed to the right and left of a bisecting line, the pattern will quickly become lopsided. Rather than try to push the stiff side to the size of the freer side, it may be necessary to compromise. In this exercise, it is the symmetry and quality of the steps that are crucial, not the overall distance traversed. If the rider does not insist on symmetry, the value of this exercise is lost. As the horse advances in its training and symmetry becomes established, the exercise can be made more difficult by incrementally increasing the sideways traverse and/or by shortening the number of strides between each change of direction.

Flying Changes

As we have noted, the flying changes are a relatively modern exercise or movement, which did not have its birth in the royal schools. It was probably fundamentally for this reason that they were not included in the modern classical repertoire without some argument. Alois Podhajsky wrote of them:

Changes at every stride are one of the most controversial exercises, as a number of experts consider them circus movements and disapprove of them for this reason. Many arguments took place at the Spanish Riding School without ever coming to a satisfactory conclusion. No one could give a reasonable explanation either for or against them. But the Federation Equestre Internationale as a ruling body on international equitation declares that they belong to the classical exercises and demands them in the dressage tests at the Olympic Games.[2]

In all fairness to the trainers who did not feel that the changes were a true classical exercise, one that is developed and improves with strength and practice, no other movement seems to be such a matter of genetics. Horses born with the ability to change can do so correctly from the first day they are introduced to the movement. Other

[2]Podhajsky, A., *The Complete Training of Horse and Rider* (Doubleday 1967).

horses have no inclination to change and training them to do the flying changes can be a long and arduous process.

I have had horses in training that executed three clean flying changes on crossing the centerline of a three-loop serpentine on the first day I asked for them. I have also had horses that have taken a year to achieve the same pattern consistently. It seems to have little to do with a conscientious preparatory training program, although control in the multiple changes definitely does.

In a single flying change, the horse canters on one lead, performs a change in the moment of suspension and lands continuing in canter on the opposite lead. The exercise can also be performed in sequence, for example, a horse canters four strides on the right lead, does a flying change and then canters four strides on the left lead, changes again and repeats the sequence. The number of strides can diminish until, in one-time changes, the horse executes a flying change at every stride, appearing to be skipping down a line.

Over the years I have noticed that two movements seem to have a mystical hold on people learning dressage. One is the piaffe, the other is the flying change. Although the counter-canter plays an important part in the preparation for flying changes, I now know not to wait too long before beginning to train them. Early in my career, I religiously heeded the advice of my teachers to make sure that the counter-canter was confirmed before attempting the flying changes; and too often the counter-canter became too concrete – so confirmed that it was difficult to get the horse out of it.

Before discussing the 'where' of the flying change, the 'how' should be clarified. Flying changes seem to be taught around the world in two distinct schools. In one, the change is initiated and controlled by strong leg aids, which predominate over the seat. In the other, the change is initiated by seat and weight aids, which predominate over the legs.

The main problem with changing with the lower legs is that, by now, the horse has been taught leg-yielding, shoulder-in, travers, renvers, half-pass, and even counter-changes of hand. If the lower legs are used, particularly if one is used more strongly and further back than the other, it will be virtually impossible to make straight changes, which are a premier requirement of classic changes. The horse will do exactly what it has been trained to do – swing the haunches away from the leg. The effect of asymmetrical leg aids in the flying change can be even more dramatic because, at the moment the change is asked for, the rear end of the horse is off the ground and therefore much easier to push out of position. When riders learn this method, or begin training this way, a whole system of defensive maneuvers ensues. They know the change is supposed to be straight but they can't stop the swing with their legs. They try to block the horse with the reins, usually grabbing the outside rein in an effort to prevent the drift. This blocks impulsion, so the rider's body gets thrown more into the movement in an attempt to produce more forward momentum. When the haunches swing out and the rider tries to change back, horse and rider are so far out of line that the horse's neck is bent back in the opposite direction. Eventually the warp is amplified. When the rider changes off the lower leg or spur, the hip and seat move. However, when they follow the leg in this way, it is almost as a ricochet or recoil. The change is late and the rider often bumps the horse in the back at the critical time of the change over, making even semi-successful clean changes hollow. I do not know why this system is still evident, and worse, practiced, but it is.

Classical, straight changes are initiated with the back, seat and hips. The hips of the rider become one with the hips of the horse. In informal practice, if one were to watch the riders who change this way, the rider's lower legs may swing. This would lead one to believe that the rider is signaling the change with the lower leg. However, if one were to look very carefully, say with a slow motion video camera (there are commercially made tapes to this effect), one would see that the lower leg is, in fact, often too late to make the change, which has already taken place. In fact, the subtle but clear actions of the hips, upper leg, thigh and back, has made the change and the lower leg is following the inertia created by the seat. (We will examine this further when discussing the tempi changes in Chapter 7.) The seat predominates: everything is in perfect timing. When changes are trained and executed in this way, the horse will remain straight. The hips of both horse and rider will change like those of a cross-country skier. The legs track in two straight lines like skis. The left hip and leg advance, then the right, then the left, etc. When the hips create the change, the seat will be pushing the change. The changes will be light and round, and when it comes to the multiple changes these will hold a straight line. In this system, the rider will never be behind the motion, grinding the horse's back down into a hollow pose, thus making the hind legs change late.

Before we go on to discuss the training of the young horse and some possible problems, we should first analyze further how the rider learns the aids on a trained horse.

Even a fairly inexperienced rider could feel which canter lead the horse is on with their eyes closed. By the nature of its mechanics, the canter has a slight twisting feel in its motion (see Photos 61–64, pages 121–122). This is coupled with a big undulation that most beginners love to feel. In the right lead, for example, the left hind leg will strike the ground first (Photo 61) once the haunches have come under. The rider feels the horse 'up in front' of the seat. In the second beat (Photo 62), the diagonal pair, the horse falls forward and down. The rider feels the dip, as the shoulders of the horse seem to begin to sink. The drop down feels slightly to the right as the horse prepares for the third beat on the single, leading, right foreleg (Photo 63). At this point the tip forward and to the right seems the most dramatic, because the hind legs are rising up off the ground. The whole horse seems balanced on the right shoulder. A split second later, the mini roller-coaster ride begins to come uphill again as the hind legs come under the center of gravity, lifting and leveling the forehand (Photo 64). The right canter continues to repeat this rise and fall along a right axis. One might imagine riding a skateboard, or a scooter, and pushing off behind with only the left leg, the right hip ahead on the board and advancing, staying out in front. Thus a slight asymmetrical pattern or twist, if you will, yields a straight line. The right hip can be kept ahead, but the rider will have to keep pushing with the left leg, as if riding a skateboard.

If the rider wanted to change driving legs, it would obviously be necessary to change hips. In a flying change from right to left, there is only one time when this change can be asked for and achieved. That is when both hind legs are off the ground and before the right hip gets ahead of the left. This corresponds approximately to the moment

Photo 65. Excelso – last beat of right canter. The rider changes her hips while the hind legs are up and in mid-air. The left hind will follow the rider's left hip up and forward to stay in the air – the right hind will come down first to be the first beat of left canter.

Photos 66 and 67. The phase of the canter stride when the change occurs.

Photo 66. The rider initiates the change with hips, seat and the lightest of leg aids. If the rider did nothing, the right hind would come down first and the horse would stay in left canter.

Photo 67. A moment later the horse follows the rider's hips and brings the right hind up with the rider's right hip. When the rider engages the right hip, seat and inside leg he picks up the horse's right leg and hip: now that leg stays in the air and the left leg will come down first to be the first beat of right canter.

when the leading foreleg is on the ground by itself (when the rider feels about to enter the deepest part of the dip in the canter undulation). Therefore, just as the rider comes up out of the dip, this is the moment to change the hips (see Photo 65). The left hip pushes straight forward, like a skier. The back gives authority to the center of gravity and the hips. The steady leg debars sloppiness. There is no throwing of the weight to one side or the other, which would unbalance the horse and make it crooked. There is no strong lower leg aid that would push the haunches into a travers, or drive the shoulder over. In a change from left to right, the process is reversed (see Photos 66, 67).

Photos 68 and 69. Front view – the last beat of left canter. The rider has brought his right hip forward – there is a slight dip in the right shoulder. The rider's body pushes forward, not side to side. The outside leg goes back almost as a reaction to the pushing aid of seat, back and hip – it is not a case of the lower leg throwing the body.

The classical rider's seat is deep, strong and light. Each seat bone is connected, centaur-like, to the corresponding hip of the horse. Thus, when the rider switches hips in a subtle but clear and powerful movement (Photos 68 and 69), the horse does the same. Since there was no lateral force (sideways-pushing leg), the horse lands straight on its track like the imaginary skier. The horse is ready, if necessary, to repeat the exercise

perfectly straight (see Photos 71–77 in Chapter 7).

Once again, the reader has to appreciate the layering of the classical system. Such a powerful but subtle movement by the rider has been in preparation from the first lessons on the longe, when Newcastle advised the rider not to 'sit upon the buttocks' but to learn to balance over the legs. The rider must master control of the center of gravity first on the straight lines, and then in the asymmetry of the lateral exercises. The seat and weight become subtler, quicker, and more responsive with balance. One day, a shift of weight, timed exactly to a fraction of a second as in the flying change, is possible.

In progressing to the training of the horse, we must, honestly, ask a key question: what if the young horse does not follow the rider's hips in the first attempts? In all honesty, the horse probably will not do so. The rider must then create a situation where the horse will perform a mechanically correct change (rear to front) in consequence.

One of the most common approaches is to go down the long wall in the counter-canter. On the corner, the rider collects the horse more than usual. The rider would almost want the horse to feel suspicious – this will not feel the same as continuing through the corner in the counter-canter. When the horse and rider are just about to enter the corner, the rider asks for the change. If it fails, the rider must wait a few strides to see if the horse will get the idea and make the change. If it does not, the rider makes a transition to the trot, or walk, and does a simple change. The rider must show the horse what is required. Very often, the horse will change in front, but not behind. In such cases, the canter should be kept short, and a touch with the whip or spurs given to excite the hind legs. If the horse feels a little bucky, that is good. The hind legs must quicken. The rider then holds the reins steady at the next attempts, avoiding any temptation to turn the head or neck into the new change. The horse's body must also be kept straight. It is almost as if the rider must prevent the shoulders from going over until the hind legs go first. The curve of the corner will do the work, because the horse will be uncomfortable in the stiff counter-canter and, if kept active and not allowed to stretch out through the turn, will probably change by itself. As soon as that happens, the rider must praise the horse and go on with the new canter.

If the horse is still late behind, the rider should do everything the same, but this time carry a longish whip. If, for example, the rider is counter-cantering on the right lead and approaching a left turn at the corner, the whip should be in the rider's left hand. As the horse approaches the corner, the rider taps with the whip toward the left hock. The horse may kick up at this, but it will initiate the hind leg and hip change. The rider should then praise the horse and repeat, trying to coordinate the seat aids with the signaling of the whip.

If, in the beginning, the horse seems to change without specific signals from the rider' seat, this is not a worry. The important thing at this stage is to get a mechanically clean change. After a few more, the rider should try the change without the whip. Remember, the key element is that the horse keeps straight. Building a little nervousness or quickness into the step and letting some of the natural change of direction offer relief, are good tools. Then, the normal canter must be resumed as soon as possible after the change. From the beginning, the rider must tell the horse, 'I will never initiate a flying change without a set up, a little collection, and a little surge of power'. Then, if the rider approaches a turn in the counter-canter with seat relaxed and back swinging, the horse will stay in the counter-canter. If, however, the rider braces the back and collects the horse, the horse is being prepared to change. The rider is telling the horse 'I may change my seat and hips, and you must follow'.

The advantage of training the change from the counter-canter to the true canter is that it is the horse's natural inclination to get out of the counter-canter to the true canter. Also, and very important, there is the fact that the wall will serve as a straight line to help keep the horse from huge sideways deviations, even when changing toward the arena. The disadvantage is that, with some horses, this method will ruin the reliability of the counter-canter for a while. A few horses will feel trapped by the wall and perform better in free space.

A common system of teaching the change in free space is to circle the horse in a figure of eight with the circles about 15 meters in diameter. On crossing the middle of the arena, make a simple change through the trot. Continue until the number of trot steps is reduced to one or two. When the horse gets used to the pattern, eliminate the trot all together. The canter is set up the same as in the previous exercises – collect, straight, firm it up, and quicken it. The whip is used on the new inside. Then everything gets calmed down again. The advantages of training on the figure of eight are twofold. First, that a very clear change of direction and rein from one true canter to the other is present. Second, since the counter-canter has been left out of the exercise, it eliminates confusion if the horse starts to anticipate the change. The disadvantage is that the horse and rider are out in the open and, if the horse becomes crooked, the change can become crooked. It is much more difficult to keep the horse straight in a free space with no wall.

A rider who does not have a lot of experience, or can't change in front of a mirror, may find it hard to feel exactly when and if the change is performed correctly. In addition, the first change may be small or ill defined. Therefore, it is important that someone with a good eye is on the ground and can tell the rider the instant the horse switches correctly. A secondary, but highly important aspect here is that a softening of the aids can reward the horse immediately.

Let me say, at this point, that I have never encountered a sound horse that could not learn to do a single flying change. Some learn in a matter of days, some take months. Some will learn to change as they feel the rider collect them and straighten them before a turn, others will need to be tapped into the new change with the whip. The process may take a lot of patience and will require discretion. This is an exercise that cannot be practiced too many times in one session without it becoming very frustrating and/or upsetting for horse, or rider, or both.

In all the years and all the problem changes I have had to retrain, I never once fixed a faulty change by riding bigger or longer. I have always had to shorten the stride – in some cases quicken the tempo – but I have always had to collect, to get the horse more on the hind legs and therefore more active. If the horse is late behind, it usually means that the rider needs more activity to shorten the length of the hind leg steps and quicken the step. It will be much easier for the horse to make a small jump than a big one. Then, after the horse has learned the change, the rider can open the canter up again. If the horse is late in front, it usually means that it is getting caught by the reins. The rider has to make sure that the neck is not locked stiff, not by bending it, but by encouraging it to reach straight into the new turn. It is very important not to bend the horse to signal the change. If you bend the neck and head into the new change, this will come back to haunt you later when you try to make straight tempi changes.

When I mentioned earlier about creating a situation whereby the horse would perform mechanically clean changes right and left in response to circumstances, this is what I meant. After this comes the point in training when the rider will ask for the changes without the help of a new bend, corner, or circle. The rider will ask for changes on a straight line. In the case of the rider who was previously using the figure of eight, this pattern can now be spread out, connecting the two circles with a longer, straight diagonal line. The rider who was using the counter-canter on the wall can now ask for a change in the middle of the wall, not near the turn. When the rider can obtain a single flying change anywhere in the arena, when it is straight, and when the horse waits for the rider to change with the seat, then the horse is ready to begin multiple changes and tempi changes.

Multiple Changes

Once the rider can place a single change anywhere – one time at the beginning of the diagonal, one time in the middle, one time at the end; one time in the beginning of a long wall, one time in the middle, etc., now is the time to try to put two or three together. Early attempts might entail riding one early on the long wall, one in the middle, etc., always remembering that even numbers of changes will leave the horse in true canter for the oncoming corner, while odd numbers of changes will leave the horse in counter-canter. At this point the intervals between changes are unimportant. What is important is that the horse waits for the rider. If, when the changes were started, they were always set up, that habit will pay off. If there is no habitual set-up, there will be no change. The rider should always prepare for the changing and should never surprise the horse. If the horse anticipates too much, the rider can stay in the counter-canter or make full transitions to the walk or halt. Having previously trained in all these movements, the rider has many options if things go wrong.

When the horse can do three changes back and forth down the long wall, horse and rider are probably ready for tempi changes. Discussion of these tempi changes has been left for the following chapter, on high school work. Although, traditionally, a horse's training has been classified into such categories they are, of course, arbitrary divisions. A horse may be more advanced in one area than another. However, it is important that a horse's training stays fairly even. If one were to go to a particular stable and see it full of specialists – one in piaffe, one in tempi changes, another in pirouettes – and none doing these movements in the context of a well-rounded, high level of performance, one would probably be seeing a stable of talented horses, and not so talented trainers.

CHAPTER SEVEN
Haute Ecole

The underlying theme of this book has been to explain how the classical system is a continuous process. There is a complex layering system of skills and a dovetailing of exercises. Unless one trains horses all the way through, it is impossible to really understand the way the training must fit together and what is more and what is less important along the way. All along, there has been the inherent warning that all theory must yield a cohesive whole, or the trainer can become infatuated with interesting but unworkable fragments. The tendency in the beginning is to want to climb the ladder as quickly as possible. Some riders think that a lot of experience at Grand Prix level will automatically fulfill the requirements for experience at the lower levels. Well, it won't. There is no substitute for experience at every level: each has its own importance and, in some cases, the lower levels are more important. So long as a rider is seduced by the glamorous notion of high school, there will be a problem. This is not just some psychological problem of too large an ego. The problem is one of pragmatic importance and it has a real physical dimension, which is that the horse knows the rider doesn't really care about the fundamentals, about doing the simple things right. The horse knows that it can wear the rider out with a little dragging of the feet. This rider will bore easily.

I cannot tell you how many times young instructors have come up to me and said, 'If I don't let my students do upper level movements, they'll go to another instructor who will. I won't have any business'. Back in the seventeenth century, Pluvinel lamented that 'The problem with

academies is that many are run by persons who are solely interested in personal gain which makes it impossible for them to perform public duty'. He went on to suggest that, if whoever ran the academy had financial security, then 'they would not be forced to pay compliments and offer other attractions to the young who are under his tutelage or sometimes tolerate vices simply to keep them or attract others'.[1]

Part of being a teacher is to do the teaching and not let the students control the curriculum. Like the horse, if the students know that the teacher doesn't really care about the fundamentals, about doing the simple things right, they also know that they can wear the teacher down with a little feet dragging. The teacher will bore easily. A student might think 'If I procrastinate a little, then I can do something that is more fun'. Any school of horsemanship that is based on such 'fun' demeans the blood, sweat and tears of such as La Broue and Newcastle and Guérinière, who gave us classical dressage. There can be great joy in riding, but it is set up with great work. The study of equitation is school, not entertainment.

Sometimes, deliberately allowing a student to do a higher-level exercise than they are really ready for can be appropriate. It may expose and illuminate a simple point, which otherwise would be too subtle for the struggling rider. A basic example might be as follows. In the very first lessons, student riders will very often try too hard to sit correctly. Often, a student ends up with too much leg

[1]Pluvinel, Antoine de, *Le Maneige Royal* (J.A. Allen 1989).

133

strength, or the wrong kind of thigh contact. If that student rides leg-yields, or is given a task which separates the use of the legs, requiring that the rider has to push the horse with one leg then the other, the student can develop the right kind of alive tonus in the legs. Now, the student may think that this wonderful sideways motion of the horse criss-crossing its legs is just grand, but as the teacher knows, in this case, the leg-yield is pretty much incidental. The teacher is interested in getting the rider's leg muscles educated; in teaching the rider not to just sit there with frozen and gripping legs, trying harder and harder to hold on. By changing the focus of attention, the teacher can obtain what is required in the rider's body.

Too many riders will try to help the teacher. They are sure they know what the teacher wants, so they keep trying harder and harder, not realizing they are getting in their own way. When the teacher lets them focus on something else, the mind is kept happy with the subterfuge of its new challenge, while the teacher does the real work on the rider's body. This is very different teaching from allowing students to skip over fundamentals. An observer may see two lessons on leg-yielding and think they are the same. In reality, one lesson is about a sub-standard leg-yield, and the other is about perfecting the fundamentals of the seat in a creative way.

Not all riders and all horses are capable of high school work. The teacher may know, statistically, that of the 'x' number of students presented, only one will make it to the elite rider status, or the elite horse status. The problem is that the teacher cannot know for sure which will be the one – in spite of all the propaganda from the horse breeding associations. Beyond some simple, obvious rules of conformation, that even a novice student of riding could learn in a few weeks, the teacher cannot tell by looking at a three-year-old horse whether it will make it to high school, and the same goes with riding students. (To me, the best breeding programs in the world hinge on performance. Thus, if a horse were a great performer, the assumption would be that this horse had the right combination of genotype and phenotype, even if the conformation says that this shouldn't work. The breeding of thoroughbred racehorses is a very good example. All the body types are let in, the subjective pre-screening is limited, and the performance should do the sorting.

Pedigree is important only because it is a history of performance. Bull-fighting horses have long been bred this way, and great jumping horses constantly defy the so-called rules of conformation.)

However, these are challenges for horse breeders. For horse trainers, the challenge is to be fair and to train all students, human and equine, the best way that the trainer knows how. Let the horse and/or the student decide how far each might want to go. It is not the decision of the teacher.

Now this comes full circle. If a teacher does not believe absolutely in the equal importance of all levels of training, then that teacher will not be able to give a novice the same quality of lesson as a Grand Prix rider. This fraudulence will prove that the teacher has not understood the classical principles and how they are woven together – the layering again.

Some Preliminary Thoughts on Spurs and the Double Bridle

At some point during the Campaign School work it was most likely that spurs were introduced (see The Exercises of the Campaign School in Chapter 4). It goes without saying that spurs should never be used to injure a horse, and any style of spur capable of wounding a horse is inappropriate. However, neither is bludgeoning a horse with dull spurs acceptable. Spurs are not implements of crudity: they are designed to engender more sophisticated feel and response in both horse and rider. In some cases horses will respond without them but now, in high school work, they have to be considered mandatory. By now, the horse must be so acclimatized to, and trusting of, the rider's leg aids that the use of spurs can be considered similar to writing with a more finely pointed pen. If there is a problem with using spurs, this points to something more fundamentally wrong with the feel of the horse or rider.

There is only one other notable change in equipment as one gets to the high school training, and that is the introduction of the full bridle. The full bridle is a fine-tuning instrument: it is not used to stop a strong horse. Transitions are used to balance a strong horse. The bridle only aids in transitions. Because the full bridle is much more sensitive an instrument than the snaffle bridle, mistakes with it are harsher, more amplified, but also nuances of lightness are available that are not achievable in the snaffle. From the point of view of a rider's education, even if a horse could do all the movements of high school in the snaffle bridle, the rider's feel must be taken to a higher level by learning to ride competently with the full bridle. In competitions, the full bridle is mandatory at the level of Prix St. Georges and above.

The first thing to consider with the full bridle is holding the four reins. Today, virtually every possible combination is used, but there are some ways better than others. There is also an historical precedent. Before we consider the different methods, for the sake of clarity, first number the spaces between the fingers. From the bottom of the hand, the space between the little finger and the next (often called the ring finger), will be 1; the space between the ring finger and the next (usually the longest finger) will be 2; the space between that longest finger and the index (pointing) finger will be 3; and the space above the index finger, which can be closed by the thumb coming down on it, will be 4.

When riding with a snaffle, the rein most commonly comes in at 1, goes up the middle of the hand and comes out at 4. When the snaffle rein runs between the fingers, it has an added delicacy that comes from the two fingers being able to close on the rein creating tension, but having 'give' in the fingers, being separated from the fist. If the snaffle rein comes in at the bottom of the hand and comes up the middle and out at 4, so that the whole fist is used, this eliminates a lot of the feel of the fingers, because there is no way to catch the rein with the friction between the fingers. I teach pupils, when riding in a snaffle, to bring the reins in at 1 with the bight (excess of the rein) coming out at 4. When picking up the reins of the full bridle, the simplest procedure (though not the most classical) is to take up the bridoon (snaffle) rein in exactly the same way as the rider has been doing with the simple snaffle bridle – in at 1, out at 4. This leaves the rider and horse with a certain calming familiarity. Next, take up each curb in at 2 and at 4. The reins will criss-cross from the bits to the rider's hands. The curb bit gets its power from its lever action over a fulcrum created by the curb chain. Its great-

est use is not lateral but longitudinal. Therefore, it needs to be kept even both left and right. (The jointed snaffle, however, is often worked one side or the other. But as the work progresses, a lot of excessive neck bend is taken out and the body is made straighter and more connected.)

The old masters addressed the issue by riding '3 in 1'. The right snaffle rein (for ease of comparison in this section, I am using the term 'snaffle' to describe the bridoon on a full bridle) remained by itself in the right hand coming in at 1, and up and out at 4 (or in around the smallest finger and out at 4). The left hand held all the rest of the reins. Traditionally, the left snaffle rein was carried around the bottom of the hand (moved down one finger). The left curb rein came in at 1 and out at 4, and the right curb rein came in at 2 (or 3, if the rider wanted to get a little more space in between), and out at 4. This left hand was carried more over the horse's neck and resulted in a very even curb. Slight twists of the wrists could produce turns, and small movements of the whole fist back and forward could slightly increase the pressure of the curb or relax it. In this system, the rider could easily bring the right snaffle rein over and place it on top of the 4 space of the left hand thus freeing the right hand for swordplay, for example. Or the rider could simply demonstrate a supreme level of control from very subtle movements of one wrist.

Over the years, I have simplified my teaching on holding the reins to one of three ways. First, for the plain snaffle bridle, the snaffle reins go in at 1 and out at 4. Second, for the full bridle, the snaffle reins again go in at 1 and out at 4; the curb reins go in at 2 and out at 4. The third and final way is probably the quietest and most sensitive for the full bridle. In the right hand, the right snaffle rein goes in at 1, out at 4. All the rest of the reins are in the left hand, as follows: left snaffle rein, in at 1, out at 4; right curb rein, in at 3, out at 4; left curb rein, in at 2, out at 4. (My own preference is that I do not put the rein around the bottom of the hand.)

Finally, there are some riders who love to switch back and forth between the snaffle and the full bridle. I have found that the full bridle is significantly complex and horses need time to learn about it and adjust to it. Therefore, I do not switch back and forth a lot, especially when I first introduce the full bridle. I ride with it for a long time. I may change the adjustments, starting with a long, mild curb chain, or even use a rubber guard if the horse is very sensitive. I may use a slightly thicker snaffle; but in general, I like the horse to become completely accustomed to it and train in it. The snaffle may be used on light days, or days when the horse is hacked. The idea of putting a fairly well trained horse back in a snaffle and then allowing it to pull or become heavy under the guise of freshening it up is ludicrous. It would be like telling a good pianist to go back and practice on a dull or poor instrument because this will somehow strengthen their skills. In a riding context, the only things that get strengthened are the rider's arms!

The Progression of High School Work

Before going on to discuss high school exercises, some of which have I have alluded to earlier, I would like to emphasize the point that there are divisions of exercises in the high school category. Not all horses train perfectly in all areas. Some may be more advanced in the trot work, for example, and take a while to catch up in the highest canter exercises – or vice versa. This is normal. In some cases, the exercises cross the divisions. While the canter pirouette belongs in the high school, some might think the half-pirouette should have been included earlier. The problem with the half-pirouette is that it is not half as difficult as a full pirouette. Indeed, if it is done correctly, it is just as difficult as a full pirouette – is simply half the number of steps. Since it is a complex exercise, to which a reasonable amount of controversy is attached, I have left it until this chapter on high school work. The underlying point here is that the rider/trainer cannot make an exact recipe that applies for every horse.

Tempi Changes

Once the horse is doing a few calm, straight, multiple changes, it is time to being the tempi changes, which are multiple changes with an exact number of strides in between. Up until now, the focus has been on waiting if

Photo 70. The horse has finished the last stride of left canter and is changing to lead on the first stride of a right canter sequence.

necessary to get the right preparation before doing a flying change. Now the preparation must be pressed to be there on demand.

One of the most troublesome aspects for riders learning tempi changes is the counting of strides. Many riders will be fine unconsciously practicing four- or five-stride changes when learning multiples, but then completely go to pieces when they have to deliberately count the number of strides in between the changes. To remedy this, the first thing is to learn a system of counting that can keep track of the total number of changes while adhering to a certain rhythm. Probably the most common system is to think in terms of clusters.

Taking changes every four strides as an example, the rider will keep track of the number of changes by assigning a sequential number to each change and adding these in to a count through the series. At the moment of the change, the foreleg(s) will be on the ground (see Photo 70). The hind legs will be coming forward. The rider then makes the change and, as the change lands, the rider counts 'one'. Remember: as the change *lands* it will be the first stride of the upcoming sequence. This stride will probably feel quicker or faster than the other upcoming strides. In this first cluster or sequence, counting 'one' for the first change will coincide with the first stride of the sequence. The rider must not be confused by that coincidence. *The count which is keeping track of the number of changes will always supercede the count that marks that stride as the first of the series.* The rider then counts 'two' for the second stride, 'three' for the third. Whilst counting, the rider is also preparing to change right after the completion of the next stride which is counted as 'four'. As stride number four is finishing, when the foreleg(s) are on the ground and the hind legs are off the ground, the rider changes. On landing, the rider counts 'two', because this is the second change. In fact, it is the first stride of the second sequence, but the change count supercedes the stride count on this stride. Remember; this landing stride will probably feel quicker at first, and the rider will have to be sharp so as not to get left behind in the counting. The next stride is the second stride so the rider counts 'two', then 'three' for the third, 'four' for the fourth. Right after counting 'four' the rider changes again. This time, initial count is 'three', once again substituting the total of the changes for the first stride of the sequence. This process simply repeats, so that this useful compromise counting system keeps track of any number of changes while making sure that they happen in an exact sequence. The count should sound like this: 1,2,3,4; 2,2,3,4; 3,2,3,4; 4,2,3,4, etc.

It has been my experience that too much help in counting from the ground will often lead to more confusion. It is best to let the rider do a line of three- or four-time changes, and then quiz the rider as to where they have made an error, if one has been made. As they get the idea, add more. In the beginning, it is important to count the big number of the change emphatically, whether mentally or physically, in order to accentuate it. That will help build each sequence to a crescendo, thus preparing each set for the change. Obviously, the counting is shortened as the sequence goes down. Three-time changes are 1,2,3; 2,2,3; 3,2,3; 4,2,3, etc.

If the rider and horse are having a lot of trouble getting the idea of repeating sequences in a rhythm, a shallow serpentine pattern up the centerline might be helpful. The rider swings out slightly from the centerline for six strides or so, and then crosses the centerline on changing from left to right, for example. Then there is a shallow right loop of six strides and back to the centerline with another change right to left, followed by a shallow loop to the left. By placing it at the change of direction and bend, the change itself will usually be easier and more definite The clear polarity will lend definition to the sequence, and it can help the rider who becomes flustered by the counting and begins missing changes in consequence. Obviously, this is very much a temporary exercise, but it can be useful, especially if the horse and rider are consistently missing the change in one direction but the other. The drawback to this exercise is that it puts off dealing with straight lines of changes.

The tempi changes will often proceed fairly systematically until the one-time changes, which are almost a gait in themselves. In the training of the one-time changes, the horse and rider need to have fairly quick reflexes. In the beginning, it is better to keep the stride a little more collected and as straight as possible. If the horse if bent too much in one direction, it will have to swing its hips way to the other side to compensate for the crookedness.

One of the easiest ways to begin training the one-time changes is to start with a couplet, just two, and to start on a circle, to the left, for example. On coming across the middle of the arena, the rider straightens the horse as if approaching the intersection of a figure of eight, but stays on the circle. Upon reaching the centerline, a change is made to the right. Immediately upon feeling the horse change, the rider applies the aids to change back left so as to coincide with the curve left. At this stage of training, there should be no concern about the first change – almost certainly, the rider will get it. The rider's focus is on getting back onto the left circle, on the left lead, as quickly as possible. Again, this is an exercise where it may be helpful to have someone on the ground with a good eye, because the first changes may be muddled or broken. If the rider sticks to the simple couplet, and keeps the horse's stride short and lively, the one-time changes will come, even if, at first, they feel like accidents.

(Very often, at this point, good students will complain that the horse is doing the changing 'by itself': the rider feels that he or she has no control over the changing. Such riders must be reminded that everything in the set-up has been under their control. The rider still does have control, but now in a more relative sense. Certainly, there is an argument that if a mouse goes through a maze constructed by a human, that is the mouse's doing; but the human has controlled the outcome by building a structure. The horse and rider will get together soon. Relative control will turn into more absolute control with practice. But, in the beginning, if one is a little ahead or behind the other, that is normal.)

The couplet exercise can also be used along the wall. The pros and cons of practicing changes in different places have been cited in the previous chapter. Riders will have to experiment and discover the most effective method for them and for each horse. Once the couplet is working regularly, the rider can either group a few of these couplets together, down the long wall, for example, or try to add a third consecutive change. When the rider and horse achieve the third change this is a psychological breakthrough, because they have broken through the sequence left, right *and* right, left, to obtain the sequence left, right, left. Once this psychological breakthrough has been achieved, the rider will be able to add more one-time changes without doing anything new physically.

Faults in Tempi Changes

SWAYING OR CROOKED CHANGES

The biggest fault of tempi changes is if they swing or sway from side to side, or are in general crooked. Every rider has been forewarned by the classical system to get the basics right (see Photos 71–77). If the strike-offs, or canter departs, are faulty, the rider should have fixed them before the changes were started. A rider who is

using too much leg should have studied and worked more on the seat and balance. I have seen the faces of old master trainers as they watched riders who swung all over in the saddle and pushed the horse's hindquarters one way and the other. Theirs is not a look you want aimed in your direction as a rider. For one thing, there really isn't a place in classical riding for the sight of two sets of haunches wagging like a cabaret show. More importantly, it evokes a kind of defiant attitude to the classical tradition, its history and its principles. It is as if to say, I can do this any way I wish.

When many of the old masters held back certain exercises from certain students, it was not just because they felt the students were not physically ready. The masters were not afraid that the student would make a mistake. No good trainer is afraid of mistakes. The fear is that the student would not by ready psychologically, or that there was not the proper respect being put into the work. Lack of respect diminishes the legacy of classical riding. A teacher takes it personally if his student is making a mockery of past trainers whom he

Photos 71–77. If the basics have been mastered the changes should be so straight that one could roll a ball down a straight line between the horse's legs. This horse is very correct – forward with no waggling in the changes.

has worshipped, or a tradition that the teacher has grown to love more and more deeply. It is difficult sometimes for a teacher to instill the proper weight for particular lessons. It is odd how success very rarely adds depth to a rider's life experience. Failure is much better at cultivating a solemnity. Failure can shatter the stiffness of confidence that may block a rider from learning new things. When failure sets up a kind of hopelessness, it has the possibility of liberating the rider. However, too much failure can break a rider's spirit. The art of teaching, then, becomes a matter of finding ways to instill in a student a kind of relentless self-questioning, which has the benefits of failure without the negative aspects of pervasive self-doubt. Then, for some people, it will not just be a matter of semantics when the question changes from: 'What is wrong with what I am doing?' to 'How can I do it better?'

ASYMMETRICAL CHANGES

Another problem is that the changes are uneven, left and right, or one is larger and/or freer than the other: these are proofs of asymmetry. The faulty side and the change have to be isolated and improved. Let us say, for example, that the change from right to left is not of the same quality as the change from left to right. The rider can take the horse to the rail or the wall, pick up the counter-canter on the right lead, continue until the balance feels fairly good, and make a flying change to the left. Now, the rider should not do a flying change back to the right – that change is fine. Instead, the procedure is to make a simple change, or a transition down to walk or trot. If the horse feels a little strong, the rider should definitely return to the walk and wait until the horse settles. When the horse feels about right (probably not perfect – the rider who waits for perfection won't get in any practice), the rider must resume the right lead counter-canter, balance it, make it very straight and then change again. The whole process is then repeated, the idea being to continue isolating the faulty change in order to polish it.

MISSING THE RHYTHM OF THE COUNT

This is essentially a lesser fault, especially if it only happens occasionally. If, however, there is a pattern developing – the horse always misses at 'X', for example,

then the rider has to look closer to find the reason and make the correction. Flying changes are relatively quick and subtle. When small problems arise, the rider has to be careful not to get consumed by them. A strong reaction by the rider can set up suspicion or anxiety in the horse, thus engendering a real problem of confidence where before none existed. A strong physical reaction almost always pushes the horse sideways, thus making it crooked. In principle, this is rather like getting after a horse excessively for shying. The horse becomes afraid of and/or anticipates the punishment, as well as the source of the shying: the whole process doubles the anxiety. However, if the basics are followed, in a year or so the horse will grow out of the problem. When faced with such difficulties, a rider who really cares about the training of horses and equestrian practice must constantly remember not to panic.

The Canter Pirouette

The canter pirouette has to be considered the ultimate canter exercise. It is the smallest of circles a horse can make while remaining cantering. With virtually no forward advance, it requires a complete collection of the stride and then, in successive canter bounds, with the hind legs practically on the same spot, it turns a complete 360 degree revolution until, from the same spot as its origin, the horse moves off forward or into a lateral movement with no apparent change in rhythm or tempo. When executed correctly, it is precise, powerful, and under such control that the rider should be able to interrupt it at any one of the six to eight strides, and ride off without hesitation.

When the rider undertakes a study of the canter pirouette, two things emerge. One is what people say about it: – different master's opinions; theories. The other is what riders actually do; what happens.

The canter pirouette is to the canter what the piaffe is to the trot – namely, an exercise which demonstrates the ultimate collection within that specific gait. It is here that so much of the controversy concerning the pirouette begins. I have stated many times that the classical consensus ties itself to the natural movements of the horse. There is a built-in loyalty to the integrity of each gait. For example, a canter on three legs will never be accepted into the repertoire of classical exercises because it is so unnatural. There is a fundamental belief that the correct trot is a two-beat gait, and the correct canter a three-beat gait. Therefore, it is quite logical to insist that all the exercises of the trot remain two-beat, and all the exercises of the canter remain three-beat. However, modern high-speed filming techniques have proven that trots are not always two-beat and canters are not always three-beat.

This scrutiny becomes similar to a scientist looking for the smallest particles of matter with instruments of ever-increasing efficiency. With more and more sophisticated observations the atom loses its place as the smallest particle when sub-atomic particles are discovered, and so the process will continue. But there is no threatening cloud of scientific discovery looming over the classical principles. The classical principles are holistic ideals, which involve aesthetics and geometry. A half-pass may meet all the requirements of lateral bend and the placing of the footfalls, but if the rider has trained the horse from force and fear then, as Xenophon said two thousand years ago, it cannot be beautiful. When the canter pirouette is proven to be a four-beat movement, this does not contradict the ideal. Rather, it defines the geometry of individual movement or groups of attempted movements, which can often help to enhance the ideal.

Many trainers have held different opinions as to whether the pirouette is a three- or four-beat exercise; but rarely, if ever, has an appraisal of the good pirouette been based on footfalls. More importantly, what is judged is the integrity of the rhythm coming to it and through it – whether it has true collection, whether it has control, and so on. Brigadier General Kurt Albrecht said, 'The canter pirouette is developed from the "school canter", which is in fact a four-time canter though the unassisted human eye is too slow to recognize it as such... Nevertheless the pirouette shows more impulsion if the illusion of the three-time canter is preserved.' [2] Thus, the ideal can seemingly be an illusion – and how

is one to measure an apparent illusion?

Both the canter and walk pirouette have been described as turns around the inside hind leg. This inside hind leg, however, must keep moving in the natural sequence of the particular gait, and not get 'stuck to the ground' so that the horse would pivot on it. (This is not the leg which makes the pirouette happen.) Because the rhythm of the gait is so important and forward impulse is such a core principle of classical riding, that hind leg is allowed to move forward somewhat. This is why a pirouette which stops – or worse, one that moves backwards – is a serious flaw. Not because something horrible happens biomechanically the moment a horse rocks backward too much, but because something very serious assaults the core principle of forward impulse first. When learning the levade, a horse will sometimes back onto the hind legs to set itself up, but good trainers discourage too much of this. In the classical pirouette the horse should step into collection with its hind legs, not back up onto them. The lifting occurs from the forward engagement and tucking under of the haunches and hind legs, not from pushing and pulling the weight back with the forelegs, neck and shoulders. (When a human physician warns a patient with back pain to flex the knees to get under the weight and lift with the legs, rather then leaning over to pull the object up with the arms and thus straining the stretched out lower back, this is the exact same advice for a good, healthy pirouette with the horse.)

The pirouette has also been described as a circle on two tracks where the radius of that circle is the length of the horse's body (see Photo 38, page 88). Imagine a carousel horse with the pole through its hindquarters rather than its saddle: if one pushed it sideways, it would swing like a gate. The hind legs and the forelegs are inscribing two circles of very different dimensions. The hind legs may be inscribing a circle with a circumference of three feet (0.9 m) – the size of a generous dinner plate, as is often described. The forelegs are stepping laterally inscribing another circle the circumference of which is about twenty-five feet (7.5 m).

When a horse enters the pirouette in a three-beat canter it is supposed to stay in the three-beat canter through the pirouette and out of it again. In theory, the canter could remain three-beat as long as the diagonal

[2]Albrecht, K., *A Dressage Judge's Handbook* (J.A. Allen 1988).

Rear views of canter pirouette.

Photo 78. If this diagonal pair breaks apart the pirouette will become four-beat. Here, the leading foreleg is leaving the ground and the left hind takes over.

Photo 79. Here, the diagonal is grounded (leading foreleg almost planted). If the inside hind does not catch the weight sent over by the left hind, the hips will sink and the pirouette will fall inward.

pairing of the second beat remains together and stays pure (see Photos 78, 79). In reality, there are two main areas where the requirements of the pirouette influence or impact on the requirements of the three-beat canter. One is the reduction in the suspension phase between successive canter strides; the other is the number of strides it takes to complete the 360 degree revolution of the full pirouette.

In a normal canter stride there are the three beats of the canter but there is, in a sense, a fourth, invisible beat of suspension between repeating strides (see Photo 64, page 122). If a rider, in trying to hold the pirouette to a small circle, pulls on the reins and/or subsequently reduces all the jump and suspension between strides by killing all the forward impulse and eliminating the power, the stride will spread out to four beats. The hind legs will have to lift off the ground to replant for the next stride, but they won't do this during a moment of complete suspension. Instead, they move when the forefeet are on the ground. Thus, like a rocking horse, the horse transfers weight back and forth, one end always supporting the other. In a similar way, the walk is a four-beat gait because there is not enough power for a moment of suspension of the stride. In both cases, the timing of the legs spreads out like uniform spokes of a

wheel, thus transmitting what impulsion was present into more even increments of thrust and support.

The second issue is the number of strides in a given pirouette. Although nowadays the consensus is that the pirouette should have between six and eight strides, as recently as forty or fifty years ago it was common to see pirouettes of four strides. If we were to refer to the approximate dimensions of a pirouette given earlier, and it is accomplished in eight strides, the hind legs would have to move some four to five inches (10–12 cm) sideways with each stride to make a full 360 degree revolution. The forelegs, in addition, would have to move about three feet (0.9 m) sideways with each stride. If, for the sake of argument, the number of strides were cut down to four, the hind legs would have to move almost ten inches (25 cm) sideways with each stride, while the forelegs would have to cover a distance of six feet (1.8 m). There comes a point when there is too much difference in the lateral distances between hind and fore legs. The torque generated and the distance that the forefeet spread out to, break up the diagonal pairing. The horse advances the pirouette in a fan-like, four-beat rotary movement. The shoulders push the horse around in a spinning movement. This is the antithesis of collection. Once the pirouette is entered at this lateral speed, it is virtually impossible to interrupt the sequence smoothly and ride out at a given stride. Riding the pirouette in this way eliminates the requirement for complete control of the sideways motion, and really violates the classical premise of forward first, sideways second.

Kurt Albrecht said that the problem with the pirouette lies in the limits of human vision. It is a fact that the person who rides a pirouette can never see it. Human vision has never been a part of the pirouette. The rider must feel it. If the movement is filmed, it will always be after the fact. If it is ridden in front of a mirror, much of the movement will be blocked from view as the pirouette is turned. The rider has to develop a feel for the pirouette, and then must stick honestly to its high standards. Most experienced riders are not fooled by the differences between a collected three-beat canter (see Photos 81–83) or a four-beat school canter, and a four-beat broken down canter. In the pirouette, the mass of the horse will be lifted onto the hind legs. It will fall forward and to the inside over its diagonal pair of legs, and onto its lone, leading foreleg before it is lifted again. Although

Photos 80–83
Canter pirouette – front views.

Photo 80 (right). The horse will use both hind legs to lift the forehand...
Photo 81 (below left). The mass will fall forward and to the inside – on to the diagonal pair – the rider must be careful not to fall forward...
Photo 82 (below middle). Finally, the third beat of the leading foreleg and then...
Photo 83 (below right). A return to the left. Good power and animation.

143

distinction of the canter beats might be blended, all phases should be present. To all intents and purposes, there should not be any reduction or acceleration of the canter tempo. A great deal of the beauty of the pirouette lies in how it fits into the regular collected canter sequence. If poor quality is detected in practice, the rider has to analyze why.

Training the Canter Pirouette

One of the most common ways to begin training the pirouette is to use a combination of the travers and a passade or a half-circle in travers position (see Figure 22, page 87). For example, the rider proceeds down the long wall in a right canter keeping straight above the horse. The rider applies the left leg slightly back and bends the horse around the quiet, steady, inside (right) leg so that the horse is advancing with the haunches in. As the corner is approached, the horse and rider will begin a turn of 6 or 8 meters but, as they get halfway round the turn, since the haunches are kept in, the haunches will be 6 or 8 meters from the wall. The rider can either straighten and head back to the same wall and then continue in counter-canter, or blend a half-pass into the finish of the half-circle and take it back to the wall and continue in counter-canter. Obviously, adding in the half-pass will ensure that the outside (left) hind leg which carries the travers will continue doing extra work to finish the exercise. Thus this exercise is a good strength builder as preparation for pirouettes.

This exercise evolves in two ways. One is that, over time, the size of the passade-type half-circle can be diminished until it is the size of a working pirouette. Second, the rider will begin to approach the pirouette-type circle with the haunches in less and less, eventually starting it from a straight line. This, of course, is preparation for making pirouettes off a straight line away from the wall.

Another common approach to training the pirouette is to spiral in on a circle, again in travers. Beginning with an 8 or 10 meter circle, the rider again places the outside leg back to increase the bend in the body and push the haunches inside. The horse can do one revolution at 8 meters then the rider can come in to a 6 meter figure, etc.,

gradually diminishing the size. It is better in the beginning to come in like this, one orbit at a time. This teaches the horse and rider control and virtually eliminates the risk of spinning. If the rider spirals down too fast, this has a tendency to encourage a kind of swirl that easily develops into a tornado, which cannot be interrupted and has a life of its own. In the orbiting system, if the horse begins to gain too much speed or loses its balance and falls onto the shoulders, the rider can easily open up the circle or hold it steady at the same orbit.

There is a whole genealogy of pirouette exercises that involve corners. These are always partial pirouettes. One example is to ride an imaginary box within the rectangle of the arena. The rider travels down a straight line of one side, collects, does two pirouettes strides to turn a right angle, then heads off straight across the second side of the box, collects for corner number two, turns the second right angle with two pirouettes strides, and so on.

Such exercises are often used with horses learning the pirouette and the reasoning is that, because they are just a couple of pirouette strides, they are a softer introduction. This is really not true. These exercises are very difficult. If a number of experienced riders were asked 'Which, in an average pirouette, is the most difficult stride – or are they all the same?', the strong consensus would be that the first step entering the pirouette off a straight line is the trickiest; and the last stride leaving the pirouette to return to the straight line is probably the second most difficult. In these corner-type pirouette exercises, the design has placed the three most difficult elements of pirouette together:

1) A straight approach, no turn, no passade, no spiral.
2) The first step, the entering stride, which has all the risks of stepping out, etc.
3) The last step, where the rider must sum up the turn and cleanly feather it into a straight line.

To repeat, the half-pirouette is not half as difficult and certainly a quarter-pirouette is not one fourth as difficult as a full pirouette! To perform the box exercise correctly, one needs a well-trained horse. Because of the difficult elements, it is not a good exercise for an inexperienced horse. It encourages horses and riders to be too quick and too sharp, and the rider to use too much rein. The lines coming in and going out are rarely straight, encouraging sloppiness. It does not give the young horse enough time to find its balance, nor the rider enough time to correct a slow or fast stride, or one that leans. In general, there are much better choices for teaching and practicing the pirouette.

There is a motto at the Spanish Riding School, which is the 'thinking rider'. This is what it means – that a rider does not blindly execute any exercises presented. The rider must understand the principles behind the exercises and must be able to discern the important parts from those less important. The rider must know the object of every exercise performed and be the first to know when it is missing the mark. This does not mean that a rider will know how to fix the problem immediately, but it does mean learning how to think. More thought will yield more solutions and less force.

Problems in the Canter Pirouette

The pirouette is still in the family of circles. As such, the outside has to be allowed to extend to cover the additional distance. Therefore, the rider has to have a very good response from the horse when using the outside leg to place the horse in a travers position around the inside leg (see Photo 84), and must keep it there, with the horse's outside hind leg stepping under the center of gravity and lifting on each successive stride. If the rider's use of the outside rein goes beyond a normal kind of support and instead tries to pull the horse sideways, several things will occur. First, the braking action of the increased rein aids will be enough to tip a precariously balanced pirouette onto the forehand. Second, by blocking the bend, the rider forces the horse onto the inside shoulder, thus stiffening the back. Third, this same destruction of bend will force the hindquarters (and especially the outside hind leg) to step out away from the center of gravity, thus forcing the load to be carried exactly opposite where it should be.

Very often in training, as the size of the circle diminishes and the workload increases, the horse will try to escape from carrying this weight by stepping out, away from the center of gravity, with the outside hind leg. The

Photo 84. When the rider uses the outside leg to place the horse in a travers position, a good response is needed from the horse.

rider feels this and responds by increasing pressure of the outside leg. This sets up a very common problem – with more muscular exertion the rider starts contracting the outside leg. Soon, the whole outside of the rider's body seems pulled over the hip in that direction. The rider's weight is now off center and leaning outside (see Photo 39, page 88). The result is a kind of isometric stand-off between the rider's aids. The rider turning the pirouette to the right, for example, squeezes and squeezes with the left leg to try to push the haunches of the horse to the right. However, the rider's weight has shifted to the left over the contracted leg, and it tells the horse to step under it to the left. Each aid negates the other. If the rider's weight is to move anywhere, it leans to the inside *slightly* (Photos 85, 86), for too much lean can tip the pirouette inside and upset its balance. The rider has to be careful on the one hand not to rush the pirouette steps and to give them time to collect, but not fall out of rhythm either. As Newcastle warned hundreds of years ago, the rider's lower legs should not clamp. If the horse resists, they should move in more of a bumping or tapping action – too much steady pressure

Photo 85. Pirouette with the weight aids – never with the reins.

Photo 86. Exemplary use of the weight to direct the pirouette.

will often tighten the sides of the horse and the movement can seize up even worse.

Another common fault occurs when the pirouette is ridden too slowly, without adequate power. The horse enters the pirouette and begins a kind of exaggerated, slow terre-à-terre. The diagonal pairing breaks down completely and the horse seems to rock slowly back and forth, hind legs to forelegs, hind legs to forelegs. This kind of pirouette is really showing no collection. The stride has been shortened by slowing down and not by gathering. One end is always supported by the other, rather than the hind end supporting the whole movement. When a pirouette is ridden with power, maintaining rhythm in the tempo in which it was started, it can, in fact, show the

highest collection in the canter, and as such is a supreme exercise of the high school.

The Piaffe, the Passage and Transitions Between Them – a Western Tantra*

*(I would ask the reader not to read this section in pieces, but to read it the first time all the way through.) *Tantra: Sanskrit: loom, weave.*

Of all the movements performed today, it is in this grouping that we see the most fundamental mistakes in understanding and execution. This is, in part, because the definitions have been changed either deliberately or through careless imitation. These movements are intricately woven together in theory and in practice. If one does not understand the craft with which they intertwine, it will be impossible to appreciate the incredible wisdom in General L'Hotte's analysis and advice, which we shall discuss in due course. More importantly, it will severely limit one's appreciation of the sublime beauty of this symphonic performance of exercises. Of paramount importance is that the rider will never be able to reproduce them consistently and correctly. This is the greatest risk. The weaver can lose the loom: this will be a setback until another can be built. If the weaver loses the tapestry, this can be a powerful and sentimental loss, but another one can be woven. But if the weaver loses the knowledge of *how* to weave, there are only memories.

The Piaffe

The piaffe is a natural evolution of collecting the trot, so in a sense it is the most collected trot. As in the trot, the diagonal pairs of limbs have the same swing time but, unlike the trot, there is asymmetry. The forefeet and legs are asked to travel higher, at least twice as high as the hind feet and legs (see Photo 87). This is possible because the object of the exercise is to move the hind legs further up under the center of balance. If this transference is accomplished, the forelegs and forehand will be lighter, freer, and able to move faster.

Historically, a very important use of the piaffe was as preparation for jumps or airs above the ground. The horse could be asked to gradually coil its hind end under. The trainer then adjusted the piaffe so the set up, the balance, the lightening of the forehand could be made just right before the singular, sometimes explosive, effort of a jump. Today, at some of the historic schools in the world, one can still see horses vigorously engaged in piaffe just before the set up in a capriole or courbette. These piaffes, made honest by the requirements of jumping off the hind legs, are of the highest quality. Jumping out of the piaffe is so accurate a proof, that one can use it in reverse to judge the quality of one's own piaffe. All that the rider has to ask is

Photo 87. Piaffe.

'could the horse levade out of this piaffe', and the answer will be an indication of whether the balance is correct.

The piaffe should not have lateral deviations (these will be discussed in depth later). If the horse's limbs begin to travel too far away from their normal way of going, this is usually a signal that there are fundamental problems of strength and balance, which are interfering with the horse's ability to balance itself in that higher collection.

Although the piaffe should not have any lateral movement, swaying or rocking, for example, it has always been allowed a little longitudinal or forward movement. In fact, except at the highest, finished levels (and even then only for short intervals), in most practice situations it *should* move forward. Allowing the piaffe to move gives the hind legs more chance to come up under but also to extend and then flex again. This can avoid the hind legs cramping, which can happen if the trainer overzealously forces them too far under, turning the engagement false. In such cases, the forelegs invariably step in to carry the load because the hind legs cannot. When a piaffe is held on the spot, it is most vulnerable to evasions. Without the purifying elixir of natural, complete cycles of muscular movement (albeit very short ones) throughout the 'ring of muscle', it is easy for the limbs to develop unnatural patterns. So, while it is true that an already schooled piaffe can be 'polished' by working on the spot in pillars, for example, it can also be ruined that way.

As the horse makes a transition into a piaffe, it steps forward into the movement with its hind legs. The rider never pulls on the reins to try to force the horse backwards, but forms a passive hand, which dams up the increased energy. As the hind legs gradually step under, the forehand is simultaneously lifted up. The horse's back is now firm and rounded, and the neck is also extended as if the whole spine curves in a 'C'-shaped, upward bow. The base of the neck raises up, and the underside contracts. This is why, in some of the old photographs when the rider shows extreme collection in the piaffe, the underside of the horse's neck will look 'pigeon-throated', or puffed out. A perfunctory glance from an uneducated eye assumes the horse to be hollow when, in fact, the deepest set haunches lift a back as strong as the deck of a drawbridge. The mid-section of the horse is completely connected. The horse's body is one muscular whole. The rider's back and the horse's back are welded together in a kind of cross. Following the balance of the rider, this solid cross is either tipped upward or lowered (see Photos 88, 89).

Shown these two photos for a brief study of the piaffe, and given a choice without the grid lines, many people selected Photo 88 as the better piaffe. Now, some right-angle lines have been placed as guidelines and reference points. A plumb-line from the point of the rump shows the hocks engaged in both photos. However, the white horizontal line shows the croup to be lower than the withers in Photo 89. (In and of itself, this cannot be the sole requirement of a good piaffe.) A look at the placement of the standing foreleg in Photo 88 shows that it is further back toward the center of gravity than in the other

Photo 88. A more horizontal piaffe.

Photo 89. A better piaffe.

photo. A vertical line from the foot intersects the edge of the saddle. This leg has crept back and is closer to its diagonal, planted, partner, thus making the distance between the two grounded feet shorter. This is a more horizontally balanced piaffe, tending toward triangulation. The weight of the horse is not significantly borne by the hindquarters.

In Photo 89, the piaffe is of much better quality. A vertical line drawn up from the planted forefoot shows it is much more forward. The distance between the grounded pair of legs is longer as they are further apart. This is possible because the neck is raised higher (see the face now much more in front of the vertical). The top line is firmer, so the hind end can lever the forehand up. This piaffe shows the hindquarters carrying more weight and the forehand being lifted and lightened. This piaffe can turn into a levade which would show more classical collection and weight shift than that in Photo 88.

One of the reasons why so many trainers have suggested always trying to teach the piaffe before the passage is because it is usually safer and easier to show the horse this round, connected, solid-back form. A lot of horses will show strong cadence in the trot. Some have a predilection for a false, hovering step which can look 'passagy' but, instead of elastically moving off deep-set joints and powerful muscles, the floating step bounds stiffly off tendons and ligaments, with little dampening of conditioned musculature. A lot of inexperienced trainers cannot seem to resist trying to train this into the passage. In general, it is precisely these horses that have the inclination to hover that should never learn the passage first. These horses usually bound up and down with a flat or stiff, hollow back. When more power is added to heighten the step, it amplifies the dropped back and pushes the hindquarters further out behind the horse as the horse flexes the wrong way at the lumbo-sacral joint (Figure 23). The haunches cannot tuck under the croup, which goes flat with the tail rising up.

Once the rider who has engrained this habit eventually tries to collect into piaffe, no amount of force or terror can bring these haunches under. The more the rider pushes the horse together, the deeper the 'U' becomes in the horse's back, and the higher the croup rises. The hind steps get higher and, instead of carrying the load, they get lighter

Figure 23. Hollow grand passage.

and lighter. The piaffe looks backward, with the hind legs rising higher than the forelegs. The transition from passage to piaffe becomes impossible without first stopping, rounding the back up, and then going into piaffe. If the horse is first shown how to tuck its hind end under, rounding its top line, the rider can avoid falling into the trap of false cadence. So how is this accomplished? And what are some of the systems for training the piaffe?

One of the most common systems for starting the training is the work in-hand (see Chapter 1, in which this preparatory work has been covered.) Then comes the time when the rider begins to ask for the beginnings of piaffe, or half steps. It is safer to train the piaffe from the walk than the trot. Think, for a moment, of a motor boat. When the boat is accelerated from an idle, the bow of the boat goes up. When the motor is cut off, the bow of the boats falls back to the water level. When the piaffe is started from the walk, the natural acceleration can help lighten the forehand and make it easier to let the horse feel those short, carrying steps. If one were to try to collect to the piaffe from the trot, there would be the added problem of a natural deceleration, which ordinarily tips the mass onto the forehand. As I have stated, it is possible for the horse to decelerate with its hind legs. This is important, but it is also difficult. Since the inexperienced horse will have enough trouble with the rhythms of the piaffe, the simpler the system the better.

If the rider has the luxury of a helper, and especially if that person has some experience, it can be very useful to have the helper support the rider's first efforts from the ground with a long whip. Since, from its early work, the horse will be familiar with being engaged from the whip, and with a person on the ground, these factors can add a certain comfort from routine. More importantly, the helper on the ground can make sure that the horse carries its hind legs forward, and rounds the back (now with the added weight of the rider). If there is no one available who can help in this respect, then it will be even more important that the rider keeps the early piaffe steps moving forward.

Remember, the piaffe is an exercise to build strength and improve balance. It develops over time. Too many riders need to see the finished piaffe, and thus try to achieve it too early. The result is the short steps get stuck too much on the spot. The horse often steps, or stamps, too quickly. It is stuck inside a nest of tension. This begins to poison the possibilities for good transitions. On the other hand, the helper on the ground (if there is one) and/or the rider can push the hindquarters too much, so that they become so engaged that they cramp up under the movement and can't carry weight. The surest sign of this is when the forelegs begin to shift backwards to get under the mass in order to carry the weight. The horse thus triangulates – that is, the hind feet and the forefeet come very close to forming a point of a triangle. (A more detailed discussion of triangulation will follow later.)

Another mistake made by too many riders in the early stages is that of trying to drive the horse into the piaffe with a heavy seat. The result is that the rider depresses the horse's back and blocks the haunches from tucking under. The seat should be light but strong, suggesting forward movement to the horse with a total body movement that projects the rider's center of gravity and distributes the weight helpfully, so there is room for the horse's back to come up as the rider presses toward the pommel.

Simultaneously, the rider urges the hind legs to come forward and under with aids from the calves, or touches of the heel or spur.

In addition to avoiding an overtly heavy use of the seat, the rider must fight the temptation to lean backward, thinking that this will push the hind end down and under. Almost always, this results in pushing the back down, and not the legs under. Such a seat is oppressive. It discourages the horse from rounding up its back and curling its hind end under. Spirited horses will often stiffen defiantly against an oppressive 'driving' seat, setting up a battle that will have no winner.

Often, in the first mounted steps (especially if the rider is working alone) it is useful to take the reins in one hand and the whip in the other. Turning the whip down, and reaching as low as possible without leaning from the saddle, the rider should tap the hind legs into the activity of the piaffe. Caution should be used not to tap as hard or so high as to get the horse jumping up behind. This is the opposite of engagement. The idea is to tap and let the hind legs carry the horse slightly forward and very 'uphill'. That is the same as was done from the ground. This time, from the saddle, the rider uses leg, seat and back aids so as to produce an association with the whip aids. Now, the rider can change the variables in training a little at a time, thus building on each previous lesson. Since the piaffe is a continuation of the forces of collecting the trot, the rider's legs are used in the same way. My preference is not to use alternating leg aids to signal or to amplify the piaffe – unless one of the horse's legs is specifically holding back. It is too easy to get a horse and/or rider learning the piaffe swaying or rolling in the back if alternating leg aids are employed (this is shown in Photo 113 on page 160).

Since the piaffe is not a trick, but rather a culmination of the collection of the trot, the collecting aids do not need to change, but should continue as a refinement of the logical steady continuum. If the rider's normal collecting aids cannot eventually produce a classical piaffe, then it is suspect whether the rider really understood collection from the beginning.

Unilateral leg aids move the horse sideways. There is an old anecdote: a visitor is watching a dressage rider practice. The horse and rider do shoulder-in, travers, renvers, half-pass. After a while, the visitor asks: 'Why do you go sideways so much?' The dressage rider answers: 'In order to teach my horse to go straight'. (The piaffe is a straight movement.) Very often, in the initial steps of piaffe, the horse will swing its haunches to avoid the hard work or to place more weight on the favorite side. The rider will need unilateral leg aids at that point to push the horse back into symmetry. This correction is possible because it follows from a logical, detailed education that has taken years. It is crucial that the movements of the high school are seen as blossoming from the nurturing of the classical system. They are simple, beautiful results of conscientious practice. They are not tricks – singular, entertaining responses to special cues. They are logical conclusions to long, careful systems of exercise and practice.

I know a man who ran a publishing company for many years: a company world-famous for high-quality educational books and for important literature. At times, the material wasn't always the most profitable but it was important. The company was taken over. Its reputation, staff and machinery were exploited. Popular books that would sell the most and the fastest became the top priority. In a few short years, morale dropped, the company's reputation was ruined, and it was put up for sale. It is easy to exploit something that works well. The hard part is to construct a mind-set that understands that a quick result is not always profitable over the long run. It is always interesting to me how, historically, these decisions seem to be fueled by the decadence of entertainment. Education is not motivated by entertainment. Classical dressage does not receive its validity or inspiration from entertainment.

When dressage becomes motivated by fun and entertainment, it invites serious fragmentation. Riders appear like idiot savants. Such people are capable of multiplying any two numbers in the world and coming up with a correct answer, playing a piece of Brahms after hearing it once, or of seemingly superhuman feats of specialization, yet they are unable to cross a street safely or feed themselves. Their entertaining feats many excite the public but, certainly, the parents of any savant would trade those brilliant skills in one moment for a more normal life for their child. A rider who can only do piaffe is not a classical rider. This was one of the strongest messages bequeathed

by Pluvinel, who proposed that if one learns to balance a horse, one might learn to balance one's own life.

Passage, Doux and Grand

Once the piaffe is developing there will come a time when one needs to begin training the passage. The final goal will be the marrying of the two movements. One of the pinnacles of classical riding is to show clean transitions in and out of these two movements.

I first learned the passage in the same way as many trainers have done – the passage grows out of a restraining of the forces used for extending the trot. If it is developed in a horse that already has high natural cadence, more power is added, thus amplifying the scope of the step and its bounding uplift. Always, though, the idea was that this is a very forward step. However, as I trained more horses, I began to see that, when horses performed passage in such a large step, their backs were too flat, too soft. The hind legs would stay camped out behind (compare Photos 90 and 91). Perhaps most obvious was the fact that I could not make good transitions into the piaffe. I began a study of the passage. I can still remember re-reading Guérinière for clues on the passage and noting:

Photo 90. Wrong way to begin passage training.

Photo 91. A better way to begin passage training.

Photos 92–95. Doux passage.

It is paramount in this movement that the horse hold its legs as long as possible in the air, one fore and one rear, diagonally opposite as in the trot; but is must be a good deal shorter, smoother and more studied than an ordinary trot; so that there be no more than the distance of twelve inches between each step taken; i.e. the hoof in the air should be placed approximately twelve inches beyond the one which is on the ground.[3]

Photo 93.

Nowhere else in his entire book did he give a specific dimension like this. I concluded that is must be very important. I found out, after years of practice, that it is indeed very important. I began to train the passage differently. The first thing I had to do was drastically reduce the size of the passage as I had been training it. I found that, when I went into this new passage, I immediately got a much firmer and rounder back, with the hindquarters more under and not behind. The feeling was more like an elongated piaffe. In fact, the way I trained this new passage was to think more of opening the piaffe, not holding back the lengthened trot. I began training the piaffe to alternately open up and shorten. And here was the secret of this great transition.

As the horse's strength and balance improved, it covered more ground, until it was covering the twelve

[3]De la Guérinière, F.R., *School of Horsemanship* (J.A. Allen 1994).

Photo 94.

Photo 95.

inches (30 cm) that Guérinière advised (see Photos 92–95). At this point, I understood why writers of the past would call the piaffe a passage on the spot (Photo 96) – a passage covering twelve inches of ground. This is a very different passage – ridden differently, trained differently, than the long passage my own contemporaries were practicing. Once I began training the passage out of the piaffe and concentrated on making transitions longer or shorter, I found for the first time, that it was indeed

Photo 96. At this point, I understood why writers of the past would call the piaffe a passage on the spot.

possible to make real transitions between the passage and piaffe without stopping, rounding the back up, and then continuing (see Photos 97–99). I also realized that, on some horses, it would be possible to go to a longer passage once the shorter passage was confirmed, and the horse would not lose the form in its back and/or hindquarters.

It was some years later that I came upon some writings on this subject by Alexis-François L'Hotte. He talked about incorrect grand passages, and about the haunches following 'regretfully'. I had a strong image of my mother

153

Photos 97–99. Transition from doux passage into piaffe.

making my brother and me get dressed on Sunday, often interrupting our games, and taking us to church. I remembered walking behind her dragging my feet and, in remembering, I knew what following 'à regret' means. I have often felt that, had I read L'Hotte's few paragraphs on the piaffe, doux passage and grand passage early in my career, it would have saved me years of struggle. In any case, I feel that they are so important and so brilliant that I asked permission to reprint Hilda Nelson's wonderful translation of L'Hotte's advice, which appears in her book *Alexis-François L'Hotte, the Quest for Lightness in Equitation*, in its entirety (so that it might save the reader some time or struggle). The extract is from the section The *grand passage*, the *doux passage*, and the *piaffe*:

In this chapter in which he compares Classical equitation with circus equitation, L'Hotte spends considerable time discussing the passage. Many horsemen, says L'Hotte, see in the passage, regardless of the quality of its execution, the official trademark of *haute école*. Not so, says L'Hotte…The passage, without lightness, that touchstone of Classical equitation, is not *haute école*.

In the past, the *écuyers* executed only the *doux passage* which entails a marked flexion of the limbs and the flexibility and pliancy of all the joints. This kind of passage emerges naturally and directly from the piaffe when the horse indicates the desire to move forward.

There is thus a difference between the former *doux passage* and the more modern *grand passage* which is an energetic extension sustained by the limbs and tension of the joints.

The *grand passage* can be obtained in two ways:

The first way is to obtain it directly. Here it is presented as a separate air, not part of any other, such as the piaffe. It can be easily obtained with energetic horses. All one has to do is contain the trot while increasing its energy. Obtained this way, the passage has little to do with Classical equitation. Furthermore, says L'Hotte, it is executed mechanically and automatically.

The second way to obtain the *grand passage* is when one lets it flow out of the *doux passage* which, in turn, flows out of the piaffe. Now, all the degrees of extension and shortening of action are available.

L'Hotte re-introduces his discussion of Ourphaly, *général* de Novital's horse mentioned in *Souvenirs*. Ourphaly's passage was full of energy, unlike those sad-looking 'passaging' horses one often sees, whose shoulders do all the work and whose haunches follow 'à regret' (regretfully) and whose hocks have lost all their springiness. With Ourphaly, due to their energetic impulsion, the haunches pushed the shoulders, raised and opened them, and give perfect harmony to the ensemble of the movements.

Yet, Ourphaly, like so many horses, had his weakness. He was not able to give all the degrees of extension and lacked the ability to go, by degrees, from the piaffe, to the most extended and energetic passage, and back to the piaffe. His movements did not flow.

Very few horses can go through the ascending and descending gamut without ever falling into brusqueness in the movements. What these horses lack is the total flexibility of the joints when the passage is carried to its greatest extension and still retain their pliancy and flexibility. Furthermore, when the passage is shortened and enters the piaffe, the hocks, while engaging under the mass, must retain their energy and the knees must be raised and carry themselves forward as though the horse wanted to gain territory. 'That is how the *grand passage*, the *doux passage* and the piaffe are joined and when the rider can, at will, modify the nature of the movements and regulate their extension.'

It is actually the *doux passage* which requires flexibility of the joints and which contributes to the schooling of the horse and to perfection, whereas the *grand passage* has detrimental effects in that it demands tension of the joints if practised prematurely, that is, before the *doux passage* has been learned [see Photos 92–96, pages 152–3].

Our former *écuyers* knew what they were doing when they first had the horse piaffe, unsaddled and unmounted, between the pillars so that he could become familiar with the air. Only later was the horse asked to do the piaffe and then the passage mounted. Rather than execute this graceless and automatic passage (graceless and automatic for both horse and rider), it would be better for the rider to do a graceful and natural trot, precise and free, which would please the real horseman (not the crowds necessarily) who has a feeling for beautiful and graceful equitation. It is up to these authentic horsemen to show the way...[4]

Some trainers do not begin training the passage with the grand passage in mind. Some riders execute a preliminary passage that is short but weak. When I have asked, 'What is the exercise?' they answered, 'The gentle passage' which, of course, was their version of the doux passage. The doux passage should not be understood to be a weak, or too soft, passage. Although it is true that it is somewhat defined by the shortness of its step, it is the quality of this step, not just its length that is significant. The shorter step of the doux passage contains the haunches in order to build strength, power and lift. The feeling has to be, as L'Hotte described, that the hindquarters push the shoulders out of the way. The rider is careful to regulate this power and then to repeat it in a rather long series of very rhythmic steps.

Problems in Piaffe and Passage

TRIANGULATION IN PIAFFE
This is probably one of the most common problems with the piaffe. Older trainers refer colloquially to triangula-

[4]Nelson, H., *Alexis-François L'Hotte, The Quest for Lightness in Equitation* (J.A. Allen 1997).

Figure 24. Triangulation in piaffe.

tion as a piaffe that resembles an 'elephant on a stool'. The horse's legs crowd toward each other as if they were trying to balance on a point (Figure 24). The legs form two sides of a triangle and the back, the third side. The interesting thing about horses that triangulate in the piaffe is that they are almost universally well engaged behind. A brief look at the hindquarters and the piaffe seems to reveal a piaffe of high quality. The haunches are often deep-set, with the legs well under. Why, then, would the horse's forelegs begin to creep and slant backwards? The answer is that they are trying to move toward the center of gravity to get under the weight and therefore carry it. Whenever the forelegs begin to creep back, the trainer has to be suspicious, no matter how good the haunches look. The hind legs are not carrying the weight and are missing the premier requirement of the piaffe.

Oddly enough, horses usually triangulate in the piaffe when the rider tries too hard for engagement. If the hindquarters are forced too far under the horse, they can get so cramped that they cannot lift. If they become too stretched, especially in learning the movement, the horse's body will compensate. If the hind legs cannot hold up the weight, the forelegs will help. I have already mentioned that master after master has warned of the need to let the piaffe move forward. Ignoring this advice contributes to triangulation, and adding forward motion helps to cure it. When the hind legs are so cramped that they cannot extend, they cannot push. One of the signs of this is that the piaffe will stall: the horse has redistributed weight off the hindquarters and is caught falsely in place without drive. Allowing the piaffe to move forward calls the hind legs back into play. They now push the shoulders forward out of the way.

Sometimes, triangulation starts when the rider allows the horse's neck to be too low. The horse curls and the back comes up too much. The rider encourages this because a round back would seem desirable. Remember, in order to balance, the back must be strong and 'solid': the neck must be solidly tied in to the back for the haunches to be able to lift the forehand. If rhythmic steps are to be repeated, the back must also undulate. When a horse keeps its head and neck too low, not only does it pull more weight onto the forehand, it also can hump up the back thus making it round but much too stiff (which is not the same thing as solid). A bucking horse has a rounded back, but it is not a desirable rounded back. (Many top-class trainers do not like too much deep work, because, overdone or incorrectly done, it can stiffen a back and make true collection difficult.) Another point to bear in mind is that a lowering of the haunches does not *necessarily* mean that they have been loaded. As far back as Newcastle, trainers have advised not to get the limbs of the horse too far from their natural positions and lines.

HIND FEET TOO HIGH

When horses piaffe, or even passage, with their hind legs higher than their forelegs, the cause almost always seems to be too much use of the whip, and particularly too much whip too high on the croup. Frankly, I have seen this a lot and I cannot understand the rationale. It seems that trainers think more whip will give more

height and activity. But the response of the horse is all wrong. The horse begins to jump from the sting of the whip the way it would buck off a biting fly atop its croup. Certainly, the result is more activity and it is unarguable that there is more height – but it is at the wrong end. The jumping hindquarters are stiff, disengaged and throw weight onto the forelegs. The incredible thing is that some trainers even lower the horse's head to aid in this 'activity' which adds further to the problem. Interestingly, there is a form of training that proceeds exactly this way. It is used at the famous school of Saumur in France, where some of the horses are taught to kick. The result is a horse that kicks high and powerfully with its hind legs, perfectly on command. It is not a system to be used to train powerful engagement which lifts the shoulders in piaffe and passage.

If the trainer has not been overactive with the whip and the horse just seems to object to the whip, more fundamental work is needed. Sometimes, however, even light use of the wrong kind of whip will get a kicking or bucking response instead of an engaging coiling of the hindquarters. Very often, if the whip is too stiff, it seems to sting sensitive horses, even if the trainer has a delicate hand. A softer whip can get a completely different and more positive response.

When the hindquarters begin bounding too high, the horse needs more collection. The whip should be used lower, toward the feet. Again, the tone or the rigidity of the whip might need to be changed. The trainer should also be careful to keep the horse's poll up, with the horse tending to move forward.

HIND FEET TOO WIDE APART OR TOO CLOSE TOGETHER

Usually two things will widen the stance of the hind legs. One is that, as in a levade, they are gaining a broader base of support so they will have the best balance to carry more weight. The other is, as in some lengthened trots, the hind legs spread out to avoid forging or hitting the forefeet and forelegs. Sometimes, this latter occurs because the rear end is too powerful and the horse hasn't learned the timing required. In other cases, the horse's forehand is lazy and the extension is too 'downhill' or disunited: the forelegs are just not getting out of the way. These fundamental mechanics also apply to the passage, and probably more so to the piaffe.

If the hind feet widen their stance to prepare to carry more weight, then, when they narrow up, one can assume they are doing the opposite. In general, the closer the feet are together, the less they are working. When the hind legs swing under the line of the spine, they are usually trying to get under the center of gravity, where support takes much less effort. The result is an efficient way of moving, but it is the opposite of collection.

Let me explain this a little more. I once had a discussion with a North American cowboy. He wanted me to agree that, really, what he was doing, and dressage, were the same thing. He kept saying, 'In the end, it's all about the efficiency of movement, isn't it?' Finally, I told him that I could not agree. The passage is not an energy-efficient way to get from Point A to Point B. The piaffe is even worse. In fact, much of dressage is the construction of purposefully inefficient exercises which have very specific effects, aimed at the strengthening, elasticizing and balancing of the horse. Trotting on the forehand with 'rope walking' footfalls is probably the most efficient way to travel, but it is not dance.

There is a physical law that, for an object to remain upright, a vertical line projected downward from its center of gravity must fall within the area of support. If the line falls outside this area, the object will topple over. When a horse widens its stance, it enlarges its area of support and makes it easier to balance, because there is more room within which that vertical line projected down from the center of gravity can fall. This, of course, is what the horse does in the levade when it has to balance on just the two hind legs.

In Newcastle's text he makes repeated references to the fact that, although the whole object of dressage schooling is to get the horse upon the haunches, he doesn't want the hind legs too far from their natural positions – neither too far under the body, nor too much 'asunder' (too wide apart).

The quality of the piaffe can be assessed by how well it can set up the horse for the airs. It is not supposed to go too far. That is, it should not start widening behind. A great part of this has to do with aesthetics, grace and taste. One can see this especially in Pluvinel's advice that riding is a meditative art. He pleads with the king that more riding academies are necessary in order to educate the young men of France. The last thing he would allow is for dressage riding to turn into a contest, or some ostentatious rivalry among his students. It was, in particular, the trend for undisciplined duels between the younger generation that was disturbing him. He was certain that riding could teach the youth of France self-control. There is a whole legacy of anecdotes formed over hundreds of years that take sharp aim at ostentation in riding. These remarks are even more pointed than in the other arts because, in our particular endeavor, the egotist drags down the horse. All true horsemen and horsewomen object when a horse is denigrated in an effort to puff up a human ego. So, when a great rider makes a brilliant piaffe, it is never held for too long. The rider seems to know when it is tasteful to stop. While trying to make it brilliant, there is scrutiny of the form. The rider watches to keep it clean and fair; watches that it does not go overboard.

BALANCÉ

This is a fault both in piaffe and passage. Although it is caused by improper collection, I don't necessarily feel it is because a horse is lazy or not trying. In most cases, it is the opposite. The horse is trying too hard, but incorrectly. The horse tries to give the rider more suspension and cadence but, since the hind legs are not carrying the load and are therefore unable to propel the forehand up, the forelegs try to do it. Even although the forelegs are not really constructed as limbs of thrust, they are still capable of it. In the case of balancé, the horse pushes off with one foreleg and, although this gives the shoulders some lift, it also pushes them to the side. At that point the other forelimb steps away from the body to stop the push and initiates a push of its own. The result is a kind of tennis match of energy (see Photos 100–103). The center of gravity is volleyed back and forth from one foreleg to the other. (Remember, the widening of the stance of a set of limbs is a tip-off that they are trying to do more work.)

Photos 100–103. Balancé – this results from the horse attempting to generate lift and thrust with the forelegs.

What has to happen here is that the horse must be relaxed a little and collected to a shorter step, so as to try to take away the work from the forelimbs. This may take time but, once the hind legs become stronger and more flexible, the forehand will be relieved of the pressure of trying to help. It is important, in the early stages of the piaffe and passage, not to try too hard for height so long as the rhythm is good. The stronger the horse gets, the more amplification will come naturally.

One always has to remember that most horses will try to do what the rider asks. If they are unable to do so because of limitations of strength or technical flaws, and the rider just keeps asking for more effort, the rider will compel the horse to do the movement any way it can. Many so-called evasions are nothing more than creative improvisations by a horse that cannot or does not know how to execute a movement correctly. It is important to pay great attention to the classical rules of technique. They are not gestures of hollow tradition. They are very practical physical directives, which have evolved from hundreds of years of practice of the same exercises. They can guide a rider even if that rider is uncertain.

ROLLING PASSAGE

The fault of rolling can sometimes be seen in the piaffe, but it is more prevalent in the passage. It is probably also much easier to see the mechanics in the passage, and understand the flaw, and thus design a solution. If one were to stand in front of a horse that was rolling in the passage, one would see its shoulders twist as the forefoot swings in to land under the line of the spine, below the middle of the horse's chest. A look at the track left on the ground would reveal one single line of hoof prints. In the worse cases of rolling, one might see two lines of tracks which might appear narrow but normal, until one realized that the left had crossed over to the right and the right had crossed over to the left. A look from behind would reveal a similar action by its diagonal partner. This is a horse with insufficient impulsion and little carrying power. The horse gets a false suspension from bounding or recoiling off the tendons and ligaments of the stiffened limbs, which try to line up under the horse's center of gravity and land under the mid-line of the horse. Unfortunately, when these legs land under the middle of the horse's body, they block the flight of the second diagonal pair of legs. These legs now swing out around each planted leg and start a sloshing roll, like a half-filled tank truck (Photos 104–107).

It is hard to say where the problem is initiated. Certainly, when the left hind leg, for example, plants in the stance phase, it stiffly shoves the left hip above it upward, while the right hip seems to drop down (Photos 108–111). The horse's back always seems stiff, so the hips twist the whole barrel of the horse. When the left

Photos 104–107. Rolling passage – front view.

Photos 108–111. Rolling passage – rear view.

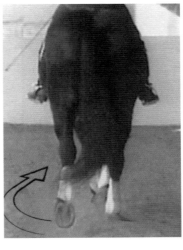
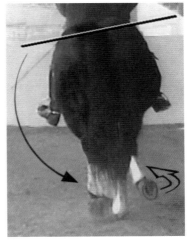
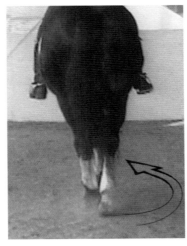
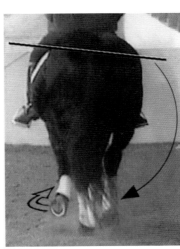

hip gets pushed up, the axial twist created forces the right shoulder down. In any case, the horse's back muscles are not working elastically on either side of the spine. You can get a feeling for this if you make some slow karate-type punches – jab the left fist and arm out while retracting the right and vice versa, to get the feeling of the back muscles and ribs, and what they are doing. Rolling horses seem to lock up their backs and ribs like toy wooden horses and slant their bodies from side to side, thus obtaining a form of suspension from a stiff recoil, instead of a powerful dampening and then extension of the muscles.

In trying to passage, when the rider feels the back stiffen and the horse begin to roll, it is imperative to ride forward into an active (not rushing) trot and get the back swinging again. Once the horse is going forward, the rider can try again to cadence and shorten the trot. It is also important that the rider's own back does not stiffen too much when entering the passage, as this can 'freeze' the horse's back Sometimes, riding shoulder-in will help free up the back of such horses between attempts of passage. Probably the most important point is not to let the horse slow the tempo way down and back off the impulsion and engagement. If a horse is not rolling in the trot, it should not roll in the passage. One last note: sometimes horses trained to passage from alternating leg aids, or unconsciously swaying weight aids, have been actually trained to roll. This is not a classic passage and it is difficult to

159

correct. Again, correction lies in powerful forward movement re-establishing swing in the back, not swing in the legs.

ROLLING PIAFFE

There can be a rolling in the piaffe which is isolated to the forelegs (compare Photos 112 and 113). This is usually a result of insufficient carrying power behind. The horse balances too much on the forehand and swings its forelegs under the torso to support the overburdened forehand. If the piaffe is encouraged to move more forward, the hind limbs will have to take on more work to relieve the shoulders. Also, the forward movement will force the forelegs to reach forward to a more normal flight pattern.

SOME GENERAL PRINCIPLES CONCERNING FAULTS IN PIAFFE AND PASSAGE

It is highly important that the rider is a very keen observer of the movement of horses throughout training, but especially so when new exercises are begun. One of my pet peeves is to watch stationary instructors give lesson after lesson from a chair somewhere in the arena. When training young horses and young or novice riders, the instructor must use mirrors, or engage assistant riders, to watch from behind and from different angles from the front and the sides.

Very few horses being trained for dressage will 'rope walk' when they trot, for example. If their movement is naturally that bad, it is doubtful that anyone would have

Photo 112. Straight piaffe.

Photo 113. Rolling in piaffe.

selected them as candidates to embark upon the process aimed at high school. However, it remains the case that a great many horses have developed impurities in the passage and piaffe that are not overtly present in the normal trot work. This means that the impurities have crept in. Trainers have to be vigilant when attempting new movements, in order to notice if and when the horse starts to improvise. All the little glitches and ticks are watched for and noticed. They are very important. Good handlers of brood mares can recount the slightest idiosyncrasies of thirty different mares when each one is coming into her heat cycle. Today, too many riders are not good enough horsemasters even to be aware when their horses begin to move differently. If the rider has little experience with the passage, that is no excuse. By this time, the rider should know the importance of the core concepts: straight, calm, and forward. Since classical dressage is a complete and logical process of layering, the rider, even if uncertain of what is exactly right, should know what is not to be accepted.

However, making allowance for the unacceptable does not always happen because the riders lack experience. It often happens because the rider wants to do the new movement so much, that what is known to be incorrect is deliberately overlooked. This contradicts the classical process and cannot speed up correct progression. The fact is, the more one trains horses in the classical system, the more one pays attention to the fundamentals – and the more quickly one will train horses.

I once heard an interview with the grandson of a very famous guitar maker. He said that, as a boy, he worked on a bench across from his grandfather. He was always watching his grandfather and thinking of ways to cut this piece faster or change the step in this or that process so as to get ahead of his grandfather. Each time, it would seem to end in a disaster. Finally, he said, his grandfather would look over at him and say, 'Take your time. We are in a hurry'.

A passage may start from the walk, but it is magical when a passage seems to pull a horse up into the air from a trot. There is a conscious interruption, with the greatest and smoothest contraction and extension of muscles. It never looks stiff, like a reflex just sprung off tense tendons and ligaments. In a good passage, the horse's back has to be supple enough to 'trampoline' the great forward force generated by the extension of the powerful legs of a high school horse. It must also be strong enough to resist the forces of torque that will try to turn the horse, like a boat rocking in its mooring.

In the classical passage the horse will take hold of the horizontal forces of pure trot and convert some of them into vertical forces. In addition to this, it will do so with no lateral deviation, and it will be symmetrical on both sides of the body and both diagonal pairs of legs. It really is a thing of beauty, and it can exalt the stature and nature of a horse. It certainly is a living, moving exaltation of the relationship between a human and a horse.

CHAPTER EIGHT
Airs above the Ground

Photos 114 and 115. From one generation to another, the body of knowledge must be passed. 'In a very real sense, each of us has to reinvent the wheel in our own time. What we must try to do is not necessarily reinvent the technological wheel with every generation. But we must reinvent the psychological wheel, the artistic wheel, the psychic wheel'. Paul Belasik *Exploring Dressage Technique*.

The airs above the ground are a series of lifts and jumps made by the high school horse. When correctly performed, they are so difficult and strenuous that today's horses usually specialize in a single air. Even at a center like the Spanish Riding School, these horses must be very carefully managed in order that the school can present examples of the different airs for the many thousands of spectators who come from around the world to see them. It is nothing for a time span of ten years to go by between outstanding jumpers. Older veterans perform prudently while young horses may be trained to as high a standard as Grand Prix before they are even tested to see if they will be suitable replacements. The investment is priceless.

The airs have often been described as originating from battle movements. This seems logical for at least certain of the airs. However, they have been ritualized for such a long time now that any connection to practical battle movements is symbolic.

In Guérinière's book, *School of Horsemanship*, there is a chapter on warhorses, in which he talks about the relationship between school training and warhorses. He cites how the passage could be useful for this, and how pirouettes could be useful for that. He goes on to say: 'If the airs above the ground offer no advantage for war, they offer at least that of imparting to the horse the agility it requires to clear hedges and ditches, which contributes to the safety of the rider'. This indicates that, by Guérinière's time, the airs were already fundamentally separated from any connection with battle. They were artistic endeavors. Even before Guérinière, this was the case for Newcastle and Pluvinel. In fact, it has been so since the first major books, which codified dressage, were written.

It is clear that, in the past, horses jumped more often and performed more different airs than is the case today. It is impossible to know at what cost. It is also clear our horses today are trained more thoroughly pre-high school, and as such, represent considerably larger investments of time, making the training and performance of the airs seem perhaps even more of a risk. Nevertheless, that the airs are the pinnacle of the 'dressed' horse's training is indisputable. The world owes a great debt to those few schools, large and small, around the world that still train these movements. They are living museums and libraries for dressage trainers and students. I don't see how a trainer's

education could be complete without studying some of these performances, and understanding these movements.

Although there has been some evolution in the airs themselves, which I will review, the biggest change has come in the way the horse is trained. Historically, all the airs were taught with the horse being confined between two pillars, or around one single, immoveable, unbreakable, pillar (Figure 25). It is one thing to groom a horse in cross ties, but imagine the claustrophobic risks of getting a horse so excited that it would attempt caprioles fixed in such unyielding restraints. It was this practice that became controversial because, although it cut down in the training time, too many horses were being ruined. One can still see pillars at most of the classical schools around the world, but in many cases they are more ceremonial. The reason is that, for a horse to be safe to work in the pillars, it has to be perfectly trained in-hand, totally confident in the highest collection, and absolutely unafraid (see Photos 116, 117). Once a horse is that well trained in-hand, the irony is that there is really no need for the pillars. Therefore, for the most part, the classical practitioners all over the world use this method of more time-consuming, careful in-hand work (often with two trainers), and then introduce the airs under saddle, with pillar work being added more for ceremony.

Training

When one begins training a horse in the airs, it is a momentous time. It is quite possible that the trainer has worked with a particular horse for many years before it is ready. The horse must be physically strong enough and psychologically grounded enough to handle the pressure of the airs.

When the trainer is standing next to the shoulders of a horse weighing perhaps half a ton (500 kg) as it makes its first attempts to balance on its hind legs, the feeling is visceral and electrifying. The muscles of the horse quiver. The hind feet plant and the hocks will flex in a way the trainer has never seen before. The breath is hard. All senses are at a pitch that would make a normal horse bolt in fear. The power seems to pass right through the trainer's body, as though the trainer had trespassed a little too close

Figure 25. Unmounted airs around a pillar. From the Duke of Newcastle's *A General System of Horsemanship.*

discussed. The piaffe is trot based; the terre-à-terre, canter based.

The Terre-à-terre

The terre-à-terre is a kind of two-beat canter that rocks back and forth going slightly forward in a jumping action. The horse, with both forefeet together, bounds off the ground with both forefeet at once, lands on both hind feet, which then jump together in a crow-hopping gesture, and back onto the forelegs. The cycle repeats while the horse slightly advances with each small jump. This can remain at the same level of impulsion, appearing like a gait in itself. The rider can also infuse a little more power with each repeating stride, coiling a little more with each successive bound onto the hind legs. If this bounding grows high enough to have a kind of mini-levade, a jump in the air so that there is a moment of suspension, then a touch down to the forelegs and then another small levade, repeating, then the terre-à-terre will evolve into the mézair. This, in turn, becomes an intermediary stage toward courbettes, or currets, which Newcastle describes as:

...an air when the horse's legs are raised more than in the demivolts being a kind of leap up and a little forward wherein the horse raises both his forefeet at once, equally advanced, and as his fore legs are

to the pure energy of Mother Nature. But if the horse rises in control, as is hoped and expected; if it doesn't bolt; if the beautiful, living muscles that the trainer has helped develop, pop and move like molten lava under a glassine skin; if the horse answers the trainer, then it feels as if some supreme Master were patting the trainer on the shoulder and validating all the years of work on collection. There is not a prize made or awarded that would make the trainer feel like that. Only standing next to the horse can provide this feeling. At that point – at least for a while – the trainer will have a very commanding view of just what he or she has been doing for so many years.

As I have mentioned, the process of introducing the airs requires that each the airs be first perfected in-hand. (Please refer back to Advanced Work In-hand, in Chapter 1.) Once these basics are reliable, a rider may be introduced, with the trainer still controlling the movement from the ground. Then, if the horse learns to cope with the additional weight and balance of a good rider, that rider will begin to take control while the trainer steps away.

There are two principal power-gaining warm-up steps to the airs. One is the piaffe; the other is the terre-à-terre. The piaffe as preparation to the airs has already been

Photos 116 and 117. These two photographs were taken in the 1940s. In both, the man in the fedora is H.L.M. van Schaik, and the horse is his Friesian, Wopke. Van Schaik was one of the author's greatest equestrian influences. A comparison of these two pictures with Figure 26 (from Newcastle's *A General System of Horsemanship*, written in the seventeenth century) shows a continuation of classical equitation down the generations. There is even some similarity in the hats!

Photo 116.

Photo 117.

Figure 26.

falling he immediately raises his hind legs, as he did his fore; that is equally advanced, and not one before the other, so that all his four legs are in the air at once.[1]

It is important to see the continuum in this work. These airs are so dramatic and distinct when they are finished, that it is sometime hard to see where they could have started.

The Pesade and Levade

The pesade and levade are the principle movements for assessing and then developing all the others. To have the best control, the pesade and levade are set up out of the piaffe. The piaffe develops the collection necessary to lift, but also allows the trainer to select the timing. Since jumps can excite the horse, a measured patience has to be trained in from the beginning, or the horse's previous training could suffer. As the horse piaffes along the wall, the trainer taps toward the hocks, or lower along the hind legs, with a long whip. This encourages the hind legs to come under

[1]Newcastle, William Cavendish, Duke of, *A General System of Horsemanship* (Winchester Press 1970).

166

for maximum engagement, the deepest piaffe possible. At the same time the rider takes a steady lift on the short rein to encourage the forehand to rise (see Photo 18, page 28). If the rider's hand jerks too harshly it can send the rise too high or out of control and into a plain rear, which is valueless. The rider or trainer can also try to tap the forelegs as a signal to fold them and hold them up for a few extra fractions of a second.

In general, if the lift is above a 45 degree angle, it is considered to be a pesade. If it is lower than 45 degrees, it is a levade. The difference, however, is not just a matter of degrees. Because the levade will show more power and more flexion in the hindquarters, it is not just a lower pesade. When it is low and the horse holds it for a few seconds, it has to be considered the epitome of collection. Over the course of history, it has become one of the most recognizable and revered forms in all of equitation.

The trainer will be able to tell a lot from this work. Some horses will stand higher (pesade) (Photo 118) in order to balance. Others will show such strength that they will squat and lift their forelegs slowly and lightly – almost tenderly – from the ground (Photo 119). Others will not want their hindquarters to stay loaded and will jump strongly forward. Yet others may kick out at the whip. Instead of frustrating themselves and the horses, by trying to plow through these obvious incompatibilities, observant trainers will note all these tendencies carefully so that the airs will be developed with each horse's natural talents and inclinations in mind.

The Mézair

The horse, of course, will not just simply step from the collection of piaffe into the perfect levade, poised as easily as a little squirrel with its dainty little forefeet perfectly folded as if it were holding a nut. More than likely, the horse will rise up a little and jump forward, and then try again. The trainer will find that the horse simply loses its balance and will touch down with the forelegs and bound up, trying again. When these initial

Photo 118. St. Graal in pesade.

Photo 119. St. Graal in levade.

levades repeat in this pattern, usually getting a little stronger and better with each successive bound, this is the mézair. (As I mentioned earlier, the terre-à-terre can also be enlarged, so that it then bounds up into the mézair.) Likewise, in attempts to perfect the levade, if the horse loses its balance and drops back onto the forehand, the movement can be repeated deliberately, so that a series of quick levades occurs, each jumping forward a little.

The Courbette

There is a little difference between the mézair and the courbette, which may lead to some confusion. Pluvinel, Newcastle and Guérinière all practiced relatively the same form of courbettes. They were larger versions with better collection; that is, they were less forward than the mézair.

A horse should not be required to perform courbettes until it is accomplished in the terre-à-terre and the mézair, for they are more than half way, to the goal of the courbette....The courbette is a jump in which the forehand is raised higher and the cadence is more sustained than in the mézair. The haunches should lower and accompany the forehand in a regular, low and cadenced gait in the instant in which the forelegs fall back to the ground. Thus this difference can be perceived between the mézair and the courbette: in the former the forehand is lower and the forward motion is greater than in the courbette, in which the forehand is higher and the haunches are under more pressure.[2]

After each leap, these courbettes all touched down with the forehand (Figure 27).

Today, at the Spanish Riding School, the courbettes are successive leaps, two to five in a row, jumping and landing on the hind legs, and jumping again. These are performed without the forelegs touching down. Obviously, these courbettes are extremely difficult and take incredible strength and balance. It would be interesting to know how and when this adaptation occurred, because it makes the courbettes much harder.

Figure 27. Courbettes, from the Duke of Newcastle's *A General System of Horsemanship*. The courbettes of Pluvinel, Newcastle and Guérinière all touched down with the forehand between successive leaps.

[2] De la Guérinière, F.R., *School of Horsemanship* (J.A. Allen 1994).

Podhajsky said that the courbette...

...must be looked upon decidedly as one of the most difficult exercises in training because, for one thing, it takes years to find a stallion with the aptitude for such work [to understand the courbette better]...it is essential to keep in mind three movements: firstly, the levade which developed out of the piaffe; secondly leaping upward in the position of the levade; and thirdly landing in the same position according to the dexterity of the horse [and then] the leaps are repeated from two to five times, and only then does the horse touch the ground again with the forefeet.[3]

[3]Podhajsky, A., *The Complete Training of Horse and Rider* (Doubleday 1967).

Figure 28. The Duke of Newcastle's croupade.

If the terre-à-terre, the mézair and the courbette are related in an evolving difficulty, the croupade, ballotade and capriole move in a similar linkage.

The Croupade

The croupade is a single, higher courbette that levels out. That is, the horse jumps. When it reaches an apex, the horse is close to being parallel to the ground. The horse's forelegs stay tightly folded toward the chest, with knees symmetrical, but the hind legs are also flexed up under the body. The impression is powerful but compact (see Figure 28).

Figure 29. The Duke of Newcastle's ballotade.

The Ballotade

The ballotade is virtually the same as the croupade only in this movement, at the apex, the horse has it hind legs stretched out. The horse is beginning to kick. From behind, one can see the horse's shoes, or the soles of the hind feet (Figure 29).

The Capriole

The capriole is set up from a single courbette which, in turn, is set up from a piaffe or terre-à-terre with as much power as possible. The horse seems to jump straight up over an imaginary high bar. When it is level, that is, horizontal or parallel to the ground, it finishes the leap

Figure 30. The Duke of Newcastle's capriole.

with a strong kick with both hind legs. (The whip of a trainer or rider signals this.) At that point it presents one of the most distinctive images in all dressage (Figure 30). And from that height the horse drops straight down onto the forefeet, and then hind. The horse is then calmed and praised.

It is clear that, historically, there were more jumps than those mentioned. Very often, slight adaptations of these standard forms occurred. I think the most important point is that one can see the progression. If one were to pull a thread in the capriole, it would end up at the first lessons on the longe line. There is something very fair in the study of dressage. One does not undertake the learning process and then, several years later, have teachers say, 'OK – well, you know what we taught you about such and such? Well, that was not quite right. From now on you will have to do it like this. Forget what we told you before'.

In classical dressage there are no magic doorways. It is not some labyrinth that needs special keys and the memorization of illogical tricks and impossible routes. It should not be full of secret societies. You cannot be sold a passage.

Classical dressage is more like a mountain. It can be kind and it can be terrible, but it is very obvious. It has a bottom, and it has a top, and one part is not necessarily easier than another. Like a good mountaineer, the rider realizes the summit has very little to do with the climb, or the mountain itself. It is all about finding excuses to keep climbing.

CONCLUSION

In an article on expert performance, which appeared in *American Psychologist*, K. Anders Ericsson and Neil Charness wrote:

Counter to the common belief that expert performance reflects innate abilities and capacities, recent research in different domains of expertise has shown that expert performance is predominately mediated by acquired complex skills and physiological adaptations. For elite performers, supervised practice starts at very young ages and is maintained at high daily levels for more than a decade. The effects of extended deliberate practice are more far reaching than ever believed. Performers can acquire skills that circumvent basic limits on working memory capacity and sequential processing. Deliberate practice can also lead to anatomical changes resulting from adaptations to intense physical activity. The study of expert performance has important implications for our understanding of the structure and limits of human adaptation and optimal learning...

...For many sport and performance arts in particular professional teachers and coaches monitor training programs tailored to the needs of individuals ranging from beginners to experts. The training activities are designed to improve specific aspects of performance through repetition and successive refinement. To receive maximal benefit from feedback, individuals have to monitor their training with full concentration, which is effortful and limits the duration of daily training.

...Deliberate practice [is] not inherently motivating like play. Nor is deliberate practice like work. Work refers to public performances, competitions and other performances motivated by external social and monetary rewards. Although work activities offer some opportunities for learning, they are far from optimal...To give their best performance in work activities individuals rely on previously well entrenched methods rather than exploring new methods with unknown reliability.[1]

In the East for hundreds of years, the Zen masters have told their students that practice will lead to mastery and enlightenment. However, it must also be the right kind of practice – 'mushotoku' — without the desire for gain or profit. To limit one's practice with preconceptions, ambition, targets, goals will only delay mastery.

In the sixteenth century in Italy, Pignatelli was training his students. One of them, Antoine de Pluvinel, went on to serve four French Kings. However, Pluvinel was not motivated by social climbing. He tried to persuade the Kings to support riding academies so that riding masters 'will not be forced to pay compliments and offer other attractions to the young who are under his tutelage or sometimes tolerate vices simply to keep them or attract others'.[2] Learning influenced by social pressure will never work. He was always talking about the individual's development as a whole. For this, riding was perfect – training the body and the mind, developing physical prowess, but also judgment, honor, courage, even virtue.

At the same time in feudal Japan, Kami-idzumi Isenokami Hidetsuna was also training his students, but in swordsmanship. The final certificate which qualified a student as a sword master was nothing more than a circle. D.T. Suzuki wrote of this:

[1]Ericsson, K.A., & Charness, N., 'Expert performance, its structure and acquisition', in *American Psychologist* Magazine, August 1984, published by the American Psychology Association, inc. vol. 49, Nov 8, pp.723–747.
[2]Nelson, H., introduction to Pluvinel, Antoine de, *Le Maneige Royal* (J.A. Allen 1969).

173

This is supposed to represent a mirror, bright and altogether free from dust…The swordsman's mind must be kept entirely free from selfish affects and intellectual calculations so that 'original intuition' is ready to work at its best…Mere technical skill in the use of the sword does not necessarily give one full qualification as a sword master. He must realize the final stage of spiritual discipline…[3]

So, spiritual discipline, not technical skill will finish making a master swordsman. Virtue, not only physical prowess, will make a master of equitation.

Today, we almost seem afraid of these words. Say them at a horse show and riders will physically wince. Winning, and figuring out how to win, are what counts. Let someone else deal with those cantankerous concepts of spiritual discipline and virtue. However, these ideals cannot be swept under the carpet. They have been a major component and raison d'être of the classical consensus of dressage from the beginning.

Why? Is classical riding so mystical? Is it some mysterious, pseudo-religious cult? I think it is almost ridiculously the opposite. It is a very practical pursuit.

Modern psychologists say that mastery requires a lot of practice, but it must be the right kind of practice. It must be 'deliberate', focused, refined. For optimum learning, there must be opportunities for creative problem solving. The effort must shift away from 'well-entrenched methods motivated by external social or monetary rewards'.

When the Zen master says, 'Don't worry about hitting the target', people get nervous. They think they need goals. The Zen master says this will only delay mastery. When ambition divides the attention, there is only half the energy needed to focus on the task at hand. This is why D.T. Suzuki wrote that the mind must be kept free of selfish affects and too much intellectualizing – so that one's 'original intuition' can work at its best.

Pluvinel told the King of France that riding is not something one can learn in the library. One must practice, train the body and mind to focus amidst noise, worry, agitation, even fear. He wanted this education to be available to rich or poor. He wanted teachers compensated well enough so that their financial security would put them above politics.

Aren't these things all the same? Teach a person how to use the mind and how to use the body, not necessarily *what* to think, or exactly what to do. The thinking person will have the best chance to do the right thing.

When a rider starts to lose 'original intuition' – the internal gyroscope, which must be very deep in our genes – the result is always the same. When one cannot find one's internal coordinates, one will replace them with external validation.

On recognizing this in a student, the master trainer will push the rider down into his or her deepest self again and again until the true self is re-formed. The masters know that societies exist at cross-purposes with the individual's development. They know that, if it can, a society will inhibit the rider's mind with its own agendas, often as propaganda for itself. (Riders should be careful, though, not to assume that the greatest assaults on their understanding and progress will come in overt form, like great demons or ogres, against which the spirited individual will readily retaliate. More often, especially when the work gets hard, the limiting forces on a rider's career are more subtle, more dangerous – the strong seduction of normality, the comforting quietness of conformity, the patronizing plaudits bestowed upon the 'well-behaved'.)

Until the practice trains the rider, the master will try to shield the student from the Mephistophelian forces of the world that wants their souls. With what do they shield them? They shield them with the example of their own practice, which is never finished. I personally don't know how to be a master, but I have known a few and been friends with them. I know they practiced until the day they died, mostly because they knew that they were not perfect people. In many cases, for me, the knowledge that they were human and imperfect was comforting, rather than disappointing. In fact, it was often the root of so much of my inspiration. Of course, they were not always approachable, but how many myths have as their core teaching that the questors' enlightenment is in direct proportion to the impediments blocking their way? Conquer your deepest fears. Understand your real self. Sacrifice. It seems that, in every generation, people cry out about the lack of real masters. But it has to be remembered that, in any one generation, there are only

[3]Suzuki, D.T., *Zen and Japanese Culture* (Bollingen Series, Princeton University Press 1970).

as many masters as there were masterful students in the preceding generation.

For me, this book is another small payment on a very big debt to those masters who have shone out like mirrors. Mirrors made so clean by the right practice, that they seem to reflect more and more light.

Photo 120. In the end, you must be friends...

INDEX